Narcissus and the Voyeur

Approaches to Semiotics

48

MOUTON PUBLISHERS · THE HAGUE · PARIS · NEW YORK

Narcissus and the Voyeur

Three Books and Two Films

Robert M. MacLean

MOUTON PUBLISHERS · THE HAGUE · PARIS · NEW YORK

ISBN: 90-279-7838-7

Cover-design by Jurriaan Schrofer

© 1979, Mouton Publishers, The Hague, The Netherlands

Printed in the Netherlands

And still deeper the meaning of that
story of Narcissus, who because he
could not grasp the tormenting, mild
image he saw in the fountain, plunged
into it and was drowned. But that
same image, we ourselves see in all
rivers and oceans. It is the image
of the ungraspable phantom of life;
and this is the key to it all.

Herman Melville *Moby-Dick*

For Edward Sowa

Preface

To 'describe' is both to 'write down' and to 'trace, represent, picture, divide into parts': so that the word 'description' is appropriate both to prose and to film. This book argues that three literary works and two films, all of which deal with the problems of reporting an experience, incorporate various aspects of an empirical epistemology: specifically, that Herman Melville's *Moby-Dick* (1851) and Michaelangelo Antonioni's *The Passenger* (1972) make use of John Locke's *An Essay Concerning Human Understanding* (1960); that James Agee's *Let Us Now Praise Famous Men* (1941) makes use of the early thought of I.A. Richards; and that William Burroughs' *Naked Lunch* (1959) and Jean-Luc Godard's *Alphaville* (1965) make use of both phases of Ludwig Wittgenstein's philosophy. Evidence for this use is cited from the relevant comments, where available, of each author, and from explicit intratextural references; it consists chiefly in showing the extent to which epistemological readings make sense of the texts in question and, more briefly, of related texts by each author. Chapter II comprises interpretive summaries of the epistemologies of Locke, Richards and Wittgenstein; Chapter III introduces the prose analyses by comparing two exemplary voyeurs, Hawthorne's Chillingworth and Melville's Tommo; and each of the other chapters analyzes one of the three books and two films as exploring the implications of its respective philosophical informant. While the interpretations in Chapter II are supported by the philosophical texts from which they are derived, it must be emphasized at the outset that they do not pretend to be definitive, but are formulated with a mind to their usefulness in specific explication.

Each work discussed deals with the fact that the faculty of

observation or attention finds no reflection of itself in the world, and that narcissistic attachment to what it takes to be that reflection is at odds with the salutary project of criticizing empirically unsound preconceptions, and with compiling an uncommitted, finally voyeuristic, report. To borrow Wittgenstein's concept, each of the texts in question might be regarded as a game played according to the rules of empiricism, a mode of thought which attempts reduction to that beyond which all else is theory. As such, it is employed as a critique of metaphysics — both of the Platonic, Cartesian and Kantian tradition of innate forms, ideas and categories; and of the realism of Aristotle, Acquinas, the Scottish Common-Sense philosophers, Kant and the American Pragmatists, the belief in the existence of 'universals', specifically denied by Locke (*Essay*, III, iii, 11-13; IV, xvii, 8), which have some unambiguous connection with a real, objective, knowable, 'outer' world. In *Coleridge on Imagination*, Richards sets up materialism and idealism as 'complementary' procedures of thought meeting in a 'self-critical process', and agrees, though he treats each as a form of metaphysics, to write 'as a Materialist trying to interpret before you the utterances of an extreme Idealist' (1934: 19). To be sure, Locke, Richards and Wittgenstein all incorporate some form of realism into their thinking: the formulation employed by each is that we cannot know 'what' the real world of objects is, but we can know 'that' it is, 'how' it behaves. And both Richards and Wittgenstein pick up Locke's distinction between 'real' and 'verbal' truth, which places the propositions which encode understanding in a digital, true-false relation to that reality; even for the later Wittgenstein, who regards the proposition as one among many language-games, 'The agreement, the harmony, of thought and reality consists in this: if I say falsely that something is *red*, then, for all that, it isn't red' (PI, 429). The question, in Godard's terms, is whether words or things come first; the recognition that it is unanswerable is the basis of the empiricist's stance.

With the exception of R.G. Peterson's 'A picture is a fact: Wittgenstein and *The Naked Lunch*', there have been no analyses of any of these works as exploring the implications of an empirical stance. *Moby-Dick* has most frequently been regarded, as in Charles Feidelson's *Symbolism and American Literature* (University of Chicago Press, 1970), as an example of Romantic American symbolism. Of the two recent epistemological readings, Paul

Brodtkorb's *Ishmael's White Whale* (Yale University Press, 1965) is phenomenological, arguing that Melville opts for Kant's position that mind actively constitutes fact (11); and while Edgar Dryden's *Melville's Thematics of Form* (Baltimore, 1968) emphasizes the self-reflexivity of *Moby-Dick*, it argues that Ishmael is a 'novelist', the author of his own destiny, who escapes from the world of 'fact' into that of 'fiction' to achieve 'a victory of art over life' (211-212): both books treat *Moby-Dick* as a novel. Michael J. Hoffman's 'The anti-transcendentalism of *Moby-Dick*' (Georgia Review XXIII (1) Spring 1968), which sees Ahab's mania as a parody of Emersonian individualism, more closely approximates my reading, though it makes no mention of empiricism.

Epistemological readings of *Let Us Now Praise Famous Men* have emphasized its realism. Alfred T. Barson's *A Way of Seeing* (University of Massachusetts Press, 1972) describes I.A. Richards' influence on Agee as Romantic, specifically Wordsworthian (33-34), and analyzes *Let Us Now Praise Famous Men* as incorporating, via the Joycean model of the epiphany, a Thomistic realism (7, 74-76, 88). William Scott's *Documentary Expression and Thirties America* (Oxford University Press, 1973) treats *Let Us Now Praise Famous Men* as a documentary work, a classification which Agee specifically rejects.

Naked Lunch has commonly been regarded as typical of the Beat culture of the fifties (see, for example, Ronald Weston's 'William Burroughs: high priest of hipsterism', *Fact*, Nov.-Dec. 1965): Burroughs himself has denied any association either with the 'literary style' or with the 'outlook' and 'objectives' of his friends in the Beat movement (*Evergreen Review* XIII, June 1967: 87). Critical treatments of the book have dealt almost exclusively with whether or not its literary merit justifies its obscenity[*]; and the above-mentioned Peterson article, showing how it is consistent with the *Tractatus*, defends *Naked Lunch* against charges of incoherence and lack of viewpoint. Peterson is concerned with the confessional form and with comparisons with De Quincey, and uses the term 'symbol' in a literary rather than a Wittgensteinian sense, so the 'Junk is . . . at last, [a] symbol of life itself'; focusing

---

[*]Eric Mottram's treatment of the oeuvre, *William Burroughs: The Algebra of Need* (London: 1977), appeared after this was written.

on the horrifying aspect of the egocentricity protrayed in *Naked Lunch*, Peterson emphasizes its satiric rather than its reportive or descriptive elements, and points up the despair and 'meaninglessness' he finds in the book more centrally than does the treatment before you.

While some notice has been taken of Godard's attention to language, there have been no related treatments of *Alphaville*, or of Godard's relation to Wittgenstein; Toby Mussman has pointed out that Godard and Burroughs deal similarly with notions of time and the association of ideas ('Duality, repetition, chance, the unknown, infinity', in *Jean-Luc Godard*, 306-08). Nothing of an epistemological nature has been written on *The Passenger*.

In this book, I am placing each of the five works in a specific context by arguing that there exists an empirical point of view that dominates Melville's prose, the shadings of Agee's arguments about description and Burroughs' pronunciations on the nature of reality, as well as the ideas of Agee, Burroughs, Godard and Antonioni on the epistemological status of the film image. These five otherwise disparate texts have in common that they are both reports and self-reflexive comments on the nature of reporting: there is herein no historical argument otherwise to tie them together, or to their respective philosophical informants, although evidence is cited of each author's awareness of empirical thought, and of Agee's and Burroughs' awareness of *Moby-Dick*. A great deal of cross-referencing and quotation of textual detail has been carried out in order to demonstrate the manner in which these texts do fit together, and this has seldom resulted in a loose or discursive style of exposition. The effort has been, not only to document the argument, but also to clarify its thorough relevance to a body of textual material. The reader is forewarned that the plethora of reference occasionally makes for a rather convoluted syntax; moreover, the larger syntax of each chapter must bear the weight of a tendency to show rather than to tell. The mode of explaining the empirical position in Chapter II, for example, is to investigate in some detail the epistemological arguments of Locke, Richards and Wittgenstein; and in Chapter III, the analysis of *The Scarlet Letter* has the force of a summary statement on literary symbols and voyeurism by virtue of its adequacy as exposition. This method, I have felt, yields maximum efficiency in a book consisting of close readings. Not only has it seemed preferable to offer detailed accounts of the relevance of specific philosophers to the literary and film texts, rather than, for example, a more general summary of the empirical stance, but nothing else has seemed as interesting.

It is a pleasure to be able to thank Peter Ohlin for his participation in this piece of work, and to acknowledge the enthusiastic help of Noreen Golfman, Bruce Greenfield, Vickie Hughes and James Wurzbach.

Thanks are due also to Penelope Houston for permission to reprint 'Opening the Private Eye', which first appeared in *Sight and Sound*; and to William Lafferty for permission to use '*The Passenger* and Reporting', which has appeared in *Film Reader*.

London, Ontario   R.M.

Contents

The Passenger and Reporting: Photographic Memory?

Someone coming into a strange
country will sometimes learn the
language of the inhabitants from
ostensive definitions that they give
him; and he will often have to *guess*
the meaning of these definitions; and
will guess sometimes right, sometimes
wrong.
And now, I think, we can say:
Augustine describes the learning of
human language as if the child came
into a strange country and did not
understand the language of the country;
that is, as if it already had a
language, only not this one. Or
again: as if the child could already
think, only not yet speak. And
'think' would here mean something like
'talk to itself'.

Ludwig Wittgenstein
Philosophical Investigations

The argument implicit in our notions of 'film realism' is that the
image on the screen corresponds in a vital way to the reality of
which it is a photograph, to what is out beyond the camera
aperture through which we peer. Since *Breathless*, however, the
film image, and the kind of analysis it makes possible, have frequently been associated with death. Godard's suggestion, via
Cocteau, that the moving camera films 'a moment when death is
working',[1] brings that forward: film atomizes 'life' and the temporal continuity of gesture as a series of discrete, not necessarily

related images – two-dimensional arrangements of shape and color which fail to embody living reality, whatever that might be. 'Photography', as Bruno says in *Le Petit Soldat*, 'is truth. And cinema is the truth twenty-four times a second.' The organic – the romanticized anthropomorphic landscape, the body – is suggestive of the symbolic, an immanent promise of unity, rooted identity in the offing; the most that the understanding, like the visual sense, can empirically do, is to analyze what is present before it into component units, working always away from the stable whole, searching out the weak link in the machine: the mysteries of the organism can be approached only by means of a model, mechanical and inelegant, which must inevitably break down, fail to work.

This decomposition – analysis and death – is often portrayed as explosion, the most violent possible rupture of context and continuity. In Jiri Menzel's *Closely Watched Trains*, for example, a photographer awakens to find that an air raid has blown his house from around him, and surrenders to laughter. The explosives expert in Leone's *Duck, You Sucker!* declares that he has given up moral judgments in favor of an exclusive belief in dynamite, and repeatedly detonates the contexts upon which his companion depends, as Leone does the myths and stock gestures which are his materials; for acceptance of or identification with any of these constitutes an uncritical failure to duck. Kubrick claims to have learned to stop worrying and love the bomb. In Michaelangelo Antonioni's *Zabriskie Point*, the killing of the young hijacker of a plane, on the side of which he has written 'NO WORDS', triggers the explosion (whether 'real' or 'imagined', of course, is not stipulated) of a house full of consumer goods which are examined in close-up as they float slow-motion before us. This is an elaboration of the earlier *Blow-Up*, wherein a photographer enlarges a casual photograph until it becomes evident that something, an aimed pistol, might be 'out there' beyond the arrangement of dots which encodes the scene, providing a context for the movements he too has 'shot' – frozen, made dead – but he is left without unambiguous answers to his questions, performing mime-troupe gestures only 'as if' in relation to a contextual substance. Explosions, literally rather than metaphorically, blow apart what words, universals, logical connections – habitual associations – hold together and make sense of. In *The Passenger*, this style of analysis is related to that which is initiated in John Locke's *An Essay Concerning Human Understanding*, in which it is for the first time proposed that all knowledge is mediated by and to be analyzed into discrete simple ideas held together chiefly by habits of language, and that it is dependent upon the perception of the agreement or disagreement of ideas – that is, on their logical compatibility. That the film works through the implications of Locke's epistomology is suggested by the name and history of its protagonist, journalist and documentary filmmaker David Locke, who was 'born in Britain and educated in America', has a 'great talent for observation'. By exploring the form of analysis set forth in the *Essay*, *The Passenger* delimits the question of what remains when habits, the vehicles of signification, have been discarded.

If it is '*wit*', according to Locke's *Essay*, to notice the 'resemblance or congruity' of ideas, '*judgement*' consists 'in separating carefully, one from another, ideas wherein can be found the least difference, thereby to avoid being misled by similitude, and by affinity to take one thing for another. This is a way of proceeding quite contrary to metaphor and allusion'.[2] It is the development of the latter faculty, which criticizes analogy and breaks complex ideas down into the irreducible simples of sensation – treats the image, as Godard put it in 1968, 'not in terms of what it signifies, but what signifies it'[3] – to which the *Essay* is devoted. While the critical faculty of attention can sometimes shift voluntarily, as when it examines remembered images, it is as passive before experience as is an open eye before light. The possibility of 'free will' is rejected in the *Essay*, 'liberty being as little applicable to the will, as swiftness of motion is to sleep, or squareness to virtue' (II,xxi, 12): to attribute freedom to the volition which apparently raises the arm is to know something about 'spiritual substance', a knowledge manifestly, empirically, impossible. To handle the problem of substances, Locke proposes, in addition to the perception of 'relations' of ideas (IV, i, 7), ideas of 'real existence', whereby we have 'intuitive' knowledge (unmediated, that is, by other ideas), through our consciousness of thinking and volition, of the real existence of self; 'demonstrative' knowledge (mediated by other ideas) of the existence of God; and 'sensitive' knowledge of the real existence of material substances, through our taking notice of 'the actual *receiving* of ideas'. The assertion of a real 'substance' which supports actual, as opposed to remembered, ideas (we 'signify nothing by the word *substance* but only an uncertain supposition of we know not what, i.e. of something whereof we have no particular distinct positive ideas, which we take to be the *substratum* or support of those ideas we do know') rests on the arguments, 1) that each organ of sense is indispensable to the production of its peculiar ideas, and that these organs do not produce ideas themselves, since we do not see colors in the dark or smell roses in winter, 2) that the attention is passive before sense perception but potentially active in memory 3) that actual ideas are often accompanied by pain, and 4) that 'our *senses* in many cases *bear witness to the truth of each other's report* concerning the existence of invisible things without us'; this awareness of a substantial world, 'though it be not altogether so certain' as intuition and demonstration, 'deserves the name of *knowledge*' in the light of these common-sense considerations (I, iii, 19; IV, xi, 1-7).

Locke leaves on both sides of the subjective screen those substances, material and spiritual, with which Berkeley and Hume respectively did away; but the presence of attention, that passenger which cannot be indicated by metaphor or allusion, is neither to be identified with substance nor considered analogous to anything apparent: perception is not the 'essence' of the soul, whatever that may be, 'but one of its operations'. While 'it is past controversy, that we have *something* in us that thinks', we do not know whether it is material or otherwise, for 'we have ideas of *matter* and *thinking*, but possibly shall never be able to know whether any mere material being thinks or no' (II, i, 10; IV, iii, 6). Whereas the 'identity of the same man', as of an animal, consists 'in nothing but a participation of the same continued life, by constantly fleeting particles of matter, in succession vitally united to the same organized body' (that to which 'the word *I* is applied'), personal identity, or '*Selfe*', is that 'consciousness' which 'always accompanies thinking', distinguishes the self 'from all other thinking things' and is limited by memory: 'as far as this consciousness can be extended backwards to any past action or thought, so far reaches the identity of that person'. 'Person' is thus a purely utilitarian 'forensic term, appropriating actions and their merit', personality extending itself 'beyond present existence to what is past, only by consciousness, − whereby it becomes concerned and accountable' (II, xxvii, 7, 19, 11, 26). Memory, moreover, is a form of habit — is defined, in fact, as *'habitual knowledge'* (IV, i, 8) — the past formation of which constrains the manner in which we interpret ideas, so that we automatically see a uniformly colored three-dimensional object 'when the idea we receive from thence is only a plane variously colored, as is evident in painting' (II, ix, 8). Conscious attention neither transcends nor can be identified with the contingencies of habit. Peter Wollen, who wrote the original but largely altered screenplay of *The Passenger*[4], sets forth in his *Signs and Meaning in the Cinema* a theory of value consonant with Locke's critique of perceptual habits — 'a valuable work, a powerful work at least, is one which challenges codes, overthrows established ways of reading and looking' — and in his rejection of 'the mystification that communication can exist'[5] approximates Locke's assertion that there can be no more exact correspondence between the thoughts of two conversants than between *'perfectly arbitrary'* words and 'things as they really are' (*Essay*, III, ii, 5-8).

'Perhaps for once', says the leader of an African government into David Locke's microphone, 'the official terminology corresponds to the actual facts; and the facts are these. . . .' No such fascistic correspondence is available to Locke: exasperated by his failure to make contact with the camp of a revolutionary army, and by his alienated situation in a third-world country, he asks David Robertson, his hotel-mate and fellow bourgeois traveler, 'How do you talk to these people? ' 'It's like this', he is told; 'you work with words and images — fragile things: I come with merchandise, concrete things; they understand that better'. Indeed, Robertson sells arms to the men to whom Locke has been trying to get through, seems to have successfully involved himself in a world beyond that in which the latter is confined, and before which he is a passive spectator. 'He believed in something', the girl played by Maria Schneider reminds him later, when he is about to give up the role of Robertson: 'Isn't that what you wanted? ' Whereas Robertson, who is 'unusually poetic for a businessman', sees a 'still' quality in the desert, 'a kind of waiting', there is nothing anthropomorphic in Locke's response: 'I prefer people to landscapes'. When he is left in the desert by one of a series of guides, he waves in greeting at a passing mounted Bedouin who returns no sign; and when his jeep breaks down there, he experiences the landscape as oppressive and unanswering rather than poetic and inviting.

This should be stressed: the jeep which breaks down and is deserted shortly before Locke discards his identity for that of Robertson, and the car which also breaks down before Locke/Robertson's death, are metaphors which undercut themselves, for neither has carried him as far as he has wished to go, enabled him to make his connection – just as, having taken over Robertson's itinerary, Locke either mismanages the appointments or is stood up by the scheduled parties. Like his successive identities – 'I used to be somebody else', he says, 'but I traded him in' – the cars are arbitrary vehicles of his frustrated quest, connected with him in no more fundamental way than by their use-value (one is pointedly 'third hand'). They can be atomized, dismantled, are amenable to the understanding: while the anonymous Schneider character recommends the landscape to him, he describes the specific malfunction of the car.

Just as the depth of his imagery is limited by the superficiality of allegorical designation, Antonioni's protagonists have always failed to make ultimate connections; but whereas in such early films as *L'Avventura* and *La Notte* the failure is to make good the promise of romantic love, the films made since his self-exile from Italy – *Blow-Up* and *Zabriskie Point* – have been explicit semiological exercises. *The Passenger* is a self-reflexive film about a self-reflexive man, for, as Locke is told by an offended interviewee who turns the camera back on him, 'There are perfectly satisfactory answers to your questions, but you don't understand how little you can learn by them: your questions are more revealing about yourself'. Locke's self-analysis yields the disparate, not necessarily related signs that we habitually regard as constituting identity – which, for John Locke, is merely a forensic device. His distinction, in the *Essay*, between actual and habitual knowledge, and his noting that a 'settled habit' of judgment operates 'so constantly and quick, that we take that for a perception of our sensation which is an idea formed by our judgment' (II, ix, 8-9), elaborate his definition by negation of the faculty of conscious attention. Attention can neither be identified with those habits of thought which guide it, nor expressed through metaphor or analogy: David Locke's point of view, he suggests to the Schneider character, is that of someone riding backward in a convertible.

Locke contemplates the dead body of David Robertson, similar enough to his own to enable him to assume Robertson's personal identity, and touches a wisp of the thinning hair as it is fanned by the desert breeze: like the landscape, the body is merely oppressive, has nothing to teach or promise. As he exchanges the photographs in their passports, he recalls Robertson's having remarked on the sameness, after a while, of all such countries as the one where they had met, to which Locke replies, 'It's us who remain the same; we translate every experience into the same old codes... we're creatures of habit' — and later: 'no matter how hard you try it's impossible to break away from the same old habits'. Keeping one of Robertson's appointments in Barcelona, Locke meets, instead of the scheduled agent, an old man who tells him as he nods toward some children: 'Ninos, I've seen so many grow up. Other people look at them and think it's a new world, but I see the same old tragedy beginning all over again. They never escape us. It's boring'. And Locke adds to his list of the elements of the identity he has left behind — 'wife, house, adopted child, successful job' — the qualification, 'everything but a few bad habits I can't get rid of'. When he expresses the wish to get beyond his habits Robertson tells him, 'It doesn't work that way', and he answers, 'It doesn't work the other way either'. For David Locke, identity is not anchored in any absolute reality; if, by the manipulation of a few signs — a set of habits and a passport — it can be exchanged, then those signs cannot logically be transcended, for in their absence 'identity' does not exist — is not, that is, recognizable: Locke first meets the girl, who becomes another kind of passenger, when attempting to avoid his television producer ('I thought someone might recognize me'); when the police ask if they 'recognize him' as he lies dead, the girl and his wife give condradictory answers.

The inability to consolidate an identity, the fact that it 'doesn't work', is as important to filmmaker Antonioni as to filmmaker Locke. We are shown the coverage of a firing-squad execution which incorporates signals of documentation — minimal green and white tones, long wide-sweeping shots with self-conscious and apparently unrehearsed adaptations of focus; but the question of its objective 'reality' ('I didn't mean to upset you', says the producer to Rachel Locke as he switches off the tape') is no more pertinent here than to the explosion in *Zabriskie Point* or to the body in *Blow-Up*. In a television eulogy for him, the producer recalls the limitations within which Locke had worked: 'David maintained that objectivity was impossible, whereas I maintained that it was both possible and necessary'. If all objects are mediated by signs, then the mosaic of conscious ideas and images, like the motion-picture screen, is an impenetrable surface, a conglomeration of accidents behind which subsists no essence that can be reached and known; thus John Locke declares it impossible to 'explain' such matters of fact as 'voluntary motions' or material 'creation' (*Essay*, IV, x, 19) – to believe in explanatory stories or context. The film opens as a vehicle enters a village square and ends with a vehicle leaving a similar square: no further-reaching context is available to clarify things. 'It sounds crazy', says David Locke of his situation, 'because I can't explain it'. To explain is to invoke context, to be able to predict and control experience, whereas the *Essay* emphasizes its inevitable instability (III, iii, 19).

Locke's producer makes a point of the unexpectedness of his death, just as the girl answers Locke's question about the impressive Gaudi building in which he has sought refuge: 'The man who built it was hit by a bus'; and when Locke, musing over some occupations to which he might proceed, suggests 'How about a gun-runner' – precisely what he has become – the girl answers, 'Too unlikely'. Rather, knowledge is limited to the interrelation of ideas, and so it is by an intricate choreography that the film proceeds: Locke is first shuttled from one guide to another in a series of disconcerting exchanges carried on out of his visual range, and ours, and then can never quite make sense of the sequence of moves plotted in Robertson's appointment book. At one such appointment we watch Locke's movements as he engages and releases passers-by to ask directions, then see and hear the rhythmic cane and feet of an old man as they encounter and respond to Locke's. He sees the girl in London; we see her in Munich; when he sees her in Barcelona they are in precisely the same postures and spatial relationship that they had briefly assumed in London: later he asks, 'Do you believe in coincidence? I never used to notice it: now I see it all around'. He is involved in, and struggles for detachment from, a kind of swirling dance over which he has no control. His present situation is 'an accident: everybody thought I was dead and I let them think so'.

And his dependence upon the coincidence of ideas informs the semantic method of the film: the camera regards Locke as he stands red-shirted in a noise filled room before Robertson's body, tilts up toward a whirling fan, the source of the noise, and returns to Locke, now in Robertson's blue shirt; again, while over the soundtrack we hear the voices, as in memory, of Locke and Robertson in conversation, the camera pans slowly from Locke as he sits working on the passports to a window looking out onto the desert as Locke and Robertson stroll into view conversing: when they return to the room, Locke leaves the frame to the left to refill their glasses, and the camera pans right from Robertson, who has continued to regard Locke off, again picking up Locke at work in the 'present'. Later, when we see him turn it off, we realize that we have been listening to a tape-recorder; through both shots, in their parallel treatments of sound, Antonioni suggests the mechanical nature of memory. Moving the actors around while the camera records the gestures and signs which mediate our perception of an event is a device patented by Lelouche in *Live for Life*, in which the camera unhurriedly pans through 720° to pick up the quarrelling lovers in successive, otherwise unrelated positions and attitudes. And such exterior shots as that which follows Locke as he moves through the maze-like interior of a simply colored building, and is completed by the covering of a window in a white wall with a green shutter, suggests Godard's style of chromatic analysis in *La Chinoise*. Here, the context of John Locke's empiricism gives the arrangement of color images an epistemological significance: sight, and photography, are modes of analysis.

That the dancer cannot be told from the dance does not imply the identity of actor and role; on the contrary, it is the nature of that passenger which finds itself alienated from role which concerns both Antonioni and David Locke. At their meeting in a Munich church, for example, the actor portraying the revolutionary leader Achebe executes a series of reactions to some xeroxed diagrams of weapons, concluding with a pleased response, while Locke struggles to improvise the role of Robertson; both are pointed exercises in acting, drawing our attention to the fact that we are watching actors at work before a camera rather than the dramatic confrontation of actual characters. As we watch, we peer through a lens at activities as detached observers, like the bellman who lingers at the door after admitting Locke and the girl to their hotel room. So does David Locke, who keeps the camera between himself and the people he interviews: 'You involve yourself in real situations', his wife complains, 'but you've got no dialogue'. His knowledge is mediated, vicarious, gained at a remove: as his wife listens to their taped conversation, we hear Robertson pause and point out to the embarrassed Locke that his tape recorder is running. And when he asks the girl, 'What kind of impression do you think you make when you walk into a room'? she replies:

'People think I'm all right — nothing mysterious. You learn more by packing someone's things.'
'Yes, it's like listening in on a private phone conversation'.

This penchant for the powerful suggestiveness of clothing and belongings, quite literal 'habits', dates back to *L'Avventura*, and is one of Antonioni's salient debts to Hitchcock: when an embassy official offers to go through Locke's things with his wife, she declines in embarrassed silence.

While meticulous attention is devoted to the soundtrack of *The Passenger* (which records, for example, the sound of the wind as it rushes past a moving car), the film is addressed chiefly to the analytic sense of sight, which is experienced as a kind of violation. Locke tells the story of a blind man who gains his sight through an operation when he is nearly forty: 'At first he was elated, really high: faces, colors, landscapes. But then everything began to change. No one had ever told him how much dirt there was. He began to notice dirt and ugliness everywhere. When he was blind he could cross the street with a stick, but once he could see he began to be afraid; he lived in darkness, never left his room. After three years he killed himself'. Most of the suggestions of self in the film are associated with the sense of sight, 'the most comprehensive of all our senses', according to John Locke, and the one to which he regularly compares the operation of the understanding (*Essay*, II, ix, 9; x, 7; IV, xiii, 1); and all of them involve the closed spaces of vehicles or rooms. It is in the outdoors that Locke conducts his interviews, invoking there the enclosed space of the camera; and he avoids confrontations with his producer, his wife and the police by ducking into buildings, racing for his car. We view the world through the windshields of three cars; find ourselves in a noise-filled air terminal and in the silence, inadvertently profaned by Locke, of a church; in the twisting, asymmetrical convolutions of Gaudi's buildings (Maria Schneider plays a student of architecture), one of which permits us the glimpse of a couple arguing violently, and the sculpted shade of an *umbracolo*; in an editing room watching video-tapes; in the glass labyrinth of a hotel lobby, a mirror-filled glassed-in bar, a glass-walled restaurant, shoe-shine stand, and Avis office; staring into bird cages, phone booths, bedrooms and through a window over the shoulder of Rachel Locke. All of our visual perceptions are mediated by the glass of the lens: 'What goes on beyond that window? ', Locke asks. 'People who read what I have to say do so because it conforms to their expectations – or worse, it conforms to mine'. Much of the choreography – the movements of people in the air terminal; a last minute decision not to enter his wife's house; the alternate interrogation and beating of a revolutionary leader in rooms partitioned by a broken plate of glass; Locke's registration at a hotel desk while his wife, beside him in a phone booth, tries to trace his whereabouts; the car chase – depends upon the bringing into relation of discrete closed spaces. When Locke switches identities with Robertson, he does so by switching rooms; and he asks a policeman who insists on checking out the registration of his car, 'Senor, are you looking for the car or the person in it'?

The comparison of the mind to a camera or room dates from John Locke's *Essay* and suggests the limitation of viewpoint that is the starting-point of an empirical semiotic: the observation that 'though it be highly probable that millions of men do now exist, yet, whilst I am alone, writing this, I have not that certainty of it which we call knowledge' (*Essay*, IV, xi, 9) is the basis of Berkeley's *esse est percipi*, and is echoed in David Locke's answer to the girl's comment that 'people disappear all the time': 'Yes, every time they leave the room'. Particularly relevant is the model of the *camera obscura*, which operates by the admission of light through a tiny aperture into a darkened room, casting an inverted moving image on the opposite wall, sharpened and controlled by a lens and corrected by a mirror: according to the *Essay*, 'the understanding is not much unlike a closet wholly shut from light, with only some little openings left, to let in external visible resemblances, or ideas of things without: would the pictures coming into such a dark room but stay there, and lie so orderly as to be found upon occasion, it would very much resemble the understanding of a man, in reference to all objects of sight, and the ideas of them' (IV, xi, 9). Such, of course, is Antonioni's camera. The situation is allegorically set up at the end of the film: the girl stands at the barred window of a hotel room – we see her only as reflected in a full-length mirror – while Locke asks from the interior, 'What can you see?' She lists 'A man scratching his shoulder, a kid throwing stones, and dust. It's very dusty here'. The procedure is repeated as Locke lies on the bed.

He has wished to leave behind the 'room' constituted by habits and a forensic definition, has leaned through the window of a cable car extending his arms as in flight, watching his shadow on the waves below; there is a quick shot, as he looks for a mechanic to repair his car, of a panting dog pacing at the end of his tether. Now, as he reclines alone on the bed, the camera moves slowly past him toward the window, the bars of which, like the wire framework in Dürer's *Draftsman Drawing a Reclining Nude*, analyze the scene on a rectangular grid: as in the first shot of Hitchcock's *Rebecca*, the camera, a nameless and unobstructed witness and dreamer, passes through the bars. Outside, it wheels slowly around in the square, registering the mundane activities and the distant expanse of landscape, following the police as they drive up with Rachel Locke and enter, with the girl, Locke's room, where – whether he has been killed by the thugs who had interrogated Achebe (we have seen them drive up and heard one of them enter behind the camera) or whether his adopted identity, like his third-hand car, simply no longer functions – he now lies dead. The camera has come around 180° to peer back into itself, the apertured room in which Locke's body lies. A room within a room, recording images from an uncomprehended source and representing to itself the decomposed elements of its identity, it remains a camera, does not transcend its own point of view – is confined, by a method that recognizes no basis for metaphysics, to the invalid but necessary terms of analogy. It is thus from its empirical limits that *The Passenger* derives the poetry of the self-reflexive experience.

NOTES

1. 'An interview with Jean-Luc Godard', in *Cahiers du Cinéma*, trans. by Rose Kaplin for reprint in *Jean-Luc Godard*, ed. by Toby Mussman. New York, Dutton, 1968: 108.
2. John Locke, *An Essay Concerning Human Understanding*, ed. by Peter H. Nidditch. Oxford: Claredon Press, 1975: II, xi, 2. Subsequent references are noted in the text (*Essay*).
3. 'Struggle on two fronts: a conversation with Jean-Luc Godard', *Film Quarterly* XXII (2) Winter 1968-1969: 23.
4. Antonioni, it is said, eliminated from Wollen's finished script most of the narrative elements and, when MGM demanded that the resultant three-hour film be cut to two hours, those portions of the film which deal with character motivation.
5. Peter Wollen, *Signs and Meaning in the Cinema*. Bloomington, Indiana University Press, 1972: 172, 163.

2

The Rules of Empiricism:
Locke, Richards and Wittgenstein

> So.
> The situation is, I agree, desperate. But fortunately
> I know the proper way to proceed. That is why I am
> giving you these instructions. They will save your
> life. First, persuade yourself that the situation is not
> desperate (my instructions will save your life only
> if you have not already hopelessly compromised it
> by listening to the instructions of others, or to the
> whispers of your heart, which is in itself suspect,
> in that it has been taught how to behave — how to
> whisper, even — by the very culture that has pro-
> duced the desperate situation). Persuade yourself,
> I say, that your original perception of the situation
> was damaged by not having taken into account
> all of the variables (for example, my instructions)
> and that the imminent disaster that hangs in the
> sky above you can be, with justice, downgraded to
> the rank of severe inconcenience by the application
> of corrected thinking. Do not let what happened
> to the dog weaken your resolve.
>
> Donald Barthelme
> *'What to do next'*

Empiricism is that mode of thought which is premised on the assumption that all knowledge is derived from experience, that there are no innate ideas or categories or structures, or pre-existent or evolving forms, which can be brought to bear on what we know: thus, as the latter part of this sentence implies, empiricism might be considered as a criticism of other, more traditional assumptions. It is usually thought of as having been invented, or at least given its first radical expression in Western culture, by John Locke. His

definition of knowledge, in *An Essay Concerning Human Under-*
standing, as *'nothing but the perception of the connexion of and*
agreement, or disagreement and repugnancy of any of our ideas'
(*Essay*, IV, i, 1), limits knowledge to the arrangements of the
particulars of sense experience: his modern successors emphasize
language as the mode of that arrangement — that ability or skill,
according to Wittgenstein, which makes having experience possible.[1]
While it has been suggested that Locke's reduction to the simples
of sensation is a quest for certainty in a form alternative to Cartesian rationalism, it is for the purpose of this discussion better
understood as a mode of criticizing vague and invalid general ideas
which mislead the understanding into unfounded habits of thought:
Locke insists upon a tentative and limited point of view, and
rejects the notion of an invisible primary order manifested in a
universe of analogies. Since analogy is invalid, the understanding,
or subjective attention which takes cognizance of ideas, is, Locke
says, 'like an eye which whilst it makes us see and perceive all
other things, takes no notice of itself' (*Essay*, 'Introduction', 1).
Wittgenstein, who uses the same comparison in the *Tractatus*
Logico-Philosophicus — 'nothing *in the visual field* allows you to
infer that it is seen by an eye' — describes the perceiving subject
as that which alone could not be mentioned in a book called
'*The World as I found it*', which included 'a report on my body'[2]
The understanding, that is, finds no reflection of itself in the
world; it is narcissistic when, like that of Melville's Ahab, it
insists upon finding that reflection, and voyeuristic when, like
Ishmael's, it confronts an impenetrable, unidentifiable surface.
For the empiricist, as for Ishmael, habits of language and configuration can neither be transcended nor identified with, are the
vain but necessary instruments of understanding. Attention is
left without a myth to guarantee the validity or continuity of its
presence, a voyeuristic tourist in its own reality, and is handled
as such in the literature and film treated in this book. Locke
defines thought as 'the condition of being awake' (*Essay*, II, i,11);
all of these works deal with that irreducibly ambiguous fact, as
well as the corresponding issues of intention, motive and free will.
For, like Actaeon, neither has the onlooker chosen to observe,
nor has he any excuse for his presence; nor can he guess — nor,
finally, is it relevant — whether the statements and gestures of
others are inhabited by an intention in any way commensurate

with its consequences. The voyeur is without myths or ultimate contexts to explain what he sees or, which is the same, his presence before it.

The response to this mythless condition, in each of the five texts, is to resort to self-reflexive modes of description or presentation. Agee's 'effort', as he calls it, 'to recognize the stature of a portion of unimagined existence, and to contrive techniques proper to its recording, communication, analysis, and defense',[3] is in many ways stylistically apposite to Ishmael's attempts at description, his going to sea ' "to find out by experience what whaling is . . . to see the world" ',[4] and shares epistemological concerns with *Naked Lunch*, wherein it is asserted that 'There is only one thing a writer can write about: *what is in front of his senses at the moment of writing* . . . I am a recording instrument. . . . I do not presume to impose "story" "plot" "continuity" . . . . Insofar as I succeed in recording direct areas of psychic process I may have limited function . . . I am not an entertainer . . . .'[5] And Agee has in common with Jean-Luc Godard, who has sought to adapt the Hollywood vocabulary of stories, plots and continuities to the effort to record actuality, strategies and techniques of formulation which are based on the empirical position that knowledge can only proceed from what is directly observed. In Godard's *Pierrot le fou*, Marianne paraphrases Ferdinand's speech: 'He spoke to them of man, of the seasons, of unexpected encounters, but he warned them never to ask what came first: words or things, or what would happen to us afterwards . . . .' In an article in *Cahiers du Cinéma*, Godard indicates that 'what was true for Marianne and Pierrot, not asking what came first, was not true for me — I was actually asking myself that very question; in other words, the very moment that I was certain that I had filmed life it eluded me for that very reason'.[6]

The pursuit of 'life', or quest for the secret source of things, and the forms into which that pursuit is forced by its frustration, is dramatized by Ahab's hunt for the white sperm whale, and for 'the little lower layer' that it symbolizes for him. ' "All visible objects" ', he says, ' "are but as pasteboard masks. But in each event — in the living act, the undoubted deed — there, some unknown but still reasoning thing puts forth the mouldings of its features from behind the unreasoning mask. If man will strike, strike through mask! How can the prisoner reach outside except by thrusting through the wall? To me, the white whale is that wall shoved near to me" ' (MD, 144). Every event is for Ahab the product of a conscious, reasoning intention. Ishmael joins the search for that lower layer, but he never finds it. In him we encounter an unrelieved struggle with the medium of language: he opens *Moby-Dick* with an etymology of the word 'whale' and a lengthy inventory of quotations on the subject (among its other forms, *Moby-Dick* is a work of scholarship: Ishmael has 'swam through libraries and sailed through oceans'), and provides chapters listing pictorial and sculptural renderings of the sperm whale, anecdotes and descriptive accounts, 'citations of items practically or reliably known to me as a whaleman' (175), and detailed computations based on the measurement of an extant skeleton, declaring himself 'omnisciently exhaustive in the enterprise; not overlooking the minutest germs of his blood, and spinning him out to the uttermost coil of his bowels" (378), all to the rhythm of his reiterated despair of ever rendering the actual whale, of making him live before us: 'I promise nothing complete; because any human thing supposed to be complete must for that very reason infallibly be faulty' (118). Unlike Ahab, whose preoccupation is completion, Ishmael has no foreknowledge of the whale, does not know what it ultimately means or essentially is, and so is forced to an account of the ambiguous and unconfigured details of his experience; a slain sperm whale, moored to the ship and methodically cut into, dismantled, atomized and reduced to so many tuns of clear oil reveals not a symbolic depth but an ineluctable surface: 'Dissect him how I may, then, I but go skin-deep; I know him not and never will' (318). The forms of *Moby-Dick* — epic, romance, tragedy — break down into episodes, accounts and words, harpoons that miss the mark of actual content; like the Pequod, that floating symbol of civilization, those forms are scuttled by the reality they are constructed to subdue. Despairing of content, Ishmael counts and recounts the items of his experience, offers that form into which experience has shaped him and which is his coming to terms with it.

Let Us Now Praise Famous Men provides an illuminating bridge between the epistemological problems of this type of prose description and those of film. By the time he wrote the work Agee was an experienced poet, fiction writer and journalist, and apparently contemplated becoming a film director as early as

1929[7]; his later screenplays, his essays on the photography of Walker Evans and Helen Levitt and his distinguished body of film criticism display that regard for photography which he records in *Let Us Now Praise Famous Men*: 'One reason I so deeply care for the camera is just this. So far as it goes (which is, in its own realm, as absolute anyhow as the traveling distance of words or sound), and handled cleanly and literally in its own terms, as an ice-cold, some ways limited, some ways more capable, eye, it is, like the phonograph record and like scientific instruments and unlike any other leverage of art, incapable of recording anything but absolute, dry truth' (234). It is this analytic precision, apposite to Godard's insistence that photography is truth, at which Agee's descriptive effort is aimed; like Ishmael, Agee self-reflexively offers himself in the process of giving form to his experience:

I would do just as badly to simplify or eliminate myself from this picture as to simplify or invent character, places or atmospheres. A chain of truths did actually weave itself and run through: it is their texture that I want to represent, not betray, nor pretty up into art. The one deeply exciting thing to me about Gudger is that he is actual, he is living, at this instant. He is not some artist's or journalist's or propagandist's invention: he is a human being: and to what degree I am able it is my business to reproduce him as the human being he is; not just to amalgamate him into some invented, literary imitation of a human being. (240)

The 'truth' of which he speaks, that is, is a subjective, empirical, merely 'relative' truth: 'Name me one truth within human range that is not relative and I will feel a shade more apologetic of that' (239). No matter how exhaustive his manipulation of words in the service of accurate representation, he is, like Ishmael and Godard, unable to render life. As with Burroughs, Agee's limited function is the recording of direct areas of psychic process, and he is unable to transcend the units — words and images — of that process, to strike through the medium of description into an objective reality: he can 'get at a certain form of the truth' about George Gudger '*only if* I am as faithful as possible to Gudger as I know him, to Gudger as, in his actual flesh and life (but there again always in my mind's and memory's eye) he is' (239). Such truth remains ambiguous and unstable, cannot be anchored in any firm context or concept of an objective world beyond its shifting forms. In a passage strikingly similar to that cited above from *Naked Lunch*, Agee — who also denies 'the obligations of the artist or entertainer' (111) – remarks on his restriction to the data of the senses:

I will be trying here to write nothing whatever which did not in physical actuality or in the mind happen or appear; and my most serious effort will be, not to use these 'materials' for art, far less for journalism, but *to give them as they were and as in my memory and regard they are*. If there is anything of value and interest in this work it will have to hang entirely on that fact. Though I may frequently try to make use of art devices and may, at other times, being at least in part an 'artist', be incapable of avoiding their use, I am in this piece of work illimitably more interested in life than in art. (242)

The aim at an absolute and comprehensive overview is given up in favour of a detailed recounting of the minutiae of experience: unable to identify 'what' these minutiae are, Agee's description addresses itself to 'how' they are known or represented – to his reader as well as to himself.

Ishmael takes the opportunity of the poised whales' heads to allegorize his objections to philosophical ponderings: 'So when on one side you hoist in Locke's head, you go over that way; but now on the other side, hoist in Kant's and you come back again; but in very poor plight . . . Oh, ye foolish! throw all these thunderheads overboard, and then you will float light and right' (MD,277). But just as Godard, despite Pierrot's summary dealing with it, acknowledges a preoccupation with the problem, so it remains central for Melville, despite Ishmael's dispatch (which is to be considered in the light of his propensity for self-negation), from *Typee* to *Billy Budd*. The empirical method which Agee explores, anguishes over, attempts to transcend and finally accepts in *Let Us Now Praise Famous Men*, and which Burroughs wields with sardonic delight in *Naked Lunch*, can be linked on the one hand to the model of *Moby-Dick*, which Agee regarded as, 'outside of *Huckleberry Finn*, the most beautiful piece of writing I know in American writing [sic]',[8] and to which Burroughs alludes repeatedly, and on the other to their respective enthusiasm for the ideas of Richards and Wittgenstein, which share much with those of Locke.

LOCKE AND MELVILLE: BEYOND THE REALM OF THE SENSES

For Locke, of course, the mind is an empty 'white paper' marked only by experience, the foundation of all knowledge, whether of external objects or of our mental operations, such as *'perception, thinking, doubting, believing, reasoning, knowing, willing'*. Ideas of the latter are supplied to the understanding by means of *'internal sense'* or 'REFLECTION', 'that notice which the mind takes of its own operations, and the manner of them' (*Essay*, II, i, 2, 4). This position of a non-transcendent critical faculty is central. *'Having ideas*, and *perceptions'*, says Locke, are 'the same thing'; 'Consciousness is the perception of what passes in a man's own mind'; *'the mind'* is spoken of as the presence of ideas in consciousness (aided by *'memory'*, 'the storehouse of ideas' or, less metaphorically, the 'ability to revive them again'), whereas 'the understanding' is what is thereby furnished 'with ideas of its own operations', so that 'mind' and 'understanding' appear to be different degrees of abstraction (II, i, 9, 19, 4; x, 2). I.A. Richards objects to Locke's inconsistency on this point: it thus appears, he says, not that the mind is present to the understanding, but 'that only *what the mind* DOES, its operations are so present. And these operations seem to be present as ideas of reflection. But his view on this is not entirely clear. Only *ideas* are present to the mind. Therefore its operations, if present to it, must be ideas. But we would expect these ideas to be ^{q} of ^{q} the operations rather than to be them'.[9] These limitations on the explanation of cognition, Locke's avowed refusal to invoke a metaphysical context (*Essay*, 'Introduction', 2), define the boundaries within which Melville and Agee operate, as is suggested by the latter's remarks on the inexplicable 'difference between a conjunction of time, place and unconscious consciousness and a conjunction of time, place and conscious consciousness' (LUNPFM, 226).

Also regarded as inexplicable by Locke is the fact that 'bodies produce ideas in us . . . by impulse', concerning which, along with the idea of *'the power of exciting motion by thought'*, if 'we inquire how this is done, we are equally in the dark': 'some motion' is 'continued by our nerves and animal spirits' from external objects 'to the brains or the seat of sensation, there to produce in our minds the particular ideas we have of them' (II, xxiii, 28; viii, 12). And since the mind 'stirs not one jot' beyond its ideas (II, xxiii, 29), understanding is 'merely passive'; the mind, however can actively combine simple ideas into compound ones, can compare ideas and thereby obtain 'all *its ideas of relations'*, and can abstract ideas from those which 'accompany them in their real existence' to form 'general ideas' (II, i, 25; xii, 1). But since the mind has no immediate object but ideas, since knowledge consists only in the perception of their agreement or disagreement, the understanding is powerless to transcend the condition of mediation (IV, i, 1).

Knowledge is either actual (present) or habitual (mnemonic); the latter is either intuitive (obvious) or demonstrative (requiring rational proof, 'the intervention of other ideas'). But in order to deal with our being left, as Richards says, 'Still shut up within the walls of our ideas' (HRP, 52), Locke hypothesizes, in the name of common sense, a substantial, physical, corpuscular world of particles 'too subtle to be perceived', which affect our senses by 'contact' (taste, touch) or by 'impulse' (sight, sound, odor): this is not a perfectly certain hypothesis, but is sufficiently so to be called knowledge. As a distinction between actual and habitual knowledge, between reality and memory, it is a common sense acknowledgment of the physical state of our affairs: for even if there is no arguable difference between being in a fire and believing so, there are consequent pains to be avoided (IV, ii, 11-14); our faculties are suited, not to perfect intellectual clarity, 'but to the preservation of us in whom they are' (IV, xi, 8). Ishmael too regards the survival imperative as the only irrefutable source of knowledge of personal identity: when the sailor who watches for whales from the masthead is a 'sunken-eyed young Platonist', he is apt to be

lulled into such an opium-like listlessness of vacant unconscious reverie . . . by the blending cadence of waves with thoughts, that at last he loses his identity; takes the mystic ocean at his feet for the visible image of that deep, blue, bottomless soul, pervading mankind and nature; and every strange, half-seen, gliding, beautiful thing that eludes him; every dimly-discovered, uprising fin of some undiscernible form, seems to him the embodiment of those elusive thoughts that only people the soul by continually flitting through it. In this enchanted mood, thy spirit ebbs away to whence it came; becomes diffused through time and space; like Wickliff's sprinkled Pantheistic ashes, forming at last a part of every shore the round globe over.

There is no life in thee, now, except that rocking life imparted by a gently rolling ship; by her, borrowed from the sea; by the sea, from the inscrutable tides of God. But while this sleep, this dream is on ye, move your foot or hand an inch; slip your hold at all; and your identity comes back in horror. Over Descartian vortices you hover. (MD, 140)

There are for Locke four 'sorts' of knowledge, that of identity or diversity, of relation, of co-existence or necessary connection, and of real existence: the first three are 'truly nothing but relations'; the fourth includes our ideas of self, God and other things (IV, i, 3, 7). Knowledge of self is intuitive, a form of Cartesian *cogito* ('If I doubt of all other things, that very doubt makes me perceive my own existence') which is nevertheless confined to empirical data, to our 'experience' of 'sensation, reasoning and thinking' which depend — again, as such pains as of hunger must convince us — on our existence as material creatures. One can only speculate on the nature of the mysterious 'something' in us that thinks; Melville scored, in his copy of Schopenhauer's *The World as Will and Idea,* a comment on 'the truth of Locke's principle that what thinks may also be material'.[10] Certainly, he makes use of Locke's notion of the mnemonically limited self. The concern, says Locke, 'that that self which is conscious should be happy' is 'the unavoidable concomitant of consciousness', so that 'whatever past actions it cannot reconcile or *appropriate* to that present self by consciousness; it can be no more concerned in than if they had never been done' (II, xvii, 7-26). This pre-Freudian model of a dynamic of repression which counteracts, by exclusion, threats to the sovereignty of the albeit arbitrarily formulated self over circumstances, informs Ishmael's speculation on his captain's madness: ' "I'd strike the sun if it insulted me" ', swears Ahab; and when he bursts from his stateroom in mid-nightmare, he exhibits the 'intensity' of the conflict between the subjected but unamenable substance (i.e. that which is beyond form, physical or spiritual) of the man, and the maniacal self formulation which is his mission:

For, at such times, crazy Ahab, the scheming, unappeasedly steadfast hunter of the white whale; this Ahab that had gone to his hammock, was not the agent that so caused him to burst from it in horror again. The latter was the eternal, living principle or soul in him; and in sleep, being for the time dissociated from the characterizing mind, which at other times employed it for its outer vehicle or agent, it spontaneously sought escape from the scorching contiguity of the frantic thing, of which, for the time, it was no longer an integral. But as the mind does not exist unless leagued with the soul, therefore it must have been that, in Ahab's case, yielding up all his thoughts and fancies to his one supreme purpose; that purpose, by its own sheer inveteracy of will, forced itself against gods and devils into a kind of self-assumed, independent being of its own.(MD, 174-175)

Words, and thus identity, are not arbitrary for Ahab, but fixed and prior to things; unlike Ishmael, he does not ' "name himself" ', but is given a name that might ' " somehow prove prophetic" ', and possesses a dualistic sense of the correspondence between mind and matter: 'O Nature, and O soul of man! how far beyond all utterances are your linked analogies! not the smallest atom stirs or lives in matter, but has its cunning duplicate in mind" ' (MD, 77, 264). Such a knowledge of mental and physical substance transcends the empirical point of view delimited by Locke. In his outrage at fate, his inability to accept his vulnerable physical condition and his consequent insistence upon returning the blow and correcting the balance, Ahab exhibits a rigidity unknown to Ishmael, who must relinquish his preconceptions, which are after all only habits of thought, and finally himself – submit that self to the random and fragmenting details of experience, and recognize the formulation of that experience as limited, incapable of an ultimate or redemptive significance. For such characters as Ahab, symmetry is primary; he has lost his and gone mad, and his whalebone leg suggests the means of its restoration.

Knowledge of the real existence of God, the second type of such knowledge for Locke, is demonstrative, put together from our intuitions that we exist, that 'nonentity cannot of itself produce any real being' and that 'incogitative' matter cannot of itself produce motion or impart cogitation to other beings. The argument rests on causality, an idea which can be present to us without our knowing the 'manner' of the operation of cause and effect, and on the notion of a Prime Mover, and does not depart from that of Hobbes, who likewise works back to the 'first cause of all causes', allowing that we 'may know *that* God is, though not *what* he is'[11] : this is as far as Locke goes. He finds no signs of a transcendent order in nature, and cites the example of changelings to show that not even the human form 'is the sign of a rational soul within, that is immortal' (IV, viii, 16); moreover, not even an immediate divine revelation could 'exceed, if equal, the certainty of our intuitive knowledge', or contradict it (xviii, 5). Nor is knowledge of God brought in to explain the observable, thereby 'to make our comprehension infinite': manual movement, for example, is caused by 'will, – a thought of my mind; my thought only changing, the right hand rests and the left hand moves . . . explain this and make it intelligible, and then the next step will be to understand creation' (x, 19).

Locke similarly disclaims any theory of sense perception, 'the certainty of our senses, and the ideas received by them', being unqualified by our lack of understanding how they are perceived (IV, xi, 2). Material substances (man, horse, gold) cannot be classified, but only defined semiologically, by listing their qualities. However, since spirits only are active, and matter passive, it must not be supposed that the power of matter to impel ideas into our mind is active, any more than is that of fire to melt wax (II, xxi, 2): a thing 'causes' in that, to use A.C. Fraser's word, it 'occasions' an idea.[12] There are 'real original primary qualities' in things ('bulk, figure, number, situation and motion or rest'), and our ideas of these are 'resemblances', for 'their patterns really do exist in the bodies themselves'; but as for ideas produced by secondary qualities ('colors, sound, smells, tastes'), 'there is nothing like our ideas, existing in the bodies themselves' (II, viii, 23, 15): so that complex ideas ('beauty, gratitude, a man') are 'not perhaps very exact copies' of their sources in nature (II, xii, 1; IV, iv, 12). And we are able neither to 'discover any connexion betwixt these primary qualities of bodies and the sensations that are produced in us by them', nor to determine which qualities of substances 'have a *necessary* union or inconsistency one with another' (IV, iii, 13, 11). There is no guarantee that ideas in the mind resemble what is in nature, nothing to substantiate Ahab's linked analogies. The distinction between primary and secondary qualities originates with Democritus, and in Aristotle is based on that between sensations of touch, which are direct, and those others which are produced 'through a medium' of other materials: since, for Aristotle, only tangible qualities are, 'in excess . . . fatal to the living animal', touch alone is indispensable, for other senses belong only to certain species and are 'the means, not to . . . being, but to . . . well-being'.[13] But Locke distinguishes primary qualities as perceived by more than one sense – sight and touch – and emphasizes the mediation even of our knowledge of the mechanisms of survival. Thus is made possible, not only the solipsism of Berkeley and the skepticism of Hume, but also the hypothesis of a world beyond our ideas of secondary qualities, visible, perhaps, but colorless.

In the June 24, 1712 edition of *The Spectator*, for instance, Joseph Addison, referring his reader to 'Mr. Locke's *Essay*', makes the following remarkable speculation:

Things would make but a poor appearance to the eye, if we saw them only in their proper figures and motions: and what reason can we assign for their exciting in us many of those ideas which are different from anything that exists in the objects themselves, (for such are light and colours) were it not to add supernumerary ornaments to the universe, and make it more agreeable to the imagination? We are everywhere entertained with pleasing shows and apparitions, we discover imaginary glories in the heavens, and in the earth, and see some of this visionary beauty poured out upon the whole Creation; but what a rough unsightly sketch of Nature should we be entertained with, did all her coloring disappear, and the several distinctions of light and shade vanish? In short, our souls are at present delightfully lost and bewildered in a pleasing delusion, and we walk about like the enchanted hero of a romance, who sees beautiful castles, woods and meadows; and at the same time hears the warbling of birds, and the purling of streams; but upon the finishing of some secret spell, the fantastic scene breaks up, and the disconsolate knight finds himself on a barren heath, or in a solitary desert. It is not improbable that something like this may be the state of the soul after its first separation, in respect of the images it will receive from matter; though indeed the ideas of colors are so pleasing and beautiful in the imagination, that it is possible the soul will not be deprived of them, but perhaps find them excited by some other occasional cause, as they are at present by the different impressions of the subtle matter on the organ of sight. [14]

This passage anticipates the setting of 'La belle dame sans merci', though it suggests that the here-and-now is the richer state and prepares for a rupture of context, whereas the winter world devoid of floral colors or the songs of birds, in which Keats's disenchanted knight palely loiters, symbolizes the fallen state of life on earth, and thus involves a context as inevitable as the seasonal round.

Ishmael's mode of doubt and vision of such possibilities is more akin to Addison's, and is similarly derived from Locke. He devotes a chapter to the analysis of what Moby Dick is to him in terms of his color, or lack of it, opening with the observation that 'It was the whiteness of the whale that above all things appalled me', thereby wittily suggesting the submissiveness, to being 'appalled' by whiteness, that distinguishes his stance from the rigid defiance of Ahab. Ishmael despairs as usual of putting his 'mystical and well nigh ineffable' horror into 'a comprehensible form' but tells us, 'and yet, in some dim, random way, explain myself I must, else all these chapters might be nought'. He refers to 'the many natural objects' in which 'whiteness refiningly enhances beauty', lists the instances of its being the sign of authority, gladness, honor, purity and divinity, and notes that these 'accumulated associations' seem incompatible with the 'elusive something' which strikes 'panic to the soul' (MD, 163-164). In *A Philosophical Enquiry into the Origin of our Ideas of the Sublime and Beautiful* (1757), Edmund Burke distinguishes between the 'passions . . . which are conversant about the preservation of the individual', which depend upon ideas of '*pain* and *danger*' and 'are the most powerful of all passions', and those which appertain to '*society*', both sexual and more general, which are the respective causes of sublime and beautiful emotions. He makes exhaustive lists of ideas productive of each (Kant produced a similar but abbreviated work in 1764, based on the notion that the sublime — tall oaks, night, understanding, men — '*moves*' while the beautiful — flowers, day, wit, women — '*charms*'[15]), noting for instance that the conjunction of 'two ideas as opposite as can be imagined reconciled in the extremes of both' (as in the combination of bright sunlight and the black spots it leaves before our eyes) is productive of the sublime.[16] Ishmael proffers the argument, based, like Burke's *Enquiry*, on the theory of the association of ideas developed by Locke and his followers, that while whiteness, 'divorced from more kindly associations, and coupled with any object in itself', produces a surpassing terror, the combination of opposite ideas is a special case:

With reference to the Polar bear, it may possibly be urged by him who would fain go still deeper into this matter, that it is not the whiteness, separately regarded, which heightens the intolerable hideousness of that brute; for, analysed, that heightened hideousness, it might be said, only arises from the circumstance, that the irresponsible ferociousness of the creature stands invested in the fleece of celestial innocence and love; and hence, by bringing together two such opposite emotions in our minds, the Polar bear frightens us with so unnatural a contrast. But even assuming all this to be true; were it not for the whiteness, you would not have that intensified terror.

There is more to the terror of whiteness than meets the eye, for it produces 'transcendent horror', 'spiritual wonderment' and 'a silent superstitious dread': 'how is mortal man to account for it? To analyze it, would seem impossible'. Yet perhaps we can approach 'the hidden cause we seek' by examining instances in our experience of whiteness 'stripped of all direct association' with terror. Ishmael warns his reader that he requires 'imagination' where 'subtlety appeals to subtlety', and that while 'some at least of the imaginative impressions about to be presented may have been shared by most men, yet few perhaps were entirely conscious of them at the time, and therefore may not be able to recall them now': like Agee, who calls LUNPFM 'an effort in human actuality, in which the reader is no less centrally involved than the authors and those of whom they tell' (xvi), Ishmael invites us to examine the details of our impressions and of our responses to them, and so presents for our meditation a number of images of whiteness which, not manifestly terrible, terrify. He substantiates his irrational fear by noting that a colt foaled far from the prairie in Vermont, despite the impossibility of a memory of 'anything associated with the experience of former perils', fears the scent of a buffalo robe: like the colt Ishmael knows that 'somewhere' the things he fears 'must exist. Though in many of its aspects this visible world seems formed in love, the invisible spheres were formed in fright.'

Ishmael goes to sea to actualize; Aristotle's connection of the primary qualities of things with the sense of touch gives force to Ishmael's credential as a reporter ('I have had to do with whales with these visible hands'); like his namesake, he has left Burke's 'society' in order to become conversant with the passions appertaining to 'self-preservation', has left Aristotle's well-being to experience the conditions of being, and so arrives at this limit to the conscious formulation of experience:

Is it that by its indefiniteness it shadows forth the heartless voids and immensities of the universe, and thus stabs us from behind with the thought of annihilation, when beholding the white depths of the milky way? Or is it, that as in essence whiteness is not so much a color as the visible absence of color, and at the same time the concrete of all colors; is it for these reasons that there is such a dumb blankness, full of meaning, in a wide landscape of snows — a colorless, all-color of atheism from which we shrink? And when we consider that other theory of the natural philosophers, that all other earthly hues . . . are but subtile deceits, not actually inherent in substances, but only laid on from without . . . and when we proceed further, and consider that the mystical cosmetic which produces every one of her hues, the great principle of light, for ever remains white or colorless in itself, and if operating without medium upon matter, would touch all objects, even tulips and roses, with its own blank tinge — pondering all this, the palsied universe lies before us a leper; and like wilful travellers in Lapland, who refuse to wear colored and coloring glasses upon their eyes, so the wretched infidel gazes himself blind at the monumental white shroud that wraps all the prospect around him. And of all these things the Albino whale was the symbol. Wonder ye then at the fiery hunt? (MD, 164-170)

The dumb blankness which is the basis of meaning is the conjectured substance which lies past the outermost boundary of experimental knowledge. It is treated as such by Wittgenstein in the *Tractatus*, for whom, 'In a manner of speaking, objects are colorless' (2.0232): since 'Death is not an event of life' (64311), 'death' is a meaningless word, marking a boundary past which experience cannot penetrate. Burroughs, who slightly misquotes the *Tractatus* in *Naked Lunch* − ' "If a proposition is NOT NECESSARY it is MEANINGLESS and approaching MEANING ZERO" '[17] − also quotes Ishmael in describing the limits of the knowable: 'Writers talk about the sweet-sick smell of death whereas any junky can tell you that death has no smell . . . at the same time a smell that shuts off breath and stops blood . . . colorless nosmell of death' (NL, 221). The Vigilante, a con man/addict who suddenly assumes the costume and mannerisms of a western sheriff, goes berserk in Lincoln Park and 'hangs three fags before the fuzz nail him', testifies at his trial, 'I was standing outside myself trying to stop those hangings with ghost fingers. . . . I am a ghost wanting what every ghost wants − a body − after the Long Time moving through odorless alleys of space where no life is only the colorless no-smell of death" '. This bare physical world lying beyond the secondary qualities perceived by the mind − 'The title means exactly what the words say: NAKED Lunch − a frozen moment when everyone sees what is on the end of every fork' (NL, 3, 8, v) − is that envisioned by Addison and Ishmael; and the Vigilante is the schizophrenic heir to Ahab, whose 'tormented spirit, when what seemed Ahab rushed from his room, was for the time but a vacated thing, a formless somnambulistic being, a ray of living light, to be sure, but without an object to color, and therefore a blankness in itself" (MD, 175). The world of the afterlife is apparently deadly dull: in the descriptive work that follows the pattern of *Moby-Dick*, the foremost fact about the present world of the senses is that (to those who are not, like the Vigilante, frustrated by their impermeability) it is endlessly, if voyeuristically, interesting: the experience formulated in LUN-PFM, says Agee, 'is worth your knowing what you can of. . . as the small part it is of the human experience in general' (246). Godard has expressed the lingering wish 'to make a movie about a wall. If you really look at a wall, you wind up seeing things in it'.[18]

Locke's empiricism suspends the question whether words or things come first: while he attributes primary qualities to the physical world and regards perception as consequence or response, he is forced to a tentative openness to either possibility, since to posit that things are prior to words is to claim, with the realists, some unambiguous knowledge of what things are. Words can form two kinds of propositons: that concerning particulars, which is empirically verifiable and thus 'the consequence of the existence of things'; and that which shows 'the agreement or disagreement of *our abstract ideas*, and their dependence on one another', consisting of '*aeternae veritates*', not because 'eternal' or 'antecedent to the understanding', but because true whenever the ideas are present from which they are abstracted (IV, xi, 13-14). It is similarly the position of the *Tractatus* that the propositions of logic are *a priori* true because they are tautological, 'say nothing' (6.1, 6.11). Since, as Locke says, there is no necessary connection among five qualities of any object, since the presence of any four does not guarantee the fifth, logic tells us nothing certain about experience; or, as Wittgenstein puts it, 'It is an hypothesis that the sun will rise tomorrow; amd this means that we do not *know* whether it will rise' (6.36311): certain knowledge is only of experience. Thinking, for Locke, is formulating propositions with ideas; truth is a matter of exhibited agreement or disagreement, and is either 'nominal' or 'verbal' ('all centaurs are animals'), or 'real', expressing an arrangement of ideas as exhibited in nature. Propositions can be either be mental or verbal; but since thinking is usually verbal, especially when words represent complex ideas, we tend to use uncritically such words as '*man, vitriol, fortitude, glory*' without reflecting on their precise meanings (IV, v, 1-7). This is the basis of Locke's concern with language, and it recurs in Melville as a critique of the forms which limit the range of Pierre's consciousness, confound the victims of the Confidence Man and define our ideas of whales, so that *Moby-Dick* opens with an etymology of the word; and in the glossaries, footnotes and parenthetical notations on the language and slang generic to cotton farmers and drug addicts in LUNPFM and *Naked Lunch*.

Locke regards words as extremely liable to 'impose' upon and cloud our understandings. Moreover, words are merely arbitrary 'marks', 'corporeal signs and particular sounds', and so inevitably fall short of perfect or 'immediate communication', no matter how well considered (IV, iv, 17; II, xxiii, 36; III, ii, 5–8).

There are also real and nominal essences in things; the former are unknowable and hypothetical, the latter dependent upon the verbal ordering of ideas: essence, as for Hobbes and for Burroughs, is purely a matter of language, for an individual might change color and shape, lose reason and memory, and would still miss nothing essential unless 'to be counted of the sort *man*, and to have the name *man* given it' (III, vi, 4). General terms, each of which names a genus of similar things, are indispensable but potentially confusing, for an idea becomes general by being abstracted from particular circumstances, as 'man' is from 'Peter and Paul', a process which leads to such 'universal terms' as 'substance', 'being', 'thing' (III, iii, 1-6, 9). Thus when he decides, having considered the arguments of Linnaeus that the whale is a mammal, to define it with Jonah as a fish, Ishmael likewise draws attention to the arbitrary and verbal nature of species; his definition of the whale as '*a spouting fish with a horizontal tail . . .* is the result of expanded meditation' on the characteristics thereby comprehended and involves the inclusion of 'all the smaller, spouting, and horizontal tailed fish' in his classification, which is subdivided among folio, duodecimo and octavo whales, each subspecies being described at length within the limits of Ishmael's experience (MD, 118-120). Locke too rejects as a false question 'Whether a *bat* be a *bird* or no': the proper way of defining, he says, is not by '*genus* and *differentia* ', which is to derive the thing from its essential name, and to attribute to language a consistency it lacks, but by 'enumerating those simple ideas that are combined in the term defined' (III, xi, 7; iii, 10).

While a simple idea can no more be defined than light can be described to a blind man, its name gives the least verbal difficulty because its reference is readily agreed upon; so with simple modes ('seven', 'triangle'); but by the names of mixed modes, 'such as for the most part are moral words', it is difficult, not only to communicate the extremely complex ideas to which they refer, but to repeatedly mean the same thing oneself. Because such ideas '*want standards in nature*' to guide their formation, there is endless wrangling over 'the interpretation of laws, whether divine or human' (III, iv, 6-10). Ishmael too avers the history of wrangling over the two superbly simple and arbitrary laws touching the 'Fast Fish', which 'belongs to the party fast to it', and the 'Loose Fish', 'fair game for anybody who can soonest catch it', and points out that they 'will, on reflection, be found the fundamentals of all human jurisprudence' (MD, 331-333). It is the very fact, however, that ideas of material substances are supposed to have precise standards in nature that confuses *their* names, which must always be 'inadequate' because the real essence and 'precise number of properties' of any substance is unknowable (II, ix, 11, 20; vi, 19, 44, 47). Again, neither does Ishmael hope to comprehend all the properties of whales in his definition and cetological system. And just as Locke considers an abuse of words, '*the taking them for things*', and so giving credence to such sophistic 'gibberish' as '*substantial forms, vegetative souls, abhorrence of a vacuum*', etc. (III, x, 14), Ishmael omits from his list of whales which have yet to be examined and incorporated into his system those names which he 'can hardly help suspecting . . . for mere sounds, full of Leviathanism, but signifying nothing' (MD, 127-128).

The whole treatment of words in the third book of the *Essay* is designed 'to make men reflect on their own use of language', to bring the reader to 'enter into his own thoughts and observe nicely the several postures of his mind in discoursing' (III, v, 16; vii, 3): if the understanding is 'tied down to the dull and narrow information of the senses' and does not even comprehend 'the extent of our own ideas', it can attain to self-consciousness only indirectly, by a critical process of negation or 'mere wary survey' of words and ideas, can know only what it is not (IV, iii, 5-6; III,v,9). Metaphor and analogy, the only direct avenues to such knowledge, are invalid, for 'all the artificial and figurative application of words eloquence hath invented, are for nothing else but to insinuate wrong ideas, move the passions, and thereby mislead the judgement' (III, x, 34); such is the effect of Ahab's eloquence on Starbuck — ' "But he drilled deep down, and blasted all my reason out of me!" ' — who is challenged, when he does oppose Ahab's will, ' " Dost thou then so much as dare to critically think of me? " ' (MD, 148, 394).

Locke ends the *Essay* by defining as the third branch of knowledge, after natural philosophy and ethics,

Σημειωτικη, or the *doctrine of signs*; the most usual whereof being words, it is aptly enough termed also Λογικη, *Logic*: the business whereof is to consider the nature of signs, the mind makes use of for the understanding of things, or conveying its knowledge to others. For, since the things the mind contemplates are none of them, besides itself, present to the understanding, it is necessary that something else, as a sign or representation of the thing it considers, should be present to it: and these are ideas . . . . The consideration, then, of *ideas* and *words* as the great instruments of knowledge, makes no despicable part of their contemplation who would take a view of human knowledge in the whole extent of it. And perhaps if they were distinctly weighed, and duly considered, they would afford us another sort of logic and critic, than what we have been hitherto acquainted with. (IV, xxi, 4)

Thus, while the mind is passive before experience, selection and recall is carried on by the '*internal sense*' of reflection, whereby we perceive 'the operations of our own mind within us', a kind of 'secondary perception', though amenable to no metalinguistic description, which can be directed by the will (II, i, 4; x, 7). But the will is in no sense free, is determined by the mind, which is motivated only by its 'satisfaction' or 'uneasiness' with a present 'state or action': will is a 'power', not an 'agent' (II, xxi, 19-29). As Wittgenstein puts it, 'I can't will willing . . . .'"Willing"is not the name of an action; and so not the name of a voluntary action either' (PI, 613). Morality may, for Locke, be logically demonstrable (III, xi, 16), but it is linked, not to a transcendent order, but, like material substance, to the survival imperative, for good and evil exist only in the context of pleasure and pain (II, xx, ii). All that can finally be said about the in-itself inconceivable faculty of attention is that it is guided and imposed upon by 'settled habit', which it opposes by attending to the manner of its operation: 'Habits, especially such as are begun very early, come at last to produce actions in us, which often escape our observation' (II, ix, 9-10). Berkeley and Hume take up the critique of habitual association begun in Locke's *Essay* (II, xxxiii, 18), likewise emphasizing the dependence of self-preservation on habits of expectation; but Berkeley argues that, in the absence of material substance, visible and tangible ideas are arbitrarily related, so that visible fire is not the cause of tangible pain, but a forewarning sign instituted by God for our benefit; and Hume reduces mental activity to three principles of association – resemblance, spacial or temporal contiguity, and cause or effect — which constitute 'a general habit whereby we always transfer the known to the unknown and conceive the latter to resemble the former',[19] an operation entirely the result of custom and without the predictive force of logical necessity.

WITTGENSTEIN'S *TRACTATUS*: CODE AND CONTENT

A major source of the emphasis on language by Wittgenstein and Richards is American Pragmatism: according to Charles Sanders Peirce, 'the word or sign a man uses *is* the man himself . . . . Thus my language is the sum total of myself; for the man is the thought.'[20] In *The Principles of Psychology*, William James cites a description by one Mr. Ballard, born a deaf-mute, of his thoughts before learning to speak or write[21]: Wittgenstein comments, 'Are you sure — one would like to ask — that this is the correct translation of your wordless thoughts into words? . . . The words in which I express my memory are my memory reaction' (PI 342-43). However, the pragmatists are committed to Darwin's theory of evolution, conceive of evolution as the effect of and response to prior things, a movement, as Peirce says, from 'indeterminacy' or 'chance' to 'a complete reign of law': 'all things have a tendency to take habits'; and mind, a condition of matter marked by the 'habit of taking and laying aside habits', is, 'by the principle of continuity', the result of matter.[22] Pragmatism is a form of realism, holding that things come before words, that conceptual universals have validity as steps in evolutionary development; it thereby gives thought the unambiguous context of an empirically unverifiable temporal continuum. In John Dewey's terms, the 'spatial' phase of 'judgment', which is the 'description' of coexistent conditions, is not in itself complete until seen in the context of 'narration', developing in time toward a more complete understanding.[23] Dewey links his psychology with John B. Watson's Behaviorism[24]; and in fact, Watson was Dewey's student in philosophy, and derives from him the opinion that thought is a subvocal, laryngeal activity. Of course, B.F. Skinner maintains the argument that understanding is explicable in terms of Darwin's 'process of selection', 'the effects of which can be formulated in "necessary laws" '.[25]

Wittgenstein rejects the context of evolution in the *Tractatus Logico-Philosophicus* — 'Darwin's theory has no more to do with philosophy than any other hypothesis in natural science' (4.1122) — and later elaborates: 'Did anyone see this [evolutionary] process happening? No. Has anyone seen it happening now? No. The evidence of breeding is just a drop in the bucket. But there were thousands of books in which this was said to be *the* obvious solution. People were *certain* on grounds that were extremely thin. . . . This shows how you can be persuaded of a certain thing. In the end, you forget entirely every question of verification, you are just sure it must have been like that.' (His objection to swallowing Freud whole is related: 'Freud asks "Are you asking me to believe that there is anything which happens without a cause?" ')[26] Moreover, Wittgenstein is later concerned to answer the charge that, in dispensing with the '*grammatical* fiction' of subjective 'inner process', he is ' "a behaviourist in disguise" ':

We talk of processes and states and leave their nature undecided. Sometime perhaps we shall know more about them — we think. But that is just what commits us to a particular way of looking at the matter. For we have a definite concept of what it means to learn to know a process better. (The decisive movement in the conjuring trick has been made, and it was the very one that we thought quite innocent.) — And now the analogy which was to make us understand our thoughts falls to pieces. So we have to deny the yet uncomprehended process in the yet unexplored medium. And now it looks as if we had denied mental processes. And naturally we don't want to deny them.(P1, 307-308)

Whereas, for the empiricists, understanding can neither transcend nor be identified with the facts of experience, the pragmatists sort it onto the linear foundation of continuous time, resolve description in narration, and project the definitive experimental findings into a hypothetical future. However, the narrators of *Moby-Dick*, LUNPFM and *Naked Lunch* are all fragmented, discontinuous personalities, devices at best, transparent yet displaying only themselves, and offering an unresolved series of sometimes contradictory descriptions. Evolution in time is one of the grids which Agee superimposes on his experience of depression Alabama, in terms both of an explanatory myth of the past and of hopes for the future; but it is unable to mitigate what he calls 'the cruel radiance of what is'. The empirical status of the evolution myth might best be indicated by its treatment in Stanley

Kubrick's *2001*, which holds a variety of grids before our eyes, and which begins as a man in an ape costume throws a bone he has just learned to use as a weapon into the air, whereupon it becomes, in the piece of horizontal – that is, narrative – montage that covers the longest time gap in film history, a futuristic space craft: a simple juxtaposition is all that is required, so automatically do we understand. The question of the nature of understanding is posed by the presence of HAL, the computer, who perhaps has 'feelings', and who attempts to affirm his analog (continuous) nature by taking over the expedition for his own purpose; as he is being dismantled, he sings in a slowing and now obviously mechanical fashion, 'Daisy, Daisy, give me your answer do': like crazy Ahab, who also takes over an expedition for his own purpose, to affirm *his* analog (continuous) nature, to assert himself as a real entity, HAL finds himself finally in a precariously digital relation to Daisy, who can only give one of two answers. Can the complex symbolism of the Pequod subdue, make amenable to its terms, the brutal threat to symmetry, and thus to signification, embodied in Moby Dick? No.

It is Dewey's objection to ' "Logical positivism" ' – properly the name of a movement that co-opted and emphasized some aspects of Wittgenstein's *Tractatus* – that it 'does not get beyond short-span, relatively isolated, temporal sequences and spatial co-existences'.[27] Whereas Dewey bases 'implication' or 'ratiocination' – the arrangement of factual evidence by means of symbols or propositions into a meaningful 'ordered whole' for empirical testing – on an 'inference' constituted by the breadth of experience, holds that when suggestions ' "pop into our heads" ' they are 'not logical' but the 'primary stuff of logical ideas',[28] logic is for Wittgenstein 'prior to every experience – that something *is so*' – that is, to description, 'to the question "How?", not prior to the question "What?" ' ' (5.552). Thus, to know an object is to know its possible contexts (2.0123). Logic contains thought and description, for we cannot think illogical thoughts, imagine an illogical world (3,3.031, 5.4731). Thought is propositional (4); and language, which 'disguises thought' so 'that it is impossible to infer the form of the thought beneath it' (4.002), is 'the totality of propositions' (4.001). Experience, however, is never *a priori*, could always 'be other than it is' (5.634). Reality is defined digitally as 'the existence and nonexistence of a state of affairs'

(2.06) described in a proposition, from which it is impossible to infer the truth or falsehood of any other state of affairs (2.062); for there is posited no such causal nexus or temporal continuum as validates pragmatic inference: 'Superstition', in fact, 'is nothing but belief in the causal nexus' (5.1361). Just as Locke distinguishes between verbal and real truth, Wittgenstein does so between understanding a proposition (knowing 'what is the case if it is true' [4.024]) and knowing whether it *is* true. Like the Behaviorists, he dispenses with Locke's psychologism, his account of verbal meaning in terms of mental process; but he maintains Locke's subjectivism: if there is 'no such thing as the subject that thinks or entertains ideas' (5.631), the world is nevertheless ' "my world" ' (5.641), the subject 'a limit of the world', an eye which cannot be seen, is not reflected in the world (5.631, 5.633). Likewise in LUNPFM and in Godard's films, nothing beyond the immediate arrangement of signs can be deduced which 'reads' them: for Godard, 'the camera that filmed itself in the mirror would make the ultimate movie'[29] — one which exhibited the mechanics of its composition and canceled the notion of the subjective 'watcher' — and Agee describes just such a shot in his scenario, 'The house'.[30] *2001* includes long takes of Keir Dullea's face, covered with patterns of colored light reflected by his instrument panel, staring into our faces, which stare back covered with the same colored patterns — shots which invite us to distinguish ourselves from our image reflection.

For Wittgenstein, the metaphysical is the meaningless; all philosophy is a 'critique of language' (4.0031), and offers no metalinguistic avenue of knowledge (though he later criticizes the *Tractatus* for trying to isolate the ideal form of language). Logic is the condition of experience, and can neither itself be experienced (5.552), nor admit extralogical knowledge of 'substance', for 'Propositions can only say *how* things are, not *what* they are' (3.221): logic is the limit of 'empirical reality' (5.5561). That 'world', 'self', 'life' and 'language' are the same and cannot be abstracted from one another (5.5563, 5.621), elucidates the search for 'life' undertaken by Melville, Agee and Godard; and the expression, '*The limits of my language* mean the limits of my world' (5.6), is the logical formulation of 'Call me Ishmael'.

The one-to-one relationship between name and thing proposed in the *Tractatus* (3.203) is criticized both by Richards and by the later Wittgenstein, who distinguishes between words and names, and between the bearer of a name and its meaning, which is usually its use and is only 'sometimes explained by pointing to its bearer' (P1, 40-45). But in both phases, Wittgenstein emphasizes context and configuration: a propositional sign might be either verbal or a composition of 'spatial objects (even as tables, chairs, and books)', so that 'the spatial arrangement of these things will express the sense of the proposition' (3.1431): one might think of the description in *Mardi* of the disarranged furniture of an abandoned ship, or of Jason Compson, Agee, Philip Marlowe and Hitchcock's camera as each registers the arrangement of objects in a deserted room. ' "The word" ', says the 'vicious, fruity old Saint' in *Naked Lunch* 'cannot be expressed direct . . . . It can perhaps be indicated by mosaic of juxtaposition like articles abandoned in a hotel drawer, defined by negation and absence' (NL, 116).

Substance, for Wittgenstein, is 'what subsists independently of what is the case' (2.024), and confirms or denies propositions: as in Locke's *Essay*, substance is distinguished from configuration (2.0271), and corresponds also to the substratum of subjective understanding, for substance is both 'form and content' (2.025). Form is constituted or determined by objects, and is what language has in common with the world (2.022, 4.094) – the possibility of structure, of an object's occurrence in states of affairs; the logical form of reality is displayed in, rather than represented by, propositions, and is perhaps best thought of as the rule of translation which governs the various 'languages' in which a piece of music can be displayed: gramophone record, musical idea, written notes, sound waves (4.014-4.0141). Content, on the other hand is that which is encoded by all these forms – the theme in music, the thinking or understanding of a proposition (3.1): 'A proposition contains the form, but not the content, of its sense' (3.13). Content is both material substance and the understanding of its forms, just as 'solipsism, when its implications are followed out strictly, coincides with pure realism. The self of solipsism shrinks to a point without extension, and there remains the reality co-ordinated with it' (5.64). Substance determines forms, but only configuration produces material properties: as in Ishmael's white world, objects may be thought of as 'colorless' (2.0232). Ishmael's mystical, well nigh ineffable horror is a precisely appropriate consideration here, for what is mystical for Wittgenstein is 'not *how* things are in the world . . . but *that* it exists', and that it is felt 'as a limited whole', as bounded by subjectivity (6.44, 6.45). The metaphysical cannot be spoken about, but makes itself manifest. Ethical and aesthetic value are likewise transcendental (as in Hume: 'Beauty, whether moral or material, is felt more properly than perceived', is not a 'fact' [*Inquiry*, 173]). It is the codification and limitation of this transcendent realm in language which informs Agee's suspicion that 'the "sense of beauty," like nearly everything else, is a class privilege. I am sure in any case that its "terms" differ by class, and that the "sense" is limited and inarticulate in the white tenant class almost beyond hope of description' (LUNPFM, 314).

RICHARDS AND AGEE: REPORTING THE ACTUAL

I.A. Richards regards judgments of beauty as emotive rather than descriptive statements, rejects the notion of continuity between the physical world and subjective consciousness and aims at a nominalistic reform of unclear and imprecise terms, such as the 'real vagues' and hypostatic judgments of Peirce and Dewey. (Likewise Wittgenstein: 'Everything that can be thought at all can be thought clearly' – 4.116.) Like Peirce, Richards employs a triadic model of the sign; like James, he conceives of thoughts or ideas as individual pointings to or references. He has recently listed James as an early influence and de-emphasized Wittgenstein[31], but it is worth noting that C.K. Ogden, co-author with Richards of *The Foundations of Aesthetics* and *The Meaning of Meaning*, and the general editor of the first English version of the *Tractatus*, is regarded by G.H. von Wright as having been 'active' in the book's translation, though to what degree is not certain.[32] According to W.H.N. Hotopf, however, 'it is highly unlikely that Ogden and Richards derived their emotive/referential distinction from either Russel or Wittgenstein. Any influence is more likely to have been the other way round.'[33] While Richards' New Critical critics have not been unanimous, they have generally divided his career at *Coleridge on Imagination*, applying to the first segment the terms 'positivist' and 'behaviorist' in a loosely conceived, occasionally epithetical fashion.[34]

In *The Foundations of Aesthetics* Richards, Ogden and James Wood deny that there is any essential condition for an aesthetic experience and suggest that a description of such an emotion would include the psychological history of the subject and the 'special momentary setting' of his 'impulses and instincts', and a 'physico-physiological account of the work of art as a stimulus', with its 'sensory effect' upon the consequent aroused 'impulses' in the subject. They list and discuss sixteen uses of the word 'beauty,' and find most satisfactory the Confucian notion of synaesthesis, involving the balance of systems of impulses which correspond, in the early stages of systematization, to emotions: the artist selects and arranges the 'elements' of experience according to 'the play of impulses which controls his activity at the moment', with the possible result 'that the same group of impulses is aroused in the spectator', this being 'the only way unless by telepathy, of coming into contact with other minds than our own'. It is only when 'emotion assumes a more general character' and 'attitude has become impersonal', when such adjustment has been found 'as will preserve free play to every impulse, with entire avoidance of frustration', that beauty is experienced, the 'equilibrium' of which is distinguished from 'passivity, inertia, overstimulation or conflict', as well as 'Nirvana, Ecstasy, Sublimation or At-oneness with Nature'. The term 'synaesthesis' includes 'both equilibrium and harmony', the former entailing 'no tendency to action', the latter a response rather to the ' "stimulative" ' than to the ' "beautiful" '. The increase in self-realization, proportionate to the involvement of impulses in responding to beauty, is self-explanatory if, 'as is sometimes alleged, we are the whole complex of our impulses': interest becomes free 'to take any direction we choose', and becoming 'more fully ourselves' is simultaneously becoming 'differentiated or isolated from the things around us'. The arrangement of the elements of experience records the interest of the artist, and of the spectator, by involving their plays of impulses, and does not seek resolution in an objective work or formulation, but transforms the ambiguity of undirected interest into a poised and available interest. This process of 'individualisation', the value of which is the involvement of 'all our faculties' and the fullest possible realization of the 'richness and complexity of our environment' [35], is worth detailing because it appears to adumbrate the description of the experience of actuality, so central in LUNPFM:

The dead oak and pine, the ground, the dew, the air, the whole realm of what our bodies lay in and our minds in silence wandered, walked in, swam in, watched upon, was delicately fragrant as a paradise, and, like all that is best, was loose, light, casual, totally *actual*. There was, by our minds, our memories, our thoughts and feelings, some combination, some generalization, some art, and science; but none of the closekneed priggishness of science, and none of the formalism and straining and lily-gilding of art. All the length of the body and all its parts and functions, were participating, and were being realized and rewarded, inseparable from the mind, identical with it: and all, everything, that the mind touched, was actuality, and all, everything, that the mind touched turned immediately, yet without in the least losing the quality of its total individuality, into joy and truth, or rather, revealed of its self, truth, which in its very nature was joy, which must be the end of art, of investigation, and of all anyhow human existence.
This situation is possible at any junction of time, space and consciousness: and just as (at least so far as we can know and can be concerned) it is our consciousness alone, in the end, that we have to thank for joy, so too it is our consciousness alone that is defective when we fall short of it. It is curious, and unfortunate, that we find this luck so rarely; that it is so almost purely a matter of chance: yet that, as matters are, becomes inextricably a part of the whole texture of the pleasure: at such time we have knowledge that we are witnessing, taking part in, being, a phenomenon analogous to that shrewd complex of the equations of infinite chance which became, on this early earth, out of lifelessness, life (LUNPFM, 225).

The concern with the influence of language that had grown in association with the intellectual reaction to the propoganda power demonstrated by the press in World War I is exhibited both in the *Tractatus* and in *The Meaning of Meaning*: but in the latter book, Ogden and Richards reject Wittgenstein's notion of a logical form shared by thought and reality, and object to the simplicity of his model. While they regard even the simplest reference, or thought, as either true or false, they also insist upon Berkeley's distinction between emotive or rhetorical language and its use to symbolize a reference to a 'state of affairs'; and they contrast their work with Saussure's semiology, which pretends to define ' "things and not words" ', fixes meanings within the context of a fictitious '*langue*', invents 'verbal entities outside the range of possible investigation' and rejects ' "symbol" ' as a term for 'linguistic sign' because it regards symbols as never ' "quite arbitrary" ' (MM, v, 5-6). Symbols, say Ogden and Richards, both direct and organize thoughts, or references, and 'record events and communicate facts' or referents ('referent', though they also

approve 'event', is preferable to 'thing' or 'object' because it does
not imply 'material substances' or entities). Symbol and thought
are causally related, as are thought and referent; symbol and referent are arbitrarily related and not, as the 'superstition' has it,
metaphysically connected by 'meaning' (9 - 15). Despite the
fact that causality is an obvious 'phantom', causal terms are used
for their 'expository convenience' and because a causal hypothesis
renders meaning 'a matter open to experimental methods' (51,
55, 73). But in their account of learning, the acquisition of habits
of perception and behavior (recurrent psychological contexts or
sets of events) which proceeds according to Hume's principles of
association, Ogden and Richards reduce 'causation to correlation',
speak of our being contextually 'directed', rather than caused, to
expect a flame when a match is struck, to respond to the dinner
bell (50-65, 127). Their chief concern is to combat our programming by hypnotic rhetoric and 'word-magic', a relic of primitive
attempts to control the environment which remains universal in
childhood, and is exemplified by Plato's idealism, Hegel's dialectic,
Whitman's celebration of the power of language and political
and commercial advertising (24, 29-31, 40).

All thinking is interpreting signs; as for Locke and Wittgenstein,
there is both verbal (because a false proposition has referents)
and real truth. Sense impressions are neural occurrences 'as to
which at present neurologists go no further than to assert that
they occur': this is not materialism, a form of metaphysics, but
simply 'the most plausible systematic account of "knowing"
that can be given'. (In *Principles of Literary Criticism*, the mind is
denominated a 'fiction', and the neurological account of mentation regarded as 'only a degree less ficticious than one in terms of
spiritual happenings'.[37]) We are, as with Locke and Wittgenstein,
unable to 'discover the *what* of referents', are limited to their
'*how*'; and like them, Ogden and Richards propose a 'critical scrutiny of symbolic procedure' to combat 'the set of confusions
known as metaphysics', emphasize definition as the means to
understanding and deny that communication takes place (MM, 80-
86, 208, 222; see also PI, 363). Language is not a signaling system
but an instrument for sorting − for thinking: in *Principles of
Literary Criticism*, Richards expands the argument that 'communication defined as a strict transference of or participation in identical experiences does not occur' (176-177). Moreover, Ogden and

Richards declare, in their handling of the interpretation of sense data, a renewed attention to the 'theory of primary and secondary qualities, which seemed to have been disposed of by Berkeley's arguments'(MM, 86). Their context theory of meaning, which stipulates that the reference of a symbol depends on its actual use, rather than on good usage or on the intentions of speaker or interpreter, is commensurate with the context theory of value elaborated by Richards in subsequent works, which disparages myths of contemplative and aesthetic attitudes and the ranking of poets or techniques, in favor of an account of the organization of the critic's impulses 'for freedom and fulness of life' (PLC, 101, 132), the breakdown of inappropriate habits of response; for 'the idle hours of most of our lives are filled with reveries that are simply bad private poetry'.[38] Man is 'not primarily an intelligence' but 'a system of interests' which directs intelligence,[39] and for which is sought the mobilized availability that is celebrated as actuality in LUNPFM.

Nor is consciousness a 'unique' relation to a proposition, or universal, or judgment (MM, 48-49). (Agee speaks of our tendency to overvalue life and consciousness as 'making a virtue of a necessity . . . being provincial . . . pleading a local cause' [LUNPFM, 227]). Sign situations mediate all perception; all experience is mental; while exclusive subjectivism is charged with leading to the '*impasse* of solipsism', and the need for behavioral observation stressed, Watson's invalidation of psychological process and introspection is rejected (MM, 18-23). That Richards' utilitarian, byproduct account of consciousness is not behaviorism is indicated in his review of Watson's *Behaviorism*: while Richards finds valuable the kind of psychological research that is strictly confined to the observable, he denies that the meaninglessness of 'consciousness', its substitution for the more ancient 'soul', follows necessarily 'from its nonobservable nature. We may not observe consciousness, but we have it or are it (in some yet undetermined sense), and in fact many of our observations of other things require it'; he agrees that stimulus-response models can account for all human behavior, that a conditioned reflex can be developed in man by only one stimulus-response occurrence, that the notion of 'instincts' is a mystification of structural contingencies upon response exhibited equally by infants and boomerangs, and that intelligent conditioning might do much to eradicate fear;

but he denies that observation can provide a complete account, and that introspection is simply invalid.[40] And as of his article, 'Structure and communication' (1965), wherein both Skinner's substitution of 'Behavior for Meaning' and Noam Chomsky's opposite method (which 'depends upon mental procedures about which as yet almost nothing whatever is known, upon innumerable "acts of immediate perception", acts of intellectual vision about which we can as yet say little more than that they are complex and various comparisons of structure and that all the rest of our mental procedure turns on them') are found insufficient,[41] Richards has not altered that view. That, coupled with his rejection in the *Principles* of the position of the 'hard-headed positivist' who 'at best suffers from an insufficient material for the development of his attitudes' (PLC, 282), seems adequate refutation of the labels 'positivist' and 'behaviorist' so often applied: Richards' arguments are those of an empiricist.

In *Practical Criticism*, he employs the experimental method 'to introduce a new kind of documentation' of the state of culture (PC, 3, 6), and elaborates the distinction between science and 'pseudostatement' set up in *Science and Poetry* along Matthew Arnold's lines: poetry is a salutary 'device' for preventing the interference of emotional beliefs with 'the logical context of our ideas', a function unhappily termed by Coleridge ' "a willing suspension of disbelief" ', since in successful poetry it is neither conscious nor arbitrary (PC, 258-261). Training in multiple definition, the careful analysis of word use, might raise criticism to the condition of a science, for when speech moves away from the 'realm of things which can be counted, weighed and measured, or pointed to, or actually seen with the eyes or touched by the fingers', precision of reference is lost (PC, 310-323).

On his way back to Cambridge from a lectureship at Tsing Hua University in Peking, according to Robert Fitzgerald,[42] Richards continued this experimental mode of teaching in a half-course in 'Practical Criticism', given with one in 'Contemporary English Literature (1890 to the Present Time)', during the second term of the 1930-1931 academic year at Harvard. James Agee attended both courses, and in December 1931 wrote Father J.H. Flye:

But altogether the most important thing in that spring was I.A. Richards, a visiting professor from Cambridge. It's perfectly impossible for me to define anything about him or about what he taught – but it was a matter of getting frequent and infinite vistas of perfection in beauty, strength, symmetry, greatness – and the reasons for them, in poetry and in living. He's a sort of Hamlet and some Dostoevsky character, with their frustration of madness cleared away, and a perfect centre left that understands evil and death and pain, and values them, without torment or perplexity. This sounds extravagant – well, his power over people was extravagant, and almost unlimited. Everyone who knew him was left in a clear, tingling daze, at the beginning of the summer. It stayed, and grew, all summer. [43]

A less 'extravagant' and more thoroughgoing indication of the extent of Richards' influence is the appearance in the May 31 issue of *The Harvard Advocate* of a story by Agee, "They that sow in sorrow shall weep", the course of which is interrupted when the narrator makes the following comment on perception and the instability of viewpoint:

The mind is rarely audience to experience in perfection; rarely is it granted the joy of emotions and realities which, first reduced to their essential qualities, are then so juxtaposed in harmony and discord, in sharp accentuation and fluent change, in thematic statement, development, restatement and re-capitulation, as to achieve in progress a continuous, and in consummation, an ultimate beauty. As a rule, experience is broken upon innumerable sharp irrelevancies; emotion and reality, obscurely fused and inexplicably tarnished, are irreducible; their rhythms are so subtly involved, so misgoverned by chance, as to be beyond analysis; and the living mind, that must endure and take part, is soon fugitive before, or else, however brave, falls to pieces beneath this broad unbeautiful pour of chaos.

The experience referred to is objective; the same difficulties hold in the case of subjective experience. The true sum of experience is, as a rule, an inconceivably complex interpenetration of subjective and objective experience. And the true sum and whole of experience is doubly chaotic.

It is therefore fortunate that most minds are constructed to float. However rigorous the weave of currents, however huge the plunge of waves, they are forever near the surface. And it is fortunate, God knows, that minds which anatomize experience are given the mercy of a million moods; these complement and relieve one another, and those which are not wholly proof against pain at least shift the weight of experience to a fresh area of the mind.

The interpenetration of contexts, the distinction, as in *The Meaning of Meaning*, between close and full, and cognitively distant and schematic experience, the inevitable discontinuity of narrative, which functions as analysis, or anatomy, the passivity of the mind before an unknowable 'pour' of experience, the notions of aesthetic experience as an achieved balance and of the artist's activity as 'selection and arrangement . . . due to the direction and accentuation of his interest' (FA, 74) – Agee's narrator goes on to comment that 'certain moods, if kept as clear as possible of deflecting intellect, reflect a selection and arrangement of experience which approaches beauty' (CSP, 93-94) – are all clear links with Richards' theory, and suggest the basis of an epistemological stance.

During that spring, according to Fitzgerald, 'Jim held the English Poetic Tradition and the American Scene in a kind of equilibrium under the spell of Richards'[44]; toward the end of a summer during which, Agee writes Flye, 'much more than I realized, these things Richards had done were fermenting', Richards told Agee that he thought the latter's poetry 'good – maybe more than good' (LFF, 54); and in his poem "Dedication" (1934), Agee includes 'Ivor Armstrong Richards' in his list of truth-tellers.[45] By 'truth' Fitzgerald suggests that Agee meant 'correspondence between what is said and what is the case – but what is the case at the utmost reach of consciousness ', and he portrays Agee as inspired by the techniques of documentary film and sociological study, responding as an artist (the 'intent of art', says Fitzgerald, 'is to make, not to state things') to 'this challenge to perceive in full and to present immaculately what was the case'. By the writing of 'Dedication' Agee was applying the 'intellect that Richards had altered' to journalism, a trade 'ostensibly and unusually in good faith concerned with what was the case', though the epistemological difficulties seem to have been Agee's preoccupation:

What was: the case in some degree proceeded from the observer. Theoretical in abstract thought for centuries, this cat seemed now to have come out of the bag to bewitch all knowledge in practice: knowledge of microcosmic entities, of personal experience, of human society. Literary art had had to reckon with it. To take an elementary example, Richards would put three x's on a blackboard disposed thus . . to represent a poem, referent and reader, suggesting that a complete account of the poem could no more exclude one x than another, nor the relationship between them. Nor were the x's stable, but variable. *Veritas* had become tragically complicated. The naive practices of journalism might continue, as they had to, but their motives and achievements, like all others, appeared now suspect to Freudian and Marxian and semanticist alike; and of what these men believed they understood James Agee was (or proposed to make himself) also aware.[46]

The coverage of any event or condition is unalterably mediated and defined by the perception of it, so that, as in *Moby-Dick*,

LUNPFM and *Naked Lunch*, the reporter's perceptions (Burroughs' persona is frequently 'your reporter') are the event, and subjective distortion the subject of the report. A report can only be substantiated by experience, by having thoughts which actually point or refer to things, whatever their context in the report; 'The source of all our attitudes', Richards says 'should be in experience itself' (PLC, 281). In the October 1934 issue of *Fortune* magazine Agee introduces a group of photographs entitled "The drought" by emphasizing the primacy of experience:

That this has been by all odds the most ruinous drought in U.S. history is old stuff to you by now. So are the details, as the press reported them, week by broiling week, through the summer. But all the same, the chances are strong that you have no idea what the whole thing meant; what, simply and gruesomely, it was. Really to know, you should have stood with a Dakota farmer and watched a promissory rack of cloud take the height of the sky, weltering its lightenings... and the piteous meager sweat on the air, and the earth baked stiff and steaming. You should have been a lot more people in a lot more places, really to know. Barring that impossibility, however, there is the clear dispassionate eye of the camera which under honest guidance has beheld these bitter and these transient matters, and has recorded this brutal season for the memory of easier time to come.[47]

And it was in order really to know that Agee and Walker Evans went to Alabama in 1936, on assignment by *Fortune*, to cover the desperate situation of the tenant farmers there, and compiled a report which *Fortune* declined to print, and which was published in 1941 as *Let Us Now Praise Famous Men*. Therein are noticeable similarities to Richards' particular concerns: the meticulous attention to word definition; the avoidance, despite the use of artistic 'devices', of the condition of 'art', which, ' "true" as it may be in art terms, is hermetically sealed away from identification with everyday "reality" ', and requires 'the killing insult of "suspension of disbelief", because it is art' (240); the insistence upon the 'process of extraordinary complexity [which] takes place between perceiving the situation and finding a mode of meeting it' (PLC, 102), reflected in Agee's strenuous effort after, and despair of, propriety of response ('It seems to me now that to contrive techniques appropriate to it in the first place, and capable of planting it cleanly in others, in the second, would be a matter of years, and I shall try none of it or little, and that very tortured and diluted, at present' – LUNPFM, 12); the notions of mentation as the occurrence of a stable poise, and of the desirability of relinquishing formulae of response in order to submit to experience, which are shown in Agee's various humiliations by the states of affairs he regards, and in his concept of the symmetry exhibited by landscape, life, consciousness and human consciousness — which is thus, as in Richards, not a unique relation — as at all times subject to the 'complex equations' of chance 'which are probably never repeated'.

Symmetry as we use it here, then, needs a little further examination. Because it is a symmetry sensitive to so many syncopations of chance (all of which have proceeded inevitably out of chances which were inevitable), it is in fact asymmetrical, like Oriental art. But also, because it is so pliant, so exquisitely obedient before the infinite irregularities of chance, it reachieves the symmetry it had by that docility lost on a 'higher' plane: on a plane in any case that is more complex, more comprehensive, born of a subtler, more numerous, less obvious orchestration of causes. This asymmetry now seems to us to extend itself into a worrying even of the rigid dances of atoms and of galaxies, so that we can no longer with any certitude picture ourselves as an egregiously complicated flurry and convolved cloud of chance sustained between two simplicities. (LUNPFM, 230-231)

On the contrary it is the present, a pointing reference to an utterly ambiguous 'that', which is 'simple', yet can be perceived only within the context which the reporter must attempt to supply. Ishmael's sword-mat, interweaving free will, necessity and chance (which has 'the last featuring blow at events'), occasions a comparable meditation. We are cut loose from the explanatory myths of ultimate context by the critical awareness Agee brings to bear, just as Richards, in "What is belief? " (1934), distinguishes between 'beliefs' ('feelings, attitudes, settings of will, concentrations of attention') and 'Beliefs', which have a 'secondary sanction', and declares himself, 'so far as I know, without Beliefs'.[48] On the other hand, while, as Agee says, words 'cannot embody' but can 'only describe', while their ability even to state a case is mitigated by both 'falsification (through inaccuracy of meaning as well as inaccuracy of emotion); and inability to communicate simultaneity with any immediacy', and while Agee values what he calls the 'cleansing and rectification of language, the breakdown of the identification of word and object', he finds it impossible to transcend attitude (as Richards says, we must always live with poetry, good or bad), the wish to obtain an unambiguous purchase on experience, to embody it in words: 'Human beings may be more and more aware of being awake, but they are still incapable of not dreaming, and a fish forswears water at his own peril' (LUNP FM, 213-215). The analog component must be hypothesized, the whale dangerously lunged at: it is Ahab's mania for unambiguous truth that brings Ishmael into the presence of what he comes back to report. Just as symbolic statements are encoded upon (and in poetry, subservient to) verbal signs, so a descriptive account, and thus the perceiving subject, are encoded upon the fragmented series of gestures and attitudes which can neither be transcended nor identified with, and which, in the absence of a stable context, are never free of the condition of self-deception.

Richards' context theory substitutes co-ordination and actualization in language for Locke's 'storehouse' of ideas; in *How to Read a Page*, he rejects the notion that we are 'wax which takes impressions from an alien world. We are so intimately interrelated with it that it is impossible to say where we stop and it begins; or whether we are more its work than it is ours'. And if he finds inadequate Locke's cautiously proceeding no further than to leave us 'still shut up within the walls of our ideas', he concurs in the difficulty of saying anything about substance (HRP, 184, 196-197). Context is controlled by language, and about the context of language itself, the relation of words to other things, nothing can be said but that a maximum awareness of definition is the condition of a self-actualizing responsiveness: 'Language', he says in 'The interactions of words' – including such linguistic 'modes' as 'pictures, music or the expressions of faces' – 'as understood, is the mind itself at work and these interdependencies of words are interdependencies of our own being'.[49]

DESCRIPTION vs. EXPLANATION: WITTGENSTEIN AND LANGUAGE-GAMES

The idea that 'mind' is a fiction remains central in Wittgenstein's work. In *The Blue Book* he defines thinking as 'operating with signs' and thus as not necessarily a mental activity: 'It is correct to say that thinking is an activity of our writing hand, of our larynx, of our head, and of our mind, so long as we understand the grammar of these statements'. To suggest that a machine can think is to take a description for an explanatory account, a 'how' for a 'what': 'It is as though we had asked "Has the number 3 a colour? " ' Like Richards in *The Philosophy of Rhetoric* (52), Wittgenstein distinguishes between a reason — having been taught supplies a *'reason* for doing what one did; as supplying the road one walks' — and a cause, an explanation why learning operates the way it does, which must always be a matter of *'conjecture'* or 'hypothesis'. In *The Brown Book* he refers to the 'general disease of thinking which always looks for (and finds) what would be called a mental state from which all our acts spring as from a reservoir', but allows that an innate 'mechanism' or ability to follow rules is a useful hypothesis.[50] Although Cecil H. Brown insists upon the centrality of this mechanism in Wittgenstein's later work as 'part of our "natural history" ',[51] it is difficult to see how this differs from Hume's admission that ideas are innate insofar as they are 'natural' as opposed to 'uncommon, artificial or miraculous' (*Inquiry*, 30), or from Watson's comparison to the boomerang's structure; moreover, in *Philosophical Investigations*, Wittgenstein disclaims interest in 'that in nature which is the basis of grammar', in the 'possible causes of the formation of concepts; we are not doing natural science; nor yet natural history — since we can also invent fictitious natural history for our purposes' (PI, *230*).

In this later phase. he challenges the assertions in the *Tractatus* which tend toward realism and toward the invention of a 'myth of "meaning" ' (PI, *147*) — the idea of a one-to-one correspondence of name (the element of a proposition) and thing, and the concomitant attempt to isolate a metalanguage, a *'super-*order between — so to speak — *super*-concepts', by reducing grammar to logic (97). On the contrary, ordinary spoken sentences exhibit no *'striving after* an ideal', are already, since they make sense, in 'perfect order' (48); and this humbler form of order is constituted by the role of a sentence in a particular 'language-game', each of which is a 'form of life', none of which has any one characteristic in common with all the others: language-games are related by unsystematically shared ' "family resemblances" ' (23, 67). Moreover, we enter the arena of any particular game, or of language itself, as David Locke enters and exits from a village square, in search of and unable to establish contact with any reality exterior to language. Language is the sphere of sense ('You learned the *concept* "pain" when you learned language'), but is not identifiable with sense: 'Where a sentence is called senseless, it is not as it were its sense that is senseless (384, 500). Language-games, or concepts (rules of procedure), are our environment, the given: 'Compare a concept with a style of painting. For is even our style of painting arbitrary? Can we choose one at pleasure? ' (*230*). Nor is reality, or assigning names to objects, prior to language (as it is for Augustine), for 'One has already to know (or be able to do) something in order to be capable of asking a thing's name' (30); the notion in the *Tractatus* of substance, which determines the logical form shared by language and the world, is replaced by the 'substratum' of the ability to speak a language (*208*).

Since a thing's existence can only be asserted by indicating the meaning of its name in a language-game, it is grammar which 'tells us what kind of object anything is' (373), and the ability to follow its rules, to know in *'particular* circumstances' how to proceed, 'go on', which constitutes understanding (154); 'The grammar of the word "knows" is evidently closely related to that of "can", "is able to". But also closely related to that of "under-stands" ' (150). Learning, acquiring the skill of language or any particular language-game, is neither the effect of a cause (466), nor based on induction, making an argument to oneself − ' "Fire has always burnt me, so it will happen now too" ' (325) − but a matter of groundless probability (480-482), exhibited in how people 'think and live' rather than logically justifiable (325). And the groundless configuarations of language offer no purchase on reality, cannot even guarantee the persistence of an object in successive references: 'we must not, in the sentence, "I see it like *this*" ', allow ' "it" ' and ' "this" 'to refer to the same thing: 'Always get rid of the idea of the private object in this way: assume that it constantly changes, but that you do not notice the change because your memory constantly deceives you' (?07). Meaning is defined as the speaker's being 'in motion': 'We go up to the thing we mean'; 'meaning something is like going up to someone' − formulations which are illustrated in and form the theoretical basis of *Alphaville*, and which deny that the subject can be abstracted from meaning, experienced in itself: 'One is rushing ahead and so cannot also observe oneself rushing ahead' (455, 457).

Understanding, knowing that 'L' comes after 'K', is neither a 'mental process' (such as a 'pain's growing more or less; the hearing of a tune or sentence') during which a 'formula occurs' to us (the understanding of the formula would then have to be explained), nor any of the 'characteristic accompaniments' of knowing how to go on, for if any common denominator could be isolated, 'why should *it* be understanding?' (152-155). As for Locke, the earlier Wittgenstein and Richards, understanding differs from real (true) knowledge, is encoded on that attitude, or 'state' of 'seeing', which makes possible thinking — interpreting or forming 'hypotheses, which may prove false' (*208, 212*). As for Richards, meaning is use; but in the absence of a model for the 'superlative fact' that we can grasp the meaning of a word in a formula, for example, an instruction to count by two's, without anticipating or predetermining its use in carrying out the order, we are 'seduced into using a super-expression' — ' "grasp it in a flash" ' — to state understanding (186-192). Attention cannot be defined except in terms of its circumstances, for thinking is not a detachable 'incorporeal process which lends life and sense to speaking' (339); but the speech necessary to thought can, like music, be attended to or not (341); and intention is 'embedded in its situation', is no more an 'experience' than is meaning (*181*): our impression of the 'intangibility' of a mental state is due to our refusal 'to count what is tangible about our state as part of the state we are contemplating' (608). Knower cannot be abstracted from known, thought from expression (317), understanding from mental state (*59*), remembering (the 'description', without 'experiental content', of a past experience) from accompanying 'memory-*experiences*' (*231*), soul from behavior or body ('My attitude towards him is an attitude towards a soul. I am not of the opinion that he has a soul' [*178*]), consciousness from brain process (412), intention from act (*217*), or self-consciousness from a particular disposition of consciousness (417): but neither can the members of these pairs be identified. Ethics, aesthetics, the 'new (spontaneous, "specific")' are always language-games (77, *224*). Like Hume, for whose principles of association he substitutes the mastery of a technique, Wittgenstein insists that 'nothing is concealed' (435), and condemns an uncritical faith in analogy: 'Where our language suggests a body and there is none: there, we should like to say, is a spirit' (36).

Richards' empiricism may be considered, in terms of its tendency to realism, as fitting between the position of a substantially determined logical form in the *Tractatus* and Wittgenstein's later insistence upon the amenability of investigation to particular examples. Whereas Richards rejects the proper name theory of meaning advanced in the *Tractatus*, he agrees that a symbol is expandable into a set of simple statements which can be clarified by means of symbol substitution (definition); the later Wittgenstein conceives of no 'final analysis' or 'single completely resolved form' for expressions (91), and rejects the schematic approach characteristic of Richards: 'Nominalists make the mistake of interpreting all words as *names*, and so of not really describing their use, but only, so to speak, giving a paper draft on such a description' (383). If the *Tractatus* anchors reference in substance, and Richards and Ogden advance a theory of signs to account for the perception and interpretation of the data of sense, make provisional use of a physiological hypothesis, the later Wittgenstein addresses the 'impression' as it can be given in a 'description' (*202-204*) as exemplified by one of the ' "aspects of organization" ' of an ambiguous diagram (*208*) – 'Above all, don't wonder "What can be going on in the eyes or brain?" ' (*211*) – denies that we make an 'inference' from 'sense impressions' to 'physical object', which are terms belonging to different language-games existing in 'complicated relation' (*180*), and thus de-emphasizes the 'pointing' function which Richards regards as basic: 'in certain circumstances, even *pointing* to the object one is talking about may be quite inessential to the language-game, to one's thought' (699). The statement ' "Red exists" ' is a statement about word use, not about the world (58). All three approaches regard symbolic statements as encoded in the arrangement of perceptible signs and thus as imprecisely communicable: 'The gesture', says Wittgenstein, '*tries* to portray, but cannot do it' (434). Thought and intention do not ' "accompany" ' speech and action, are 'neither "articulated" nor "non-articulated" ' (*217*).

A juxtaposition of the approaches of the *Tractatus*, of Richards and of the later Wittgenstein shows an increasing emphasis on the subjective, a progression from the logical form shared by object and description through the hypothetical account of association to the consideration of difficulties that become 'surveyable by rearrangement' when 'theory' and the 'hypothetical' – the notion of an *'essence'* lying 'beneath the surface' of language — are eliminated: 'We must learn to do without *explanation*, and description alone must take its place' (PI, 92, 109). This purest form of analysis is exhibited in the films of Sergio Leone, which tell stories, or subvert story conventions, by means of clichéed episodes, images, landscapes, acting styles, sound effects, ritual events and codes of honor, the whole game of western-movie signals, saliently dubbed and edited, and addressed to the ability to speak a language, to knowing 'how to play', as it is put in *The Good, the Bad and the Ugly* and in *Once Upon a Time in the West:* the elements of a mental state can be listed, counted up — as the bountyhunter counts corpses at the end of *For a Few Dollars More* — set up as a game. Wittgenstein speaks literally rather than metaphorically of the 'language' of 'sense-impressions', which 'like any other is founded on convention' (PI, 355) and of the 'use' of a sign as its 'life': 'Every sign *by itself* seems dead . . . . In use it is alive' (PI, 432). It is in this sense that Godard objects to structuralism ('structures, without images and without sounds — how can one speak of them?'), and to Barthes's decoding of fashion as though it were a 'dead language' rather than as 'something you live': 'But we're the sons of a *filmic* language; there's nothing in the Nazism of linguistics we have any use for. Notice: we always come back to how hard it is for us all to be talking about "the same thing" '.[52] Yet if Locke's substantial colorless world of contingency, brain-process and the imperative of survival is present in Melville and Burroughs, and if Richards' hypothetical causality informs the experience in LUNPFM, Godard too posits 'realism' — 'If you didn't rely on realism you'd never be able to do anything. If you were on the street you wouldn't dare to get into a cab — if you'd even risked going out that is' — as the precondition of experience lying beyond the understanding of the witness, thinks of himself as making movies which are evidential, will frustrate glib assertions about history by 'future Foucaults'.[53]

For 'empiricism' might be substituted 'critique of metaphysics'. But, unlike thinkers associated with Logical Positivism, Locke, Richards and Wittgenstein are not concerned to deny such metaphysical entities as reality, God or the thinking and intending subject, but simply insist that such entities are not experiential, cannot be described, are outside the sphere of language. True, as A.J. Ayer points out, [54] the later Wittgenstein operates with a theory of meaning that is less than empirical, since it does not follow from the linguistic prerequisite for experience that experience is impossible without language. But in reducing experience to linguistic situations which are amenable to no covering body of rules, and in showing that one cannot get outside language with language, Wittgenstein proffers that assumption in order to cancel out of consideration what cannot be examined and analyzed, and thus carries empiricism to its logical conclusion as boldly as, in his way, does Hume.

Despite varying degrees of realism, Locke, Richards and Wittgenstein have in common a context theory of meaning: what is present before the understanding, whatever that may be, is a relation or arrangement of signs which constitutes a sense or comprehensibility, and which seeks stability, hypostasis, universal applicability and a consequent reduction of the ambiguity of experience – of the tentativeness of understanding; for everything, says Locke, is 'liable to change' (*Essay*, III, iii, 9). These empiricists criticize the notion of a mysterious gap between understanding and the arrangement of signs, between sense and code. And derived from this critique are the textual cutups of Agee and Burroughs, and the attention of each of the authors herein discussed to the mere elements of signification: it will be recalled that, in the final shot of *The Passenger*, the 'ghost' of David Locke overhears a conversation in Spanish – a language, it has been established, that he does not understand.

The issues around which these texts revolve are, on the one hand, the status of the reality reported, and on the other, the interrogation of the perceiving subject's motives and intentions, and the critique of related explanatory myths. The salutary project shared by each of these men is the direction of critical attention to habits of understanding – to the linguistic environment – in order to loosen our narcissistic hold on those habits, to show that they are not, in fact, our reflections.

NOTES

1. Ludwig Wittgenstein, *Philosophical Investigations*, trans. by G.E.M. Anscombe. Oxford, Basil Blackwell, 1972: 208-209. Subsequent references are noted in the text by proposition; page references are italicized (PI).
2. Ludwig Wittgenstein, *Tractatus Logico-Philosophicus*, trans. by D.F. Pears and B.F. McGuinness. New York, Humanities Press, 1961: 5.631, 5.6331. Subsequent references

are noted in the text by proposition (TLP).

3. James Agee and Walker Evans, *Let Us Now Praise Famous Men*. Boston, Houghton Mifflin, 1960: xiv. Subsequent references are noted in the text (LUNPFM).

4. Herman Melville, *Moby-Dick*, ed. by Harrison Hayford and Herschel Parker. New York, Norton, 1967: 70. Subsequent references are noted in the text (MD).

5. William Burroughs, *Naked Lunch*. Castle Books, 1959: 221. Subsequent references are noted in the text (NL).

6. Jean-Luc Godard, 'Pierrot mon ami', in *Cahiers du Cinéma*, trans. by Joachim Neugroschel and reprinted in *Jean-Luc Godard*, ed. by Toby Mussman. New York, Dutton, 1968: 242.

7. Dwight Macdonald, *Against the American Grain*. New York, Random House, 1962: 160-161.

8. James Agee, 'Letter to a friend', in *James Agee: A Portrait*, ed. by Father J.H. Flye. Caedmon Records, 1971: side 2.

9. I.A. Richards, *How to Read a Page: A Course in Effective Reading with an Introduction to a Hundred Great Words*. New York, Norton, 1942: 193-194. Subsequent references are noted in the text (HRP).

10. Jay Leyda, editor, *The Melville Log*, volume II. New York, Harcourt, Brace, 1951: 832.

11. Thomas Hobbes, 'Human nature, or the fundamental elements of policy', in *The English Works of Thomas Hobbes of Malmesbury*, volume IV, ed. by Sir William Molesworth. London, John Bohn, 1899: 60.

12. Alexander Campbell Fraser, editor, *An Essay Concerning Human Understanding*, volume II. New York, Dover, 1959: 326, n.2.

13. Aristotle, *De Anima*, trans. by R.D. Hicks. Cambridge, Cambridge University Press, 1907: III, 12-13, 159-163.

14. Joseph Addison, *Critical Essays from The Spectator*. New York, Oxford University Press, 1970: 182-183.

15. Immanuel Kant, *Observations on the Feeling of the Beautiful and Sublime*, trans. by John T. Goldthwait. Berkeley, University of California Press, 1965: 47, 51, 97.

16. Edmund Burke, *A Philosophical Enquiry into the Origin of our Ideas of the Sublime and Beautiful*, ed. by J.T. Boulton. London, Routledge and Kegan Paul, 1958: 38, 40, 81.

17. William Burroughs, *Naked Lunch*. Castle Books, 1959: xiv. The quotation is an amalgam of two statements in the *Tractatus*: 1) 'If a sign is *useless*, it is meaningless' (3.328); and 2) '*unnecessary* units in a sign-language mean nothing' (5.47321).

18. Jean-Luc Godard, 'Struggle on two fronts: a conversation with Jean-Luc Godard', *Film Quarterly* xx ii (2) Winter 1968-1969: 23.

19. David Hume, *An Inquiry Concerning Human Understanding*, ed. by C.W. Hendel. New York, Bobbs-Merrill, 1955: 32, 114. Subsequent references are noted in the text (*Inquiry*).

20. Charles Sanders Peirce, 'Some consequences of four incapacities', in *Philosophical Writings of Peirce*, ed. by J. Buchler. New York, Dover, 1955: 249-250.

21. William James, *The Principles of Psychology*, volume I. Dover, 1950: 265-269.

22. Charles Sanders Peirce, 'Synechism, fallibilism, and evolution', in *Philosophical Writings of Peirce*, ed. by J. Buchler. New York, Dover, 1955: 358-360.

23. John Dewey, *Logic: The Theory of Inquiry*. New York, Holt, 1938: 241-251.

24. John Dewey, 'The development of American pragmatism', in *The Philosophy of John Dewey*, volume I, ed. by John J. McDermott. New York, Putnam's, 1973: 52.

25. B.F. Skinner, *Beyond Freedom and Dignity*. Toronto, Bantam, 1972: 194-195.

26. Ludwig Wittgenstein, *Lectures and Conversations on Aesthetics, Psychology and*

Religious Belief, ed. by Cyril Barrett. Oxford, Blackwell, 1966: 26-27, 49.

27. John Dewey and A.F. Bentley, 'Interaction and transaction', in *Knowing and the Known*. Boston, Beacon Press, 1949: 115.

28. John Dewey, *Logic: The Theory of Inquiry*. New York, Holt, 1938: 230-237, 115-117.

29. Jean-Luc Godard, 'Struggle on two fronts: a conversation with Jean-Luc Godard', *Film Quarterly* xxii (2) Winter 1968-1969: 22.

30. James Agee, 'Notes for a moving picture: the house', in *The Collected Short Prose of James Agee*, ed. by Robert Fitzgerald. New York, Ballantine, 1970: 187. Subsequent references are noted in the text (CSP).

31. Reuben Brower, 'Beginnings and transitions: I.A. Richards interviewed', in *I.A. Richards: Essays in His Honour*. New York, Oxford University Press, 1973: 26-28.

32. G.H. von Wright, 'Introduction' to Wittgenstein's *Letters to C.K. Ogden*. Boston, Routledge and Kegan Paul, 1973: 2, 9.

33. W.H.N. Hotopf, *Language, Thought and Comprehension: A Case Study of the Writings of I.A. Richards*. London, Routledge and Kegan Paul, 1965: 164.

34. See particularly John Crowe Ransome, *The World's Body*. Baton Rouge, Louisiana State University Press, 1968: 146-147; Allen Tate, 'Literature as knowledge', in *The Man of Letters in the Modern World, Selected Essays: 1928-1955*. New York, Meridian, 1955: 39, 51, 57; S.E. Hyman, *The Armed Vision*. New York, Alfred A. Knopf, 1948: 312; Manuel Bilsky, 'I.A. Richards' theory of metaphor', *Modern Philosophy*, L, November 1952: 137; Murray Kreiger, *The New Apologists for Poetry*. Minneapolis, University of Minnesota Press, 1956: 118, 123-125; W.K. Wimsatt and Cleanth Brooks, *Literary Criticism: A Short History*. New York, Alfred A. Knopf, 1967: 623-624, 641; Richard Foster, 'The romanticism of I.A. Richards', *ELH* 26, March 1959: 95-97 (Foster supplies a thorough bibliography on the subject of Richards' imputed 'conversion'); and G.W. Graff, 'The later Richards and the new criticism', *Criticism* IX, Summer 1967: 229-230, 240.

35. I.A. Richards, C.K. Ogden and James Wood, *The Foundations of Aesthetics*. New York, Lear, 1925: 63, 65, 72-79. Subsequent references are noted in the text (FA).

36. I.A. Richards and C.K. Ogden, *The Meaning of Meaning: A Study of the Influence of Language upon Thought and of the Science of Symbolism*. London, Routledge and Kegan Paul, 1972: 243-258. Subsequent references are noted in the text (MM).

37. I.A. Richards, *The Principles of Literary Criticism*. London, Routledge and Kegan Paul, 1925: 82-90. Subsequent references are noted in the text (PLC).

38. I.A. Richards, *Practical Criticism: A Study of Literary Judgment*. New York, Harcourt, Brace and World, 1929: 300. Subsequent references are noted in the text (PC).

39. I.A. Richards, *Poetries and Science: A Reissue of Science and Poetry (1926, 1935) with Commentary*. New York, Norton, 1970: 30, 33, 44, 65. Subsequent references are noted in the text (SP).

40. I.A. Richards, 'Behaviorism', *The New Criterion* IV (2) April 1926: 374-377.

41. I.A. Richards, 'Structure and communication', in *Structure in Arts and Science*, ed. by Gyorgy Kepes. New York, George Braziller, 1965: 130-131.

42. Robert Fitzgerald, 'A memoir', in *The Collected Short Prose of James Agee*. New York, Ballantine, 1968: 13.

43. James Agee, *Letters of James Agee to Father Flye*, ed. by J.H. Flye. New York, Balantine, 1971: 53-54. Subsequent references are noted in the text (LFF).

44. Robert Fitzgerald, 'A memoir', in *The Collected Short Prose of James Agee*. New York, Balantine, 1968: 14.

45.James, Agee, 'Dedication', in *The Collected Poems of James Agee*, ed. by Robert Fitzgerald. New York, Ballantine, 1970: 11. Subsequent references are noted in the text (CP).

46.Robert Fitzgerald, 'A memoir', in *The Collected Short Prose of James Agee*. New York, Ballantine, 1968: 29, 30-31.

47.James Agee, 'The drought', *Fortune* X, October 1934: 11.

48.I.A. Richards, 'What is belief?' in *Poetries: Their Media and Ends*, ed. by Trevor Eaton. The Hague, Mouton, 1974: 238.

49.I.A. Richards, 'The interactions of words', in *The Language of Poetry*, ed. by Allen Tate. Princeton University Press, 1942: 73.

50.Ludwig Wittgenstein, *The Blue and Brown Books*. Oxford, Basil Blackwell, 1960: 14-15, 143, 97.

51.Cecil H. Brown, *Wittgensteinian Linguistics*. The Hague, Mouton, 1974: 80-81, 85-86.

52.Jean-Luc Godard, 'Three thousand hours of film', trans. by Jane Pease, in *Jean-Luc Godard*, ed. by Toby Mussman. New York, Dutton, 1968: 299; Jean-Luc Godard, 'Struggle on two fronts: a conversation with Jean-Luc Godard', *Film Quarterly* XXII (2) Winter 1968-1969: 79.

53 Jean-Luc Godard, 'Struggle on two fronts: a conversation with Jean-Luc Godard', *Film Quarterly* XXII (2) Winter 1968-1969: 32, 26.

54.A.J. Ayer, *The Central Questions of Philosophy*. London, Weidenfeld and Nicolson, 1973: 54.

3

The Symbol and the Voyeur:
Chillingworth and Tommo

> I approached the symbol, with
> its layers of meaning, but when I
> touched it, it changed into only a
> beautiful princess.
>
> Donald Barthelme
> *'The glass mountain'*

A symbol is a word, image or gesture which represents a verbally organized context, and is thus an abstraction. Even for Locke, making one simple idea stand for many, as the whiteness of milk agrees roughly with that of snow and chalk, is a verbal activity, accomplished by naming (*Essay*, II, xi, 8-10). The names of 'mixed modes', or abstract ideas, he says, have 'perfectly arbitrary' meanings, while those of substances are arbitrary to a degree, referring 'to a pattern, though with some latitude', and the reference of names of simple ideas, which are 'determined by the existence of things', is 'not arbitrary at all' (III, iv, 17). That is, 'meaning', a term derived from Latin and Teutonic words for 'mind', whether it be equated with referent (object, fact, event) or the act of referring (thought, intention), is grounded in substance, the unknowable.

OED says that words were spoken of as the 'signs and symbols of things' as early as 1686. But David Hartley is the first of Locke's followers to use 'symbol' in an epistemological sense, suggesting that, in association, 'the visible Idea, being more glaring and distinct then the rest, performs the Office of a Symbol of all the rest, suggests them, and connects them together'; and in his 'Art of logic', he recommends the "use of Words in the way of mathematical Symbols'.[1] Wittgenstein, who regards a proposition as a symbol, also calls 'any part of a proposition that characterizes its sense or expression (or symbol)' (TLP, 3.31). And for Richards, meaning occurs when one item in a context, usually a word, substitutes for or symbolizes — means — other members, which can thus be omitted in recurrence.

The idea that a symbol represents a context has affinities with literary uses of the word. Erich Auerbach speaks of the symbolic or 'figural view of human life' fostered by Christianity, which brings figure forward from ground by making particular sets of gestures, as of the hero, traitor or saint, 'appear as exemplary, as models, as significant, and to leave all "the rest" in abeyance'.[2] Coleridge emphasizes the nonarbitrary, organic nature of the symbol, as opposed to mere allegory:

Now an allegory is but a translation of abstract notions into a picture-language which is in itself nothing but an abstraction from objects of the senses.... On the other hand a symbol . . . is characterized by a translucence of the special in the individual, or of the general in the special, or of the universal in the general, above all, by the translucence of the eternal through and in the temporal. It always partakes of the reality which renders it intelligible; and while it enunciates the whole, abides itself as a living part of that unity of which it is the representative.[3]

This notion of an organic link between symbol and context, and thus between Symbol and eternal context, persists in such opinions as T.S. Eliot's, that allegory is 'a lazy substitute for profundity',[4] and carries over into linguistic considerations, informing Ferdinand de Saussure's rejection of the term 'symbol' for verbal sign: 'One characteristic of the symbol is that it is never wholly arbitrary; it is not empty, for there is the rudiment of a natural bond between the signifier and the signified', as, for example, between a pair of scales and justice.[5] Ogden and Richards are therefore careful to distinguish their science of Symbolism from the Symbolism of the French poets of the 1890s, 'who were in revolt against all forms of literal and descriptive writing' (MM, v).

Newton Arvin is representative — symbolic — of those critics who insist that Melville is a Symbolist: according to Arvin, while the 'word "symbolism", in its literary bearing, had not come into use at the time *Moby-Dick* was written', the works of Poe, Hawthorne and Whitman show that 'the poetic mind in America was already symbolist in everything but the program'. And Melville is co-opted by the program: Ahab's pasteboard-masks and linked-analogies speeches are identified as 'Melville's personal vision of the doctrine of correspondences that lay below so much romantic and symbolist writing' (this despite Melville's indictment, in one of his letters, of 'transcendentalisms, myths and oracular gibberish'[6]), and the 'leading images' of *Moby-Dick* are defined as 'symbols in the sense that their primal origins are in the unconscious, however consciously they have been organized and controlled; that on this account they transcend the personal and local and become archetypal in their range and depth; that they are inexplicit, polysemantic, and never quite exhaustible in their meanings'.[7]

Northrop Frye also treats the symbol as Symbol, the representative of an ultimate and meaningful context. The only story, he says, and the 'framework of all literature', is that of 'the loss and regaining of identity'. Literature, which aims at 'identifying the human world with the natural world around it, or finding analogies between them' is a universe or family of derivative stories, and 'can only derive its forms from itself': the 'content' of 'experiences' may change, but the vocabulary of forms remains constant. Art is always constructed according to 'some principle of repetition or recurrence': rhythm in music and pattern in painting provide the basis for the sought identity with what is recurrent in the natural cycle.[8] For Frye, a symbol is 'any unit of any literary structure that can be isolated for critical attention. A word, a phrase, or an image used with some kind of special reference (which is what a symbol is usually taken to mean) are all symbols when they are distinguishable elements in critical analysis'. Like Saussure, he refers to words in terms of their 'external meaning' as '*signs*, verbal units which, conventionally and arbitrarily, stand for and point to things outside the place where they occur'; the 'inward' direction of meaning, which words have in 'all literary verbal structures', is the context in which they are non-arbitrary symbols. Metaphor, 'the unit of relationship of two symbols', is a hypothetical 'statement of identity' ('A is B') opposed to 'ordinary descriptive meaning' and most powerfully realized in 'the anagogic aspect of meaning': 'The literary universe, therefore, is a universe in which everything is potentially identical with everything else' – grows out of everything else, as a man is identical with the boy he once was.[9] In *Moby-Dick*, however, something is left over when the quest for identity is finished. The myth of intention, the inveterate will to re-establish rhythm or symmetry, is a version of Frye's one great Story, which may be paraphrased, 'I want to go back to sleep'; but the asymmetrical presence of Ishmael permits no such neat conclusion. Cases in point are Burroughs' exhortation in *The Soft Machine* – 'Will the gentle reader get up off his limestones and pick up the phone? – Cause of Death: completely uninteresting'[10] – and, in Antonioni's *Blow-Up*, the photographer's looking into the camera, ostensibly addressing his models as they strike various attitudes, and shouting, 'Wake up! '

Whereas, for Frye, literature is independent of experience, a body of hypothetical thought and action, Melville, Agee and Burroughs treat literature as experience, and treat experience as vicarious, as mediated by signs. Symbols, as Richards says, are the mind itself at work; but they are misleading, for they suggest the possibility of a symmetry, a uniform recurrence of contexts, which cannot empirically be realized, in the light of the empiricists' emphasis on a universal liability to change. Symmetry, that which Ahab has lost, has the two subdivisions of beauty and knowledge (beauty and meaning, for Ogden and Richards), as is suggested by the double quest in *Mardi*, Taji's for the former, Babbalanja's for the latter. Melville's texts undercut myths of identity and the hypnotic forces of rhythm, metaphor and symbolism which reinforce them. It is the Condifence Man's insistence that symmetry is immanent and trustworthy: like Burroughs and Antonioni, Melville exhorts us to wake up, to be aware that the necessary and vain symmetry of language implies no redemption from the condition of ambiguity.

CHILLINGWORTH'S EMPIRICAL EYE

The redemptive force of the Symbol, its establishment of an ultimate Context, and thus of an ultimate Understanding, can be illustrated by a consideration of Nathanial Hawthorne's *The Scarlet Letter*. As the 'representative' of his witch-hunting ancestors, Hawthorne tells us in 'The custom House', 'I . . . take shame

upon myself for their sakes, and pray that any curse incurred by
them may now henceforth be removed': so deep go the 'aged
roots' of his family in Salem, so numerous are the ancestors who
'have mingled their earthly substance with the soil', that his
'inevitable' attachment to the place is not one of 'love' but of
'instinct', 'the mere sensuous sympathy of dust for dust'; and
despite dreary appearance and climatic and social chill, the 'spell
survives . . . just as powerfully as if the natal spot were an earthly
paradise'.[11] But neither door of the Custom House, breeding-
place of 'evil and corrupt practices', where Hawthorne serves time
as if in expiation of the ancestral curse, 'opens on the road to
Paradise': here he puts 'Literature, its exertions and objects',
aside, is separated from 'Nature . . . and all the imaginative delight,
wherewith it had been spiritualized', and, as to 'human nature',
is an observer rather than one involved, is 'fond of standing at
a distance and watching' the dreaming face of the old collector
rather than of conversing with him (11, 24, 21).

He is conscious that his 'transitory life' at the Custom House is
subject to political contingency, and his assertion that 'the past
was not dead' refers both to his temporarily shelved literary ambi-
tion and to his ancestral environs – makes of them one concern
(24, 26). Exploring a room filled with ancient documents, he
discovers the historical researches of Jonathan Pue, a predecessant
Surveyor, among which is a gold embroidered cloth scarlet 'A'.
These records of the 'internal operations of his head', along with
the 'imperfect skeleton, and some fragments of apparel, and a wig
of magestic frizzle', constitute the physical remains of Surveyor
Pue, but do not, it is insisted, define the 'limits' of Hawthorne's
art: 'in the dressing up of the tale, and imagining the motives and
modes of passion that influence the characters who figure in it',
he has allowed himself 'as much license as if the facts had been
entirely of my own invention' (28, 31). The gap between the stark
fact of record (Hawthorne measures the letter, finding 'each limb
. . . to be precisely three inches and a quarter in length') and the
world of imagination (context and 'motives') is bridged by the
power of the 'A', on which his eyes have 'fastened' as if entranced:
'Certainly, there was some deep meaning in it, most worthy of
interpretation, and which, as it were, streamed forth from the
mystic symbol, subtly communicating itself to my sensibilities,
but evading the analysis of my mind.' Placing it on his breast, he

experiences 'a sensation not altogether physical, yet almost so, as of burning heat'; the 'scarlet symbol', with its explanatory manuscript, is a direct exhortation (an intentional gesture) by Pue to bring the story 'before the public', thereby to remedy a soon to be terminated income, so that Hawthorne's mind is 'recalled . . . in some degree, to its old track' (30-32).

Setting to work, he again confronts the gap between lifelessness and life, for his imagination has become 'a tarnished mirror', its creations retaining 'all the rigidity of dead corpses'; like Wordsworth and Coleridge, he laments the loss of creative power, and repairs for its renewal to the 'invigorating charm of Nature' and meditation by moonlight, 'a medium most suitable for the romance-writer to get acquainted with his illusive guests', rendering mundane details 'spiritualized', so that 'they seem to lose their actual substance and become things of intellect', in a 'neutral territory, somewhere between the real world and fairy-land where the Actual and the Imaginary may meet, and each imbue itself with the nature of the other'. The mirror image becomes an in-depth 'repetition of all the gleam and shadow of the picture, with one remove further from the actual, and nearer to the imaginative': the forms at the top of Plato's hierarchy are to be found in the 'haunted verge' of the mirror (33-35). But these recourses fail: enter 'Providence' and the 'guillotine' ('one of the most apt of metaphors') of political change, which severs Hawthorne from his debilitating dependence upon government office, leaves his 'figurative self' in a happliy 'decapitated state' and thus permits him to become again a full-time 'literary man' (39-41). He could once, had he 'the insight and . . . the cunning to transcribe it', have recorded the daily life of the Custom House and preserved the 'picturesque style' of description of one of the old story-tellers, producing what, 'I honestly believe, would have been something new in literature'; but he is dead to that world now, 'writes from beyond the grave', and the Custom House is no longer 'a reality of my life. I am a citizen of somewhere else' (35, 42-43). He has moved through fall, expiation and redemptive encounter with the power of the symbol, back to the world of 'literature'; and his movement from dead record to living romance, the analogy of which is his reconstruction of the character of the old General (as difficult a task as to trace out and build up anew, in imagination, an old fortress . . . from a view of its gray and broken

ruins'), is the activity and frame of reference to which the symbol
has drawn him.

So it is in the resulting romance: if the utopian vision of the
founding colonists has been forced to give way to the necessity for
cemeteries and jails, then Hester Prynne's appearance in the door
of the prison house before the 'intently fastened' eyes of the onlookers, and her mounting the scaffold (she has later 'a sense . . .
too ill-defined to be made a thought . . . that her whole orb of
life . . . was connected with this spot, as with the one point that
gave it unity') in order to endure the 'intense consciousness of
being the object of severe and universal observation' (45, 233, 56),
is potentially salvatory: figure comes forward from ground, focuses
the universal gaze and suggests the possibility of a deeper reality.
Just as the town beadle 'prefigured and represented in his aspect
the whole dismal severity of the Puritan code of law', Hester's
ignominy both recalls the defiling of 'virgin soil' with prisons and
cemeteries and suggests a mode of redemption, for the rose from
the bush by the prison door, which might 'symbolize some sweet
moral blossom' in the story, is analogous to the symbols on
Hester's breast, the infant and the scarlet 'A'; the latter has 'the
effect of a spell, taking her out of the ordinary relations with
humanity, and enclosing her in a sphere by herself' (48, 44-45,50).
Hester's isolation is defined in terms of a dualistic separation
between objective fact and subjective experience, for the 'no
great distance' she travels from prison to scaffold, 'measured
by the prisoner's experience . . . might be reckoned a journey
of some length', a separation which is resolved by her elevated
position on the platform, 'a point of view that revealed to Hester
Prynne the entire track upon which she had been treading since
her happy infancy': she escapes 'from the cruel weight and hardness'
of the present reality into a train of remembered images that
lead inevitably back to the present again, her memory of her
husband giving place to his deformed shape in the crowd. Her
epiphany on the platform brings together, makes meaningful,
the inner and outer (temporal and spatial) worlds of past and
present journeys, symbolizes an overview which, through the
narrator's knowledge of her 'memory's picture gallery', is also
ours. And when she touches the 'A' 'to assure herself that the
infant and the shame were real' (51, 54-56), it is as when the
photographer in *Blow-Up* touches the body in order to verify

its existence, but for the fact that when he looks again it is gone.

If in this first scene we are presented with what Agee calls the cruel radiance of what is, then the moral blossom Hawthorne offers us from the rose bush, and the pattern of symbolic imagery in which it figures, are nevertheless destined to place that reality in a context which justifies and from which springs Hester's, and by implication the narrator's, comprehensive and epiphanic point of view. The flower, for example, has its counterpart in the prison, 'the black flower of civilization': Hester's sin, to which Chillingworth refers as a 'black flower', is what binds her to Salem, 'the roots which she had struck into the soil'; passionate red figure and Puritan black ground are Hester's heraldic colors ('On a Field, Sable, the Letter A, Gules'), the rose bush amid the 'unsightly vegetation' in front of the prison (44, 165, 74, 251): flowers suggest beauty and morality. Roger Chillingworth is a gatherer of herbs ' "of a dark and flabby leaf" ', and Hester wonders whether the earth, 'quickened to an evil purpose by the sympathy of his eye [might] greet him with poisonous shrubs' (123, 166). Chillingworth, the scholarly analyst and expert at herbal concoction, discourages thoughts of death in Arthur Dimmesdale, which would withdraw the latter from under his inhuman (he is 'an unhumanized mortal') gaze and scrutiny: ' "Youthful men, not having taken a deep root, give up their hold of life so easily!" ' (247, 155). Pearl is both the 'A' on Hester's breast (Hester gives 'many hours of morbid ingenuity, to create an analogy between the object of her affection and the emblem of her guilt and torture. But in truth Pearl was the one as well as the other; and only in consequence of that identity had Hester contrived so perfectly to represent the scarlet letter in her appearance') and a child of flowers, 'a lovely and immortal flower' who cries 'for a red-rose' in the Governor's garden (95-96, 83, 100); she is named 'Red Rose' by John Wilson, and answers his catechistic question 'that she had not been made at all, but had been plucked by her mother off the bush of wild roses that grew by the prison door' (103, 105).

Pearl is the demonic result of 'lawless passion', a child of the forest whose ' "principle of being" ' is ' "the freedom of a broken law" ', (158, 126); when Dimmesdale confesses his 'nameless horror' of Chillingworth, Pearl offers to reveal the old man's identity, whispering a 'gibberish' which only 'sounded . . . like human language' into the minister's ear, though she earlier demonstrates that she knows what Chillingworth is up to: ' "Come away, mother . . . . or yonder old Black Man will catch you! He hath got hold of the minister already" ' (148, 127). An aspect of the symbolic 'A', Pearl knows it is worn for the same reason that Dimmesdale keeps his hand over his heart, her fascination with the symbol seeming 'an innate quality of her being' (169-171). In the forest, she insists that her mother resume it (' "Dost thou know thy mother now, child? " '); her function is to embody the hidden, to accost Dimmesdale for not being sufficiently ' "bold" ' and ' "true" ' to acknowledge Hester and herself in the light of noon, to be 'the living hieroglyphic in which was revealed the secret they so darkly sought to hide, – all written in this symbol, – all plainly manifest, had there been a prophet or magician skilled to read the character of flame! And Pearl was the oneness of their being . . . how could they doubt that their earthly lives and future destinies were conjoined, when they beheld at once their material union, and the spiritual idea, in whom they met, and were to dwell immortally together? ' (202, 149, 197). Pearl transcends the conventions of significance, is a connection with the hidden source of things, and so shares a 'kindred wildness' with the forest creatures: her 'errand as a messenger of anguish' is 'all fulfilled' at the moment when the 'A' on Dimmesdale's breast is revealed, and she proceeds to a happy-ever-after life in Europe (197, 244).

Pearl's significance as Word among words, pointing to the source of things as she stands pointing at the spot where Hester's discarded 'A' should be (200), is the logical extension of her father's role as ' "pious minister of the Word" ': while other clergymen are more learned or possessed of greater practical understanding, Dimmesdale's is 'the gift that descended upon the chosen disciples at Pentecost, in tongues of flames: symbolizing, it would seem, not the power of speech in foreign and unknown languages, but that of addressing the whole human brotherhood in the heart's native language' (230). He expresses 'the highest truths through the humblest medium of words and images', is for the people 'the mouthpiece of Heaven's messages' (134-135). His forte is what Ogden and Richards call the emotive rather than descriptive or small-'s' symbolic use of words: when he publicly exhorts Hester to reveal the name of Pearl's father, 'The feeling that [his voice] so evidently manifested, rather than the direct purport of the words, caused it to vibrate within all hearts, and brought the listeners into one accord of sympathy'. His final sermon has for Hester 'a meaning . . . entirely apart from its indistinguishable words', which, 'if more distinctly heard, might only have been a grosser medium, and have clogged the spiritual sense'. His preaching transcends all such mediation, achieves perfect communication, so that his hearers are entranced by 'the high spell that [transports] them into the region of another's mind' (63, 232, 236). Through Dimmesdale, words manifest a prior order, having fixed and ordained meanings; it is a mark of his fallen condition that he publicly addresses Hester in a kind of double talk, to which, when threatened with losing Pearl, she responds in kind: ' "Thou wast my pastor, and hadst charge of my soul, and knowest me better than these men can" ' (106). Dimmesdale has fallen into duality, scourges and fights for control of his body, bemoans the ' "contrast between what I seem and what I am" '; he regards falsehood as 'shadowlike', and, like Ahab, must know wherein identity consists: 'what was he? — a substance? — or the dimmest of shadows? ' A life of falsehood such as Dimmesdale's, Hawthorne comments, 'steals the pith and substance out of whatever realities there are around us. . . . To the untrue man, the whole universe is false, — it is impalpable, — it shrinks to nothing within his grasp. And he himself, in so far as he shows himself in a false light, becomes a shadow, or, indeed, ceases to exist' (182, 135, 138). This is precisely how Melville sets up Ahab's quest: substance must be uncovered, its symbol made manifest, verbal meanings brought into proper alignment with things. The empiricist's reality is the romantic's nightmare; Dimmesdale's duplicity, his failure, by keeping his 'A' covered, to give expression to his experience in the forest, has 'eaten into the real substance of his character' and made of him, as Mistress Hibbins seems to have guessed, as much a demon as Chillingworth: ' "Once in my life I met the Black Man!" ' Hester tells Pearl; ' "This scarlet letter is his mark!" ' (205, 176).

It is the function of the literary symbol, in fact, both to suppress and to bring forth, to oppose figure to ground: Dimmesdale is a minister of the Word who, exhilerated by his interview with Hester in the forest, can hardly resist teaching 'some very wicked words to a knot of little Puritan children who . . . had but just begun to talk'; he is a black man with the palest of exteriors, and it is his embodiment of these opposites that fits him as a symbol. ' "Be it sin or no" ', says Hester of Chillingworth, ' "I hate the man" '; yet hate and love are, according to Hawthorne, 'the same thing at bottom' (210, 167, 248). His inclination toward a re- demptive synthesis keeps Dimmesdale from leaving New England, for whereas Chillingworth (alias Master Prynne), like Ishmael, names himself (a demonic act, as is implied by Mistress Hibbins' reference to ' "Somebody" ', the nameless one, and by repeated mentions of Hester's and Arthur's 'ignominy') and is charged with a contradiction between his merciful ' "acts" ' and terrible ' "words" ' (230, 63), the minister rejects Hester's exhortation to ' "Give up this name of Arthur Dimmesdale, and make thyself another" ', confesses his sin at the moment of his 'very proudest eminence of superiority' (189, 237), and thus keeps and fills in the reference of his identity, redeems signification by anchoring it in substance: the 'A' is literally 'imprinted in the flesh' according to some accounts, though the narrator deems it 'irreverent to describe' the spectacle (245, 243). In the 'closing scene' of this 'drama', elevated on the scaffold while the people look on 'as knowing that some deep life-matter' is revealed, figure comes forward from the ground which it is both opposed to and repres- entative of, symbolizing the day of judgment and defeat of Satan which Dimmesdale had prophesied as ' "the dark problem of life made plain . . . . the complete solution of that problem" ' (242, 124). By his act, appearance and reality are reunited.

The symbol transforms contradictions into an emblazoned heraldic poise of ultimately identical opposites; the 'A' is the synthetic hub of radiating spokes of meaning, standing for adulteress, 'Arthur', 'Able', 'Affection' and 'Angle' (153-155, 150); and if Chillingworth, again like Ishmael, describes himself as ' "a stranger, and . . . a wanderer, sorely against my will" ', he is Cain to Hester's Abel, for she transforms the mark 'more intoler- able to a woman's heart than that which branded the brow of Cain' into an acceptable sacrifice (57, 78). The 'A' offers her means to ' "work out an open triumph over the evil within . . . and the sorrow without" ', to gain 'another' and 'more saint- like' purity (63, 75). Less happily, it affords her an 'estranged point of view' from which to criticize 'human institutions . . . with hardly more reverence than the Indian would feel', an ex-

clusion and freedom from society's approval which 'had made her
strong, but taught her much amiss' (190): Hester too is in a dualistic situation, for the 'thought' in which she indulges — the trans-
atlantic 'freedom of speculation', a 'moral wilderness' in which
she wanders — must suffice 'without investing itself in the flesh
and blood of action', so that the intellectual energy that might
have made her another Anne Hutchinson is channeled into the
education of Pearl. Hester later closes the gap between thought
and act as a dispenser of counsel, an 'angel and apostle', though
she denounces the role, of the 'new truth' that would rectify
relations between the sexes: like Dimmesdale, Pearl and the people
of New England, that is, Hester experiences a symbolic closure of
the 'breach' created by guilt, although it is 'never, in this mortal
state, repaired' (156, 251, 191).

Only Chillingworth's exclusion is unmitigated. The critical
detachment of which Hawthorne disapproves in Hester (Pearl,
who exemplifies another kind of disjunction, is finally no more
to 'do battle with the world, but be a woman in it') corresponds
to Chillingworth's learnedness, just as Dimmesdale's duplicity
parallels his demonism (244). Chillingworth is a 'scholar', an al-
chemist and a physician, 'a man of skill in all Christian modes of
physical science, and likewise familiar with whatever the savage
people could teach; he is a learner of ' "secrets" ', both in the
forest and in Salem, for there are, he says, ' "few things hidden
from the man who devotes himself . . . to the solution of a mystery" ' (55, 65-70). Dimmesdale, on his part, contemplates the
dark problem of life, and like Hester, on whom the 'shadow of
the curtain' falls so that she is 'partially concealed' during Pearl's
catechism exercise, is withdrawn, a   man of veils, is 'partially
concealed' by the same curtain, lives behind the 'noontide shadow'
of heavy curtains, scourges himself in a 'secret closet' and holds
his cloak 'before his face' as he leaves the forest (102, 119, 137,
210): the luminous celestial 'A' that marks his midnight self-
revelation burns 'duskily through a veil of cloud' (147). Their
moments of truth, moreover, are those of deep eye-contact, which
Hester dreads with Chillingworth, and which transcend the duplicity of Dimmesdale's public addresses to Hester, who answers
Reverend Wilson without removing her eyes from those of the
minister (159, 63-64); the latter 'seldom, nowadays, looked
straightforth at any object, whether human or inanimate', but

must nevertheless ' "meet so many eyes" ', which see him as the saint he doubts he is (123, 182); Hester forces him to 'look her sternly in the face', exercises 'a magnetic power' through their eye contact: at his final moment of victory he meets Chillingworth's eyes 'fearfully, but firmly' (185, 241).

For Chillingworth, however, everything is obvious: his ' "plainness of speech" ' is counterpoised against Dimmesdale's deceitful eloquence, and he is capable of subjecting the personal to critical examination, of bringing studious attention to bear in a situation of interpersonal involvement: 'With calm and intent scrutiny, he felt her pulse, looked into her eyes, – a gaze . . . so familiar, and yet so strange and cold, – and, finally, satisfied with his investigation . . .' (128, 68). Eye-contact is not redemptive for him: Chillingworth is not interested in, in fact seeks to avoid, showdowns. Eye confrontations are associated, in the equations of literature, with mirror imagery, as when Ahab gazes into the water and meets Fedallah's reflected eyes (MD, 445): the mirror in 'The custom house' brings Hawthorne from actual to imaginative, and the imagination is a mirror become tarnished; Hester is a youthful mirror gazer, and finds the 'A' disproportionately emphasized in the 'convex mirror' of a breast plate, which thus reflects truth rather than distortion (55,99); Hester and Arthur mirror one another in eye-contact; but when she contemplates 'her own image' reflected in Pearl's eyes, it turns 'fiend-like, full of smiling malice' (181,91). If the demonism embodied in Pearl resists the mirror-image correspondence that Hester and Dimmesdale have, then it may be wondered, given the satanic imagery with which he is portrayed, whether Chillingworth can be seen in a mirror: having told Hester of the torture he has inflicted on the minister, Chillingworth 'lifted his hands with a look of horror, as if he had beheld some frightful shape, which he could not recognize, usurping the place of his own image in a glass' (163). Chillingworth is an empiricist for whom nothing is hidden; he anticipates Sam Spade's relentlessness and Agee's voyeurism; he is an orphaned Ishmael, comparable to Burroughs' alienated, arch, cruelly wry private investigators, allowing his observations to speak for themselves; and like all of these characters, he knows how to wait.

However, Chillingworth's alertness to the obvious is not to be confused with the omniscience of Hawthorne's narrator: occasionally the latter hedges this omniscience, qualifies his speculations with 'perchance' or 'perhaps', as he does his illustration of Pearl's redemptive effect on Hester with, 'if we suppose this interview . . . to be authentic and not a parable' (51, 240, 110). He wonders whether Mistress Hibbins, having extinguished the light by which she is visible, 'Possibly . . . went up among the clouds', and suggests that the celestial epiphany of light is due to a meteor, imputing Dimmesdale's vision of the 'A' 'solely to the disease of his own eye and heart', though he proceeds to show the vision corroborated by the sexton's report (141-147, 150). But Hawthorne thereby questions, not his own authority, but that of the record contained in Pue's account, through which 'we seem to see' a purpose for Hester's ignominy, and which might, should anyone undertake 'the unprofitable labour', be 'worked up' into a history of Salem (191, 29); the difference between record and romance is that between the various 'theories' of how the letter came to Dimmesdale's breast, along with conflicting reports as to its actual presence there and the substance of the minister's final speech, and its 'deep print', due to 'long meditation', in the narrator's brain — between the 'more than one account of what had been witnessed on the scaffold' and the symbolic moral resolution or metastory which it is the narrator's business to portray. He protests, when a wolf offers his head to be patted by Pearl, that 'here the tale has surely lapsed into the improbable', dispensing with the fabulous but gleaning the 'truth' of Pearl's 'kindred wildness' with the forest (245-246, 195). 'When an uninstructed multitude attempts to see with its eyes', says Hawthorne, 'it is extremely apt to be deceived. When, however, it forms its judgement . . . on the intuition of its great and warm heart, the conclusions thus attained are often so profound and so unerring, as to possess the character of truths supernaturally revealed' (119-120). The only thoroughgoing eyewitness is the villain of the piece.

Hawthorne, transcending multiplicity and distortion, is spokesman for the heart. Melville, who would also 'rather be a fool with a heart, than Jupiter Olympus with his head',[12] has a strikingly different approach to records, not transcending their limitations but elaborating their ambiguity and the impermeability of appearances, as in 'Benito Cereno', suggesting in *Moby-Dick* that the account is the event, unmitigatedly distortive of the 'reality' that occasions its taking shape, and emphasizing, at the close of *Billy*

Budd, the incompatibility of event and report – or more correctly, of event and event, report and report. In *Mardi*, King Donjololo sends a pair of independent observers, 'honest of heart, keen of eye, and shrewd of understanding', to foreign islands, who infuriate him by contradicting each other ' "before our very face. . . . How is it? Are the lenses in their eyes diverse-hued, that objects seem different to both? for undeniable is it, that the things they thus clashingly speak of are to be known for the same; though represented with unlike colors and qualities".[13] Hawthorne's paraphrase of his characters' thoughts, as of Hester's subintellectual 'sense' of destiny, constitutes a freedom from his documents, so that he coyly suggests, rather than plainly states, his meaning: he is (and the reader is) that 'preternaturally gifted observer' or 'spiritual seer' who alone would detect the new expression on Hester's face on election day, as well as that 'imagination . . . irreverent enough to surmise' a connection between Hester and the minister (233, 216, 235-236). It is Dimmesdale's office to ' "hold communion, on your behalf, with the Most High Omniscience" '; and when Hawthorne says of the minister, standing on the scaffold at midnight, that 'No eye could see him, save that ever-watchful one which had seen him in his closet, wielding the bloody scourge', there could be no clearer indication that the narrator's eye also communes with that transcendent omniscience (136,139).

On the other hand, Chillingworth's point of view is as limited as that of the crowd of 'silent and inactive spectators', out of which he does not rise to the overview of the scaffold until the day of judgment (election day, when the elect come forward): he first appears when Hester, 'under the heavy weight of a thousand unrelenting eyes', discovers that he has been watching her for 'some time' from the midst of the crowd (241,53,56). (Burroughs, describing the indescriminate police clubbing of 'Yippies newsmen and bystanders' at the Chicago '68 riots, comments: 'There are no innocent bystanders. What are they doing there in the first place? The worst sin of man is to be born'.[14]) Being watched is the most unbearable kind of punishment: Hester 'had always this dreadful urgency in feeling a human eye upon the token'; and Dimmesdale lets loose a shriek when, safely in the dark, he is suddenly 'overcome with a great horror of mind, as if the universe were gazing at a scarlet token on his naked breast' (80, 140). And

Chillingworth fills that office, is a kind of psychoanalyst digging 'into the poor clergyman's heart' in search of the 'animal nature' beneath the latter's ' "all spiritual" ' appearance, urging him to expose ' "the dead corpse buried in his own heart" ' (117, 121-124). Medical men in the colony, we are told, are usually so preoccupied with the 'wondrous mechanism' of the body as to have 'lost the spiritual view of existence' (111-112), and Dimmesdale's analyst is no exception:

If the latter possess native sagacity, and a nameless something more, − let us call it intuition: if he show no intrusive egotism, nor disagreeably prominent characteristics of his own; if he have the power, which must be born with him, to bring his mind into such affinity with his patient's, that this last shall unawares have spoken what he imagines himself only to have thought; if such revelations be received without tumult, and acknowledged not so often by an uttered sympathy as by silence, an inarticulate breath, and here and there a word, to indicate that all is understood; if to these qualifications of a confidant be joined the advantages afforded by his recognized character as a physician, − then, at some inevitable moment, will the soul of the sufferer be dissolved, and flow forth in a dark, but transparent stream, bringing all its mysteries into the daylight.

Chillingworth scrutinizes every aspect of the minister, lives with him so that all details 'might pass under [his] eye', waits for indications to appear on Dimmesdale's 'surface' (116-117). Couched as he is in the language of romance (he has a 'penetrating power' of glance, plans to discover Pearl's father by 'a sympathy that will make me conscious of him', is associated with the black arts [55, 70, 120]), he nevertheless displays the skepticism of an empiricist, versed in ' "the kindly knowledge of simples" ' (67). If Hawthorne suggests that eventually 'words embody things', Chillingworth refutes any amenability to symbolism: ' "Ye that have wronged me are not sinful, save in a kind of typical illusion; neither am I fiend-like, who have snatched a fiend's office from his hands" ' (214,165). He is unregenerate, refusing any kind of redemption (' "It is our fate. Let the black flower blossom as it may!" '), as is appropriate to one limited to the sphere of mechanism, controlling the 'engine' of Dimmesdale's tortures, carrying out 'machinations', bringing a 'terrible machinery . . . to bear', tampering with 'the delicate springs of Mr. Dimmesdale's nature' (132-133, 151, 158); but the minister gains 'new energy' on the scaffold at midnight, forming with Pearl and Hester 'an electric chain' (145).

Again at this point, Chillingworth is discovered watching from ground level, his malevolent expression remaining 'painted on the darkness' when the light of the meteor has vanished (148). The hideous metamorphoses to which he is subject — horror twisting 'across his features, like a snake gliding over them', the 'something ugly and evil' in his face after it has studied Dimmesdale, and the 'transformation' brought about by several years' devotion to torture (55,120,161) — are comparable to the contortions through which Agee is put by his guilty voyeurism, and to the uncontrollable mutations to which Burroughs' characters are subject. Voyeurism and impersonal analysis — 'the constant analysis of a heart full of torture, and deriving his enjoyment thence, and adding fuel to those fiery tortures which he analyzed and gloated over' — are the weapons of Chillingworth's 'intimate revenge'; Dimmesdale must, says Hester, remove himself from ' "under his evil eye" ' (161, 187). And when Chillingworth wonders aloud if it would be possible ' "to analyze that child's nature, and, from its make and mould, to give a shrewd guess at the father" ', he is acting in his capacity as diagnostician, as when he addresses the ' "symptoms" ' of Dimmesdale's infected conscience — is, in the original sense of the word, a semiologist (109, 128). Like Ishmael and Agee, Chillingworth is both actor in and viewer of the drama in which he is involved; his finally joining the others on the scaffold is an acknowledgment that Dimmesdale has escaped, for without the suppression of a secret there can be no spy: in the redemptive scheme of the romance, guarded obscurity gives way to sunlit clarity and perfect shamelessness, and dissolves the role of the voyeur. But in the absence of such a scheme, Chillingworth, unlike the other characters, remains interesting: he enters a room in which Dimmesdale lies sleeping before an open work 'in the somniferous school of literature' (perhaps it would not be perverse to compare him with the photographer in *Blow-Up* as he moves among the hypnotized shapes of rock-fans and among the stoned inmates of a party: like him, Chillingworth is unquestionably awake), steps directly to his side and uncovers the breast on which he bears the 'A'; the combination of joy and horror in Chillingworth's comportment is comparable to Satan's at the loss of a soul. 'But', Hawthorne comments, 'what distinguished the physician's ecstasy from Satan's was the trait of wonder in it!'

(130-131).

PEEPING TOMMO AND THE INCONCLUSIVENESS OF EXPERIENCE

The remarkable difference between Hawthorne's work and Melville's is that the latter offers no certain pattern of redemption into which to incorporate and by which to justify experience. Whereas Hawthorne, whose narrator partakes of divine omniscience, regards the collector of facts and analyst of appearances as villainous, Melville's narrative personae are often unredeemed voyeurs, and the romantic hero who insists upon ultimate symmetry is, as in *Mardi* and *Moby-Dick*, merely mad. The salient example of this narrative voyeurism is *Typee: A Peep at Polynesian Life*, which bears out its subtitle with introductory promises of exciting peeps at '*heathenish rites and human sacrifices*', and such stories as of the Polynesian natives' stripping and de-deifying a missionary's wife, the immodesty of the native king's consort before the French officers, descriptions of native girls – their innocence of clothing and enthusiasm for such frolic as reveals 'glimpses of their forms', their playful transgression of the narrator's sexual 'feelings of propriety', and their enticing dancing – *à la National Geographic*, and especially the descriptions of Fayaway in 'the primative and summer garb of Eden', and spreading her robe as a sail for Tommo's boat.[15] Nonsexual 'visions of outlandish things' are also recorded, such as the numerous visions of beautiful sky - and landscapes which might not flippantly be compared to postcard scenes, and which make the narrator a 'spectator' in the 'enchanted gardens' of paradise (5, 49). Tommo is something of an anthropological field-observer among the natives, 'occupied . . . either in watching the proceedings of those around me or taking part in them myself', himself submitting to 'scrutiny' by the natives who marvel at the whiteness of his unexposed skin, going 'so far in their investigations as to apply the olfactory organ' (151, 71). And, like Agee, he feels that his 'inquiring, scientific moods' are somehow profane, as when Kory-Kory whirls an 'idol about most profanely, so as to give me the opportunity of examining it on all sides' (73-74, 178-189).

Repeatedly reminding us of his status as an eyewitness, Tommo provides a geographical description of Nukuheva and accounts of its 'natural history' (climate, animal population, vegetation, diseases), the medicinal waters of Arva Wai (though, 'As I am no chemist, I cannot give a scientific analysis of the water'), and the mysterious arrangement of huge and apparently antique blocks of stone into a gradation of terraces (23-24, 210-213, 153-155). He gives extensive attention to the food and culinary skills of the natives, to their language (including frequent glosses translating and elaborating particular terms, and a description of the 'vocal telegraph' system of information conveyance), to details of their physical formation and traces of European-introduced diseases, and to their political, economic, sexual and religious forms of practice, concentrating especially on the observance of 'taboo' people and situations — which, for the observer at least, are not governed by any predictable system, and thus impossible not to bungle against. Chapter 20 is devoted to 'the history of a day' in the valley. A notable amount of prescriptive information appears in LUNPFN (steal out in the middle of the night, take a certain path, and this will happen; pick cotton in a certain posture for so long, and see if this happens); Burroughs refers to *Naked Lunch* as 'a blueprint, a How-To Book . . . Abstract concepts, bare as algebra, narrow down to a black turd or a pair of aging cajones' (NL, 224). *Moby-Dick* is such a book, telling how to find, catch and process whales; and in *Typee* we learn how to make a fire Typee-style, how to manufacture 'tappa', the native cloth, how to prepare 'arva' -root juice, how to prepare breadfruit, how to climb coconut trees, how to tattoo and how to obtain coconut oil. But while Tommo misses nothing obvious to inspection, he is 'baffled in . . . attempts to learn the origin' of particular festive customs, and does not know 'what to make of the religion of the valley', daily ceremonies being 'very much like seeing a parcel of "Free-masons" ' making secret signs to each other: 'I saw everything but could comprehend nothing'. And the Typees' concealment from him of evidence of their cannibalism leaves him dubious as to what they intend for him. What is not obvious, that is (and this applies also perhaps to the Typees, whose indecisive behavior on the day of his escape makes dubious whether they know what they want to do with Tommo, who is also 'inclined to believe' that they have 'no fixed and definite ideas whatever on the subject of religion'), is intention, purpose, a stable context of meaning (169, 177). And this ambiguous situation informs his report on it, and his editorial comments: 'those things which I have stated as facts will remain facts', he says in defence of missionary practices; 'any reflections, however, on those facts may not be free from error' (199).

Tommo's limited point of view, is precisely the subject of the book. And it is the source of the excitement of the adventure. As the sounds of shouting and musket fire in the hills reach their ears, Kory-Kory interprets them 'as if he were gifted with second sight, going through a variety of pantomimic illustrations, showing me the precise manner in which the redoubtable Typees were at that very moment chastising the insolence of the enemy'; but Tommo subsequently discovers that the Typee leader had 'rather inclined to the Fabian than the Bonapartian tactics', and can report the issue of the skirmish only 'as far as its results came under my observation' (129-130). Melville constantly denies his narrator a comprehensive point of view, involving him in a subjective struggle with details, the attempt to configure ideas meaningfully. From his first thoughts of desertion he is deluded, 'picturing myself seated beneath a cocoanut tree on the brow of the mountain, with a cluster of plantains within easy reach'; he and Toby successively find themselves 'shut . . . out from the view of surrounding objects' by a forest of reeds, and so unable to determine their direction, attaining the 'lofty elevation' of a mountain crest and a corresponding 'sense of security', but beholding, not a valley like the one they have left, but a 'series of ridges and inter-vales, which as far as the eye could reach stretched away from us', and which provide the setting for subsequent misconstructions of the terrain, and of each other's behavior (31, 38-41). The 'Important Question' of their geographical position, relative to the inhabitants of the valley below, is a bivalued one: '*Typee or Happar?* '; annihilation or friendly reception? Pointing out that 'it was impossible for us to know anything with certainty', Tommo persuades Toby to avoid the valley, the country offering them 'little choice' but by turn to descend into the canyons in their path and climb the intervening ridges, Tommo suffering alternately from 'ague and fever', and thus driven alternately by thirst and repulsion from water, descending from each rise not knowing 'whether I was helplessly falling from the heights above, or whether [his speed is] an act of my own volition' (50-53).

Deciding to risk the valley and agreeing (Toby is 'overjoyed at my verification of his theory') that all the canyons must lead there, they arrive at a sheer precipice down which they lower themselves by long roots, Tommo 'taking care to test their strength before I trusted my weight to them', but finally reaching a point at which all the roots within reach snap off at being tried, so that he must take the 'frightful risk' of jumping for an untested root; descending a second cliff and again faced with ' "no other alternative" ', he must follow Toby's example ('I could scarcely credit the evidence of my senses') and leap from cliff to precarious treetop (54-63). When they approach two natives of the valley with the question "Typee or Happar? " and then put 'together in the form of a question the words "Happar" and "Mortarkee", the latter being equivalent to the word "good", they proceed on the assumption that they are addressing the friendly Happars and receive emphatic affirmation of their formulation: in fact the natives are Typees, frightened by the strangers' use of their enemies' name; moreover, their basic assumption is false, for the Typees are gentle, while the Happars later seriously wound Toby (69).

The suspicion persists, however, 'that beneath their fair appearances the islanders covered some perfidious design, and that their friendly reception of us might precede some horrible catastrophe'; nor, given the 'fickle disposition of the savages', is the answer to questions formulated by two-valued logic ever binding, for death is an immanent possibility 'under all these smiling appearances' (76, 97). Tommo is frightened by the ambiguous (' "What can all this mean, Toby? " '), repeatedly finds Typee behavior 'unaccountable', 'unpredictable', suspects by taste that he is eating human flesh, only to discover by taper that it is pork, and forms his 'conclusion . . . from my own observations, and, as far as I could understand, from the explanation which Kory-Kory gave me' (93-97, 235); about Toby's disappearance, 'All their accounts were contradictory', and with narrative hindsight Tommo notes that all his 'speculations were in vain' (107- 109). As for his own motives, when he remembers 'the numberless proofs of kindness and respect' on the part of the natives he can 'scarcely understand how it was' that he should indulge 'dismal forebodings', though he acknowledges the 'mysterious disease' in his leg, an 'unaccountable malady' that comes and goes unpredictably until after he has left. As for the motives of the Typees, while Tommo has some evidence of their 'intention' to keep him prisoner (is jerked alert out of his eagerness to meet a European ship: 'It was at this moment, when fifty savage countenances were glaring upon me, that I first truly experienced I was indeed a captive'), he knows nothing of their 'object', the possible 'treacherous scheme' behind their kindness (118-120, 142, 239). He is continually, that is, hanging by an untested root, just as his report must repeatedly exclude knowledge of the 'purpose' behind customs. And he closes the account with a confession of ignorance as to the 'mystery' of Toby's fate (153). Ultimate proof, the confirmation or not of all his suspicions, is unavailable: his understanding is confined to sets of words and gestures with only the most precariously guessed contexts, and is undercut by further observations.

Edgar Allan Poe's *The Narrative of Arthur Gordon Pym of Nantucket*, while it does not record a nonliterary event, is a comparable work in that it relates a series of episodes, each involving a shift in perspective which undeceives the narrator by modifying his point of view. 'In no affairs of mere prejudice, *pro* or *con*', Pym says, 'do we deduce inferences with entire certainty, even from the most simple data': awakening from a dream of being devoured by a lion, he discovers his dog's paws on his chest; stowed away in the hold of a ship, he forms 'a thousand surmises' as to why he has been deserted, only to learn that a mutiny has occurred above deck; marooned at mid-ocean, he is approached by a brig over the bow of which leans a man making 'encouraging' gestures, 'nodding to us in a cheerful although rather odd way, and smiling constantly so as to display the most brilliantly white teeth' — a lipless corpse, in fact, shaken from behind by a gull devouring his liver. But Pym's narrative differs from Tommo's peep in pointing toward a resolution of the ambiguous in perception: the suggestion in the appended editor's 'Note' that the Antarctic fissures mapped by Pym have the form of Ethiopian, Arabic and Egyptian words takes us from a close-up of the confusion and 'utter darkness' of the chasm to an elevated and meaningful overview[16] — the point of view of the 'earth-angels', as it is put in 'The domain of Arnheim', that ' "class of beings, human once, but now invisible to humanity, to whom, from afar, our disorder may seem order — our unpicturesqueness picturesque" '.[17] No such point of view is suggested in *Typee*; Kory-Kory's invocation of a creation myth to explain the ancient stone structures on the island 'at once convinced me that neither he nor the rest of his countrymen knew anything about them'; Tommo reckons that the 'monument' is 'doubtless the work of an extinct and forgotten race', though there are 'no inscriptions, no sculptures, no clue, by which to conjecture its history'; they do 'establish the great age of the island' and eliminate the possibility that it is the work of 'the coral insect'. It is 'as possible as anything else' that the island, and for that matter the whole of America, has been thrown up by volcanic eruption: 'No one can make an affidavit to the contrary, and therefore I will say nothing against the supposition' (154-155). The ambiguity of a situation uncontrolled by an informing myth is most vividly illustrated by the effigy of the dead warrior-chief, seated in a canoe and 'holding his paddle . . . in the act of rowing, leaning forward and inclining his head, as if eager to hurry on his voyage', the direction of which is commented on by the 'polished human skull, which crowned the prow of the canoe', so as to glare 'face to face' at the warrior (172): the illustration is repeated in 'Benito Cereno' by the mutinous Babo, who replaces the San Dominick's figurehead of Christopher Columbus with a skeleton, beneath which is inscribed, *Follow your leader*'.[18]

Marheyo's use of Tommo's old shoes as a pendant necklace illustrates this lack of fixed context or meaning, the fact that 'things unserviceable in one way, may with advantage be applied in another . . . if one have genius enough for the purpose' (146), just as the students in Godard's *La Chinoise* remark the cleverness of a passer-by who makes handlebars and a bicycle seat out of their discarded, Picassoesque bull's head. This is consonant with Tommo's account of the Typee language, similar to other Polynesian dialects in that it features the duplication of some words, and in 'the different senses in which one and the same word is employed', so that 'one brisk, lively little word is obliged . . . to perform all sorts of duties . . . the particular meaning being shown chiefly by a variety of gestures and the eloquent expression of the countenance'. And while he regards these dialects as less sophisticated than civilized languages, he notes their extreme 'intricacy', the complete blackboard conjugation of a Hawaiian verb covering 'the side of a considerable apartment' (224-225). Here as elsewhere, Tommo treats words simply as other things, as visible tabulated marks, or as sounds, noting the 'labial melody with which the Typee girls carry on an ordinary conversation, giving a musical prolongation to the final syllable of every sentence', and the 'rough-sided sounds' issuing from the men when in the midst of their peculiar sort of 'wordy paroxysm' (277). And he gives similar descriptions of gestures, Toby on various occasions 'throwing himself into all the attitudes of a posture-master, vainly [trying] to expostulate with the natives by signs and gestures', at one point 'opening his mouth from ear to ear, and thrusting his fingers down his throat, gnashing his teeth and rolling his eyes about' in order to indicate hunger (80,69): the problem with which Tommo and Toby consistently struggle is how messages are communicated, how things are known.

Names are arbitrarily connected with things. The Washington Group of islands is 'arbitrarily distinguished' from the Marquesas, for inclusion within which Tommo offers an argument based on dialect, laws, religion and customs (11). The name 'Typee' means 'a lover of flesh', remarkable in its application to one out of many cannibalistic tribes; and in fact Marnoo points out that, with reference to the French, 'as yet the terror of their name had preserved them from attack' (24-25, 138). Tommo repeatedly deplores the exposure of the natives to Europeans in order to become '*nominal* Christians', 'enjoy the mere name of Christians without experiencing any of the vital operations of true religion' (195,182). He notes that 'the term "Savage" is . . . often misapplied', and suggests that it is by civilized intruders that the Polynesians 'are made to deserve the title' (124, 26). References are ostensive ('Ned, pointing with his hand in the direction of the treacherous valley, exclaimed, "There — there's Typee" ') and language learned by association: establishing that his dinner is not human flesh but 'puarkee', Tommo declares that 'from that day to this I have never forgotten that such is the designation of a pig in the Typee lingo' (25,95). Thus the language of the descriptive report does not embody but refers to things, just as (as in Berkeley) physiognomy is 'indicative' of emotion, which is 'depicted' in the countenance (214, 351, 142). It is emphasized that 'description' is inadequate to 'beauty', to 'a scene of confusion', to 'a sensation of horror', to the feeling of 'wretchedness' and to the vividness of recollections (12, 15, 13, 125, 237, 120, 91): as in Locke, these simple ideas, which enter the mind 'by all the ways of sensation and reflection' (*Essay*, II, vii, 1), can only be named. 'I may succeed', says Tommo, 'in particularizing some of the individual features of Fayaway's beauty, but that general loveliness of appearance which they all contributed to produce I will not attempt to describe' (86). Like Agee, Tommo offers lists of particulars, records of events and fallible calculations, leaving their realization to his reader: when, in Chapter 31, he proposes 'to string together, without any attempt at order, a few odds and ends not hitherto mentioned' (226) he displays that insouciance as to an organizing superstructure that also characterizes LUNPFM and *Naked Lunch*. Tommo is a kind of Adam bestowing his own names on the ' "Feast of the Calabashes" ' and on ' "Fayaway's Lake" ', and on Mehevi 'the title of king' (160,171,189). And like Chillingworth and Ishmael, Tommo and Toby name themselves: Toby is 'the name by which he went among us, for his real name he never would tell us'; and since Toby is the name actually used by Melville's companion, there is no reason not to assume that when the narrator says he 'hesitated for an instant, thinking that it might be difficult for him to pronounce my real name, and then with the most praiseworthy intentions intimated that I was known as "Tom" ', he is withholding from Mehevi the name 'Herman' (31, 72).

This attitude toward words is to be distinguished from that of the captain from whom they escape, who 'has registered a vow' not to return home without a full cargo of sperm oil, and at the writing of *Typee* is still in the Pacific, and from that of Christian navies who 'burn, slaughter, and destroy, according to the tenor of written instructions' (22-23, 27). Both are associated with oratory, the captain delivering a specious harangue on the evils of Nukuheva; and the replacement by merciless subjugation of native idolatry with a disinterested mercantilism would make a fit 'subject for an eloquent Bible-meeting orator' (34-35, 196). The taboo Marnoo gives a 'powerful . . . exhibition of natural eloquence . . . during the course of his oration', exhorting the Typees to resist the French by suggesting that their ferocious 'name' has real meaning — addressing their faith in words. By speaking 'a few words of their language' to the first frightened Typees he meets, Tommo instills in them 'a little confidence'; and when he finally succeeds in formulating the desirable message, ' "Typee Mortarkee" ', his hosts are suddenly ecstatic, shouting 'again and again the talismanic syllables, the utterances of which appeared to have settled everything' (137-138, 68, 71). While singing is unknown to them, they are 'remarkably fond of chanting', the rhythmic and hypnotic repetition of patterns which Agee, when he speaks of Gudger's adopting 'a saving rhythm' of movement (whereas LUNPFM is a 'dissonant prologue'), defines as a psychological security device. Words and forms have immutable significance for the Typees, and 'An exchange of names is equivalent to a ratification of good will and amity among these simple people', who live in an unquestioned world of analogy, describe heaven in terms of finer mats, lovelier women and more plentiful breadfruit (227, 72, 172).

'The penalty of the Fall presses very lightly upon the valley of Typee', for there is no strenuous labour and an admirable 'social order' without the aid of 'municipal police' or 'established law' — an 'enigma' which Tommo can 'explain' only by supposing an 'indwelling' and 'universally diffuse perception of what is *just* and noble', precivilized and 'distorted by arbitrary codes': 'It must have been by an inherent principle of honesty and charity towards each other . . . that sort of commonsense law which, say what they will of the inborn lawlessness of the human race, has its precepts graven on every breast' (200-201). Locke rejects the idea of any such innate principle (*Essay*, I, i-ii), allowing for a 'law of nature' (a law, as opposed to a right, is 'what enjoins or forbids') which is 'implanted by nature in all men', discoverable in each independently of his fellows by the rational 'arranging together of the images of things derived from sense perception', and evidenced by the presence of conscience and men's regard for virtue; but, while he holds that the law of nature is 'perpetual and universal' in its 'binding force', he denies that it is 'inscribed in our hearts' (or derived from 'tradition') and holds that human society is impossible without 'a definite constitution of the state and form of government'[19]: so that Tommo is describing a form of myth of original identity with some hold on him, and thus comparable to that of the White Whale which at times captivates Ishmael, to Agee's communal experience and feeling, with the Gudgers, of having come home, and to the manic phase of Burroughs' fantasies.

While Locke rejects the notion of 'golden ages in the past' and the obscuring of an innate law by a 'Fall',[20] the honesty and fraternal feeling of the Typees suggests to Tommo an edenic alternative to the depravity fostered by arbitrary codes, life as it

was meant ('intended') to be lived. Repeatedly, European intruders are denounced for their corrupting influence on the 'unsophis-
ticated and confiding' natives (15), political manipulations resulting in 'out-rages and massacres' (18), the introduction of the
mosquito and syphilis (192,212) and the hypocritical champion-
ship of 'the progress of the Truth' (195). In Typee there are no
snakes, birds do not fear men, and 'the whole year is the long
tropical month of June just melting into July' (211-213); Mehevi
is twice referred to as 'the noble savage', and Rousseau is invoked
as an authority on 'the mere buoyant sense of a healthful physical
existence' (90, 189, 127); Malthusian theories are inapplicable
here, for there are none 'of those large families in arithmetical
or step-ladder progression which one often meets with at home'
(192). Early in his adventure, Tommo finds sleep a 'state of happy
forgetfulness', and for the Marquesans 'it might almost be styled
the great business of life . . . . To many of them, indeed, life is
little else than an often interrupted nap' (48, 192). The myth of
paradise is the possibility of somnolence, the young girls living
'in one merry round of thoughtless happiness', the Polynesian
enjoying 'an infinitely happier, though certainly a less intellectual
existence, than the self-complacent European' (204, 125): Tommo
is a man awake confronted by a vision of sleep, a recorder of
events who is in that interstitial space in which Burroughs and
Godard locate the reporter figure, between two contexts or
languages, able to identify with neither.

Tommo speaks of his supposition of an innate principle as
theoretical – how else 'are we to account for the social condition
of the Typees?' – and subject to contradiction by further experience: 'I formed a higher estimate of human nature than I had
ever before entertained. But alas! since then I have been one of
the crew of a man-of-war, and the pent-up wickedness of five
hundred men has nearly overturned all my previous theories'
(203). And he must argue that the Marquesan belligerence toward
whites has 'ample provocation', except intertribal enmities as out-
lets for 'evil passions' and mitigate cannibalism as a bellicose
practice among people otherwise 'humane and virtuous': 'Truth',
he says, criticizing both complete incredulity and the exaggeration
of accounts of cannibalism, 'who loves to be centrally located, is
again found between the two extremes' (205). His ambivalence
is focused on the effigy of the warrior-chief, paddling his canoe

to the undiscovered country, his 'impatient attitude' mocked by
the reversed skull: 'I loved to yield myself up to the fanciful
superstition of the islanders, and could almost believe that the
grim warrior was bound homeward.' Tommo sees 'with the eye
of faith' the 'shores of Paradise' towards which the canoeist
paddles; but he immediately dispels the enchanting fantasy with
the anthropological remark, 'This strange superstition affords
another evidence of the fact, that however ignorant man may be,
he still feels within him his immortal spirit yearning after the
unknown future' (173). Faith is both vision and 'superstition', the
'evidence' of an attitude; and Typee suggests but does not perfectly correspond to Paradise, never completely resolves Tommo's
ambivalence – a condition comparable to Ishmael's maintenance
of an equal eye. If Tommo wonders how he could ever have
thought of leaving, he also recalls clutching at 'a chance of deliver-
ance' and striking Mow Mow with a boathook – 'Even at the
moment I felt horror at the act I was about to commit' – in order
to make good his escape (246,252). Like Chillingworth, and
like Agee among the innocents, he is an observer who is not absorbed by the myth of redemption.

Written words function, according to Burroughs, 'as extensions
of our senses to witness and experience through the writer's eyes'.[21]
In his lengthy accounts of the outrages perpetrated by whites
in Polynesia ('These things are seldom proclaimed at home; they
happen at the very ends of the earth; they are done in a corner
and there are none to reveal them' [26 - 27]), Tommo is certainly
the writer of an exposé; but more pertinent is the distance between his personal contact and involvement with the natives and
the written text which records them, in which they are present to
us (Tommo frequently uses the present tense in extended accounts,
especially [175-176]), occasionally in the form of straightforward
catalogue, and of which the Typees are innocent. The reader's
point of view, the shape of his experience, the itemized elements
of his subjective consciousness, are, while he attends to his reading,
encoded upon the arbitrary marks of that written text which,
encoding also the experiences of the narrator, fails to make any
fixed, unambiguous connection with the reality it describes.
What Tommo calls his 'interest' (131, 141) and 'curiosity' (41,
45) guides the reader's attention to the details of Typee habits
and environment, posing only the most tentative relations or con-

texts to the understanding: it is this blueprint of attention, together with frequent reminders of its instability, which constitutes the record of the experience, the vicarious reconstruction of something remote. [22]

F.O. Matthiessen has shown that White-Jacket's weirdly subjective account of his fall from the masthead is not a description of Melville's experience but the embellishment of a passage from Nathaniel Ames's *A Mariner's Sketches*. [23] And Melville himself acknowledges the 'verbatim' incorporation of sentences from Porter's *Voyage into the Pacific* in 'The encantadas', except where 'facts conflict' (GSW, 146). But Leon Howard has pointed out that, while there are topographical inconsistencies in the account of Nukuheva, several of the observations are 'recorded by Melville for the first time' — not derived from other texts — and display a familiarity 'which could only have been gained by personal experience'[24] Indeed, Tommo frequently cites an 'impression produced upon my mind' so as never to be 'effaced' (28, 29, 40, 45, 49, 207, 243, 244, 252), and traces each 'idea', and each certainty, to 'seeing' (189, 183-185, 193). Almost as frequently, he insists that 'this picture is no fancy sketch; it is drawn from the most vivid recollections' (86, 204, 186). While he invokes the records made by Mendanna, Cook, Steward, Fanning and Porter in support of his appraisal of the beauty of the islanders, and cites Cook, Carteret, Byron, Kotzebue and Vancouver on the unavailability of data on Polynesian religion (183-184, 177), he is constantly questioning 'the truth of . . . reports' that do not tally with observation, attacks the 'unintentional humbuggery in some of the accounts we have from scientific men concerning the religious institutions of Polynesia', and the deceptive write-ups of native conditions which 'are sometimes copied into English and American journals' ('Not until I visited Honolulu was I aware of the fact . . . .'); and he adds an appendix, arguing from his eyewitness experience of the behavior of the English commander Paulet against 'the distorted accounts and fabrications' which circulated in Boston (170, 188, 196). The shortage of reliable reports is a major source of Tommo's suspense, for 'It is a singular fact, that in all our accounts of cannibal tribes we have seldom received the testimony of an eye-witness to the revolting practice', the only 'evidence' being either 'second-hand' or based on admissions of civilized natives. Tommo's 'suspicions' are strengthened by his catching sight of three shrunken heads and by the circumstances surrounding a victory celebration following a battle, but it is not until he actually sees — 'the slight glimpse sufficed; my eyes fell on the disordered members of a human skeleton, the bones still fresh with moisture and with particles of flesh clinging to them here and there' — that he can be said to know: 'the full sense of my condition rushed upon my mind with a force I had never before experienced' (232-238).

The scarlet 'A' imbues Hawthorne with the vision necessary to tie up all the threads of his history, to leave no element unplaced in the symbolic pattern; but no such perfection of structure appears in Melville's writing. The narrator of *The Confidence Man* despairs of any 'consistency' in 'fiction based on fact',[25] and the narrator of *Billy Budd* argues that 'The symmetry of form attainable in pure fiction cannot be so readily achieved in a narration essentially having less to do with fable than with fact. Truth uncompromisingly told will always have its ragged edges.'[26] And none so ragged as the narrative device that is Ishmael: the anticlimactic terminations of *Typee*, *Moby-Dick* and *Billy Budd* all work against the closed symmetry of fiction. Yet facts have no existence apart from being reported or experienced, from being arranged in a narrative: a fact, for Melville, is textual, contextual, linguistic.

Not only does an empirically conceived eyewitness report yield only a relative truth, as Agee says, but it can never claim to be exhaustive. Ishmael's prayer to be prevented from ever completing anything is the opposite of the omniscience of Hawthorne's narrator, of the omnipresence of Whitman, and of the Cartesian geometric perspective of Edgar Poe's Dupin, who misses no detail, formulates perfect hypotheses and even, in 'The mystery of Marie Roget', makes literary fiction applicable to reality. It is also to be distinguished from the later, Darwin-derived movement of naturalism (although *Moby-Dick* has been labeled a 'naturalistic novel'), which is exhibited in almost all American descriptive prose from Twain and Dreiser down to Faulkner, Baldwin and Mailer; which invariably, if only implicitly, invokes the evolutionary continuum as guarantor of narrative consistency; and which in its earlier phase is preoccupied with exhaustive presentations of determinant data. In LUNPFM, Agee argues specifically against ' "naturalism" ', ' "realism" ', modes of description false to experience, as in the following prescription for handling a city street:

You abjure all metaphor, symbol, selection and above all, of course, all temptation to invent, as obstructive, false, artistic. As nearly as possible in words (which even by grace of genius, would not be very near) you try to give the street *in its own terms:* that is to say, either in terms in which you (or an imagined character) see it, or in a reduction and depersonalization into terms which will as nearly as possible be the 'private', singular terms of that asphalt, those neon letters, those and all other items combined, into that alternation, that simultaneity, of flat blank tremendously constructed chords and of immensely elaborate counterpoint which is the street itself. You hold then strictly to materials, forms, colors, bulks, textures, space relations, shapes of light and shade, peculiarities, specializations, of architecture and of lettering, noises of motors and brakes and shoes, odors of exhausts: all this gathers time and weightiness which the street does not of itself have: it sags with this length and weight: and what have you in the end but a somewhat overblown passage from a naturalistic novel: which in important ways is at the opposite pole from your intentions, from what you have seen, from the fact itself. (LUNPFM, 235)

Interestingly enough, Walker Evans has recently denied that there is any truth to Agee's description of a shared consciousness of frustrated sexual urgency between Emma and each of Gudger, Evans and Agee before her departure, a contradiction which points up Agee's subjective limitations and the tenuous nature of proof, the question how either of them knows. The 'anxious desire to speak the unvarnished truth' asserted by Melville in the preface to *Typee* involves alerting us to the tentative nature of description, a condition frequently reinforced by accounts of Tommo's suspenseful situation: like the reader, Tommo is caught in a subjective world of language and impressions in which anything can happen, the whole shell of experience slip into an unforeseen meaning. His attempts to understand, and ours, are the subject of the book. In the absence of a stabilizing symbolism, there can be no more unambiguous contact with things than the impulse to survive. It is the extent of Melville's realism, as of Locke's, that we may credit a substantial reality behind Tommo's report, for he is the eyewitness who has been there to see and touch it, and come back to tell; but his account emphasizes spatial or descriptive formulations of experience, the exploration of individual sequential situations, rather than their narrative or temporal context. His narrative is a stringing together of events, sometimes in list form, no one of which necessarily implies the next; and there is nothing in *Typee*, or anywhere in Melville (despite the host of critical opinion to the contrary, especially regarding Ishmael and Pierre), that can be called 'character development'. Time points in no necessary direction — is, as the warrior-chief's effigy in *Typee* and the skeletal figurehead in 'Benito Cereno' suggest, only metaphorically spatial. Like Chillingworth, Agee and Burroughs, Tommo must learn to wait. And he too is a voyeur, for inconclusive evidence is evidence for its own sake.

NOTES

1. David Hartley, *Observations on Man, his Frame, his Duty, and his Expectations*, volume I, ed. by T.H. Huguelet. Gainesville, Scholars' Facsimiles and Reprints, 1966: i, 2, prop. 12, cor, 7; iii, 1, prop. 83.
2. Erich Auerbach, *Mimesis: The Representation of Reality in Western Literature*, trans. by W.R. Trask. Princeton University Press, 1968: 116, 317.
3. Samuel Taylor Coleridge, 'The statesman's manual', Appendix B in *Complete Works*, volume I, ed. by G.T. Shedd. New York, Harper, 1884: 437-438.
4. T.S. Eliot, 'Henry James', in *Literature in America*, ed. by Philip Rahv. New York, Meridian, 1957: 228-229.
5. Ferdinand de Saussure, *Course in General Linguistics*, trans. by W. Baskin. Glasgow, Collins, 1974: 68.
6. Herman Melville,'To Evert A. Duychinck', *The Letters of Herman Melville*, ed. by M.R. Davis and W.H. Gilman. Yale University Press, 1960: 78-79.
7. Newton Arvin, 'The whale', in *Literature in America*, ed. by Philip Rahv. New York, Meridian, 1957: 168-169.
8. Northrop Frye, *The Educated Imagination*. CBC, 1974: 19-21.
9. Northrop Frye, *Anatomy of Critisism: Four Essays*. Princeton University Press, 1957: 71-74, 123-125.
10. William Burroughs, *The Soft Machine*. New York, Ballantine, 1966: 173. Subsequent references are noted in/ the text (SM).
11. Nathaniel Hawthorne, *The Scarlet Letter*. New York, Rinehart, 1960: 8, 6-7, 9, 10. Subsequent references are noted in the text (SL).
12. Herman Melville, 'To Nathaniel Hawthorne', in *The Letters of Herman Melville*, ed. by M.R. Davis and W.H. Gilman. Yale University Press, 1960: 129. Subsequent references are noted in the text (LHM).
13. Herman Melville, *Mardi and A Voyage Thither*, volume I. London, Chapman and Dodd, 1923: 225-227. Subsequent references are noted in the text (M).
14. William Burroughs, *Exterminator!*. New York, Viking, 1973: 94.
15. Herman Melville, *Typee: A Peep at Polynesian Life*, ed. by H. Hayford, H. Parker, and G.T. Tanselle. Chicago, Newberry Library, 1968: 5-8, 14-15, 90, 110, 131, 77, 152, 134. Subsequent references are noted in the text (T).
16. Edgar Allan Poe, 'The narrative of Arthur Gordon Pym of Nantucket', in *The Complete Poems and Stories of Edgar Allan Poe*, volume II, ed. by A.H. Quinn and E.H. O'Neill. New York, Alfred A. Knopf, 1970: 732, 738-739, 745-748, 782-783, 832, 853-854.
17. Edgar Allan Poe, 'The domain of Arnheim', in *Introduction to Poe: A Thematic Reader*, ed. by E.W. Carlson, Atlanta, Scott, Foresman, 1967: 315.

The symbol and the voyeur: Chillingworth and Tommo 91

18.Herman Melville, 'Benito Cereno', in *Great Short Works of Herman Melville*, ed. by W. Berthoff. New York, Harper and Row, 1966: 241. Subsequent references are noted in the text (GSW).
19.John Locke, *Essays on the Law of Nature*, ed. by W. von Leyden. Oxford, Clarendon Press, 1965: 111, 117, 119-121, 127-129, 133, 147, 193.
20.John Locke, *Essays on the Law of Nature*, ed. by W. von Leyden. Oxford, Clarendon Press, 1965: 227, 139.
21.William Burroughs, *The Job*. New York, Grove, 1974: 104. Subsequent references are noted in the text (J).
22.For a reading of *Typee* which suggests that Melville imposes a distance between himself and his morally reprehensible narrator, see David Williams, 'Peeping Tommo: *Typee* as satire', *Canadian Review of American Studies* VI, 1975: 36-49.
23.F.O. Matthiessen, *American Renaissance: Art and Expression in the Age of Emerson and Whitman*. Toronto, Oxford University Press, 1941: 390-395.
24.Leon Howard, *Herman Melville: A Biography*. Berkeley, University of California Press, 1951: 82, 90-91, 324-327.
25.Herman Melville, *The Confidence Man*. New York, Lancer, 1968: 107. Subsequent references are noted in the text (CM).
26.Herman Melville, *Billy Budd, Sailor (An Inside Narrative)*, ed. by Harrison Hayford and Merton M. Sealts, Jr. University of Chicago Press, 1963: 128. Subsequent references are noted in the text (BB).

4

Locked Out: *Moby-Dick* and
the Flotsam of Narrative Continuity

> Often, when I was young, last year, I walked out
> to the water. It spoke to me of myself. Images
> came to me, from the water. Pictures. Large green
> lawns. A great house with pillars, but the lawns
> so vast that the house can be seen only dimly, from
> where we are standing. I am wearing a long skirt
> to the ground, in the company of others. I am witty.
> They laugh. I am also wise. They ponder. Gestures
> of infinite grace. They appreciate. For the finale,
> I save a life. Leap into the water all clothed and
> grasping the drowner by the hair, or using the cross-
> chest carry, get the silly bastard to shore. Have to
> bash him once in the mush to end his wild panicked
> struggles. Drag him to the old weathered dock and
> there, he supine, I rampant, manage the resuscitation.
> Stand back, I say to the crowd, stand back. The
> dazed creature's eyes open — no, they close again —
> no, they open again. Someone throws a blanket
> over my damp, glistening white, incredibly beautiful
> shoulders. I whip out my harmonica and give them
> two fast choruses of "Red Devil Rag." Standing
> ovation. The triumph is complete.
>
> Donald Barthelme
> *The Dead Father*

The handling of empirical data in *Typee*, its lack both of Romantic symbolism and of its mirror image, realism (what Richards, in
Coleridge on Imagination, calls the 'realist and projective doctrines'),
anticipates the subsequent descriptions of Sperm Whales, economi-
cally depressed cotton farmers and heroin addiction. Chillingworth and peeping Tommo are exemplary voyeurs, reporters who

are excluded from and offer critiques of the machinery of redemption, of alignment with an extrasubjective reality. *Moby-Dick* develops, more fully than *Typee*, the implications both of that voyeurism which corresponds to Locke's inexpressible understanding, the eye which cannot be inferred from the visual field, and of the concomitant limitations of empiricism. *Moby-Dick* makes of Locke's two-fold notion of substance, that which supports material qualities and that which supports attention, a single, self-reflexive issue. When Ishmael names himself, he names the text, the visible form which encodes the content of his attention, of the reader's, and of what is described.

ISHMAEL: THE TEXT AS VOYEUR

The name, as has frequently been pointed out, is appropriate to a dispossessed orphan: as a child he is already an orphan, sent to bed for the day by a 'stepmother' and awakening in the dark, though still 'half steeped in dreams', to an unverifiable sense of touch: 'nothing was to be seen, and nothing was to be heard; but a supernatural hand seemed placed in mine'; he is unable, in his fearful paralysis, to disengage from 'the nameless, unimaginable, silent form or phantom' which 'seemed' seated beside him. In *Mardi*, Yillah is the veiled figure of whiteness, the suggestion of substance and object of a relentless quest, and 'the hand of Yillah in mine seemed no hand, but a touch'.[1] Ishmael's problem, like Locke's, is to distinguish dream from waking reality: 'afterwards I lost myself in confounding attempts to explain the mystery. Nay, to this very hour I often puzzel myself with it' (MD, 33). Ishmael is cut off from unambiguous knowledge of what his impressions mean, is without a firm context: 'Our souls are like those orphans whose unwedded mothers die in bearing them: the secret of our paternity lies in the grave, and we must there to learn it' (406). Ahab's quest resolves nothing for Ishmael, who remains, when the Pequod has gone down, 'another orphan' to be found by the Rachel (470). It is to be noticed, however, that Ahab is also an orphan, son of a ' "crazy widowed mother, who died when he was only a twelve-month old" ' (77); he addresses the corposants, 'But thou art but my fiery father; my sweet mother I know not' (417). The differences between their responses to this lack of context, to being ' "turned round and round in this world" ' (445). as Ahab says, give shape to the book — the differences, that is, between Ishmael's acceptance of 'the universal thump' (15) and Ahab's rage against it.

Ishmael's name, then, has also the import of its Hebrew meaning, 'God hears', in the sense of 'overhears', wordplays on which occur in Genesis (Hagar is given Ishmael 'because the Lord hath heard thy affliction . . . . And she called the name of the Lord that spoke unto her, Thou God seest me: for she said, Have I also looked after him that seeth me? ' — 16: 11-13; 'And as for Ishmael, I have heard thee' — 17: 20; 'and God heard the voice of the lad' — 21: 17). Ishmael's narrative function is that of a hearer or eavesdropper, and by implication of a voyeur, who, unlike Hawthorne's narrator, does not transcend but reflects upon the limits of his world: he is the formulation of his experience, the record of what he has seen and overheard. The implications of narrative omniscience are a pronounced issue for Melville: in *Mardi*, Babbalanja points out that the belief that God 'is not merely a universal onlooker, but occupies and fills all space' yields the conclusion that 'he cannot be perfectly good' (M,II, 90-91). White-Jacket attributes it 'to the fact of my having been a maintop-man. . . that I am now enabled to give such a free, broad, off-hand bird's eye, and, more than all, impartial account of our man-of-war world; withholding nothing; inventing nothing' — so that he qualifies his paraphrase of Claret's thoughts with the postscript, 'there is no knowing, indeed, whether these were the very words in which the captain meditated that night; for it is yet a mooted point among metaphysicians, whether we think in words, or whether we think in thoughts'.[2] The same limitation is noted in 'Bartleby', for 'What my own astonished eyes saw of Bartleby, that is all I know of him, except one vague report . . . .'[3] And the narrator of *The Confidence Man* regards the empirical stance as simultaneously limiting and indispensable: 'Experience is the only guide here; but as no man can be co-extensive with *what is*, it may be unwise in every case to rest upon it. When the duck-billed beaver of Australia was first brought stuffed to England, the naturalists, appealing to their classifications, maintained that there was, in reality, no such creature' (CM, 107-108).

Moby-Dick teaches the distinction between restriction to and reliance upon experience: like White-Jacket, Ishmael regards the

masthead as an 'almost omniscient' vantage point, borne aloft by
whale ships that, like Agee's prying hands, search 'into the remotest
secret drawers and lockers of the world', though the dreaming
sailor is apt to be shocked by its instability (382). In Melville,
as in Burroughs, the reader witnesses and experiences vicariously
through the writer's eyes: 'where', asks Ishmael, 'will you obtain
a better chance to study practical cetology than here? '; 'have a
peep down the mouth'; 'Look at that hanging lower lip! '; 'Look
your last, now. . . '; 'But mark . . . . See . . . .' He speaks to the
contingencies of viewpoint, presenting a 'Contrasted View' of each
whale head, estimating oil yield 'at a passing glance', noting that
'as you come nearer to this great head it begins to assume different aspects, according to your point of view . . . . Then, again,
if you fix your eye. . .' (278-284). Nor is his narrative function
distinct from his scopophilia and its aural counterpart: from the
beginning we find him peeking through the windows of inns —
'Too expensive and jolly, again thought I, pausing one minute to
watch the broad glare in the street, and hear the sounds of tinkling
glasses within. But go on, Ishmael, said I at last. . .' (17-18) — and
confessing to rudely 'staring' at Queequeg 'and watching all his
toilette motions; for the time my curiosity getting the better of
my breeding' (34). He goes whaling ' "to see the world" ' (69)
and is, as he suggests in Chapter One, a veritable tourist at sea,
catching sight of such marvels as the giant squid: 'we now gazed
at the most wondrous phenomenon which the secret seas have
hitherto revealed to mankind' (237). His 'quick observant eye'
notes the hieroglyphic aspect of the marks on the whale's skin,
though it suggests no interpretation (260); and at the heart of the
whale community, 'Some of the subtlest secrets of the sea seemed
divulged to us . . . . We watched young Leviathin amours in the
deep' (326).

   Our view of what Ishmael sees is vicarious, for his 'special
chance to observe', as when he is fastened to the monkey rope by
which he keeps Queequeg clear of the sharks among which he
works, involves an exposure to danger; but even here Ishmael's
experience is mediated and indirect, the description of an unstable situation, a point of view which might at any moment be
undercut (271). If Ahab insists on a face-to-face showdown relationship with the elements (' "Forehead to forehead I meet
thee. . . Moby Dick! " '), the sailors rowing toward 'the life and

death peril so close to them ahead' sit backward and are forbidden to turn their heads, reading the imminence of danger 'on the intense countenance of the mate in the stern' (461, 193-194); like Ishmael, they are stabbed from behind with the thought of annihilation. But Ahab covets omniscience; he leans over the Sperm Whale's head so as to face it and deplores his exclusion from its knowledge: ' "O head! thou hast seen enough to split the planets and make an infidel of Abraham, and not one syllable is thine! " ' (264). And he demands of the sun, ' "Where is Moby Dick? . . . These eyes of mine look into the very eye that is even now beholding him; aye, and into the eye that is even now equally beholding the objects of the unknown, thither side of thee, thou sun! " ' (411-412). Ishmael too would find out, by mounting the constellation Cetus, 'whether the fabled heavens with all their countless tents really lie encamped beyond my mortal sight' (234), but neither can he transcend his eyes.

Voyeurism is impossible, moreover, in a face-to-face situation (unless, like old Roger, one returns diagnostic scrutiny for a soul-searching glance): Ishmael is in the background, or rather in the extreme foreground, and unobserved, as is the narrator of 'The encantadas' when, prompted not by 'curiosity alone, but, it seems to me, something different mingled with it', he watches Hunilla's prayer at her husband's grave: 'She did not see me, and I made no noise but slid aside and left the spot' (GSW, 136). And there is a similar furtiveness attached to the 'terrific, most pitiable, and maddening sight' of the dying old whale, for it has no relation to the merciless slaughter: 'pitiable to see. But pity there was none' (298, 301). An extended shame game, however, requires two players: on the one hand, the witness is detached yet parasitic, critical and uninvolved — is left 'floating on the margin of the ensuring scene, and in full sight of it' in an embarrassed anti-climax to the conclusion of the heroic quest (470). ' "Dost thou then so much as dare to critically think of me? " ' Ahab demands of Starbuck (392). Ishmael does: with 'greedy ears' he absorbs the story of the 'monstrous monster' and partakes in the enthusiastic oath (155), but he listens to what he hears, and finally is not true to his word to hunt Moby Dick to the death. There are no conclusions to be drawn from his experience: like the narrator of 'Poor man's pudding and rich man's crumbs', like Agee among the cotton tenants, and like the bystanders who, Burroughs says,

are never innocent, Ishmael is without justification for his presence
as an observer. His only reliable contact with reality, or context,
is the survival imperative; he searches the empirical world in vain
for an excuse.

On the other hand, the only person liable to demand an excuse
is one who resents being observed, who has something to hide:
when Radney of the Town-Ho's story, for example, flinches at
Steelkilt's drawing attention to his mulish ugliness – ' "Damn
your eyes! what's that pump stopping for? " ' – he anticipates
the latter's revenge as Moby Dick devours him before Steelkilt,
who, ' "calmly looking on... thought his own thoughts" ' (212,
222). Ahab is just such a one, a man of obscurity and secrets,
like Dimmesdale, knowing 'that to mankind he did long dissemble,
in some sort, did still': when Starbuck interrupts his rallying the
crew to ask if it ' "was not Moby Dick that took off thy leg" ',
Ahab cries, ' "Who told thee that? " ' before acknowledging the
fact (142-143). From the first he is closeted from view, neither
sick nor well, but since the loss of his leg 'desperate moody, and
savage sometimes', so that Ishmael's attempt merely ' "to see him" '
is frustrated, and he feels 'impatience at what seemed like mystery
in him' (76-77). Ahab does not appear until the cruise is well
under way, and keeps Fedallah and his boat crew out of sight until
the first whale hunt, but his groin injury, the 'secret' behind
Ahab's reclusiveness (his associates 'had all conspired. . . to muffle
up the knowledge of this thing from others') finally reaches the
ears of the crew, and is 'divulged' by Ishmael (385-386). Accordingly, like Dimmesdale, Ahab cannot bear to be watched. ' "Take
off thine eye! " ' he commands Starbuck when the latter objects
to his plan of vengeance: ' "more intolerable than fiends' glarings
is a doltish stare! " ' (144). Ishmael, however, not only sees
Fedallah when he is otherwise 'unobserved' and hears what Stubb
has 'soliloquized' (412, 360), but watches Ahab's most private
moments: 'did you deeply scan him in his more secret confident-
ial hours; when he thought no glance but one was upon him;
then you would have seen that even as Ahab's eyes so awed the
crew's, the inscrutable Parsee's glance awed his' (438).

Ishmael explores the implications of listening in when he
describes the vast busy noise of life, 'the message-carrying air',
as the hum of the weaver-god's loom, by which we 'are deafened;
and only when we escape it shall we hear the thousand voices

that speak through it. . . . Ah, mortal! then be heedful; for so in all this din of the great world's loom, thy subtlest thinkings may be overheard afar' (374-375). This is precisely Ahab's terror; when he invites the carpenter to place his leg where Ahab's is no more, so that 'here is only one distinct leg to the eye, yet two to the soul', he suggests that there might therefore be an invisible inter-penetrating and unfriendly 'thinking thing' standing also in the carpenter's place: 'In thy most solitary hours, then, dost thou not fear eavesdroppers? ' (391). Ishmael, whose name means 'God hears', hears.

Interest may be defined as the suspicion of story or pattern, a speculation (in *Mardi* all thought is represented as speculation) on the shape of things. The Confidence Man solicits interest by suggesting that one must hold to a ' "symmetrical view of the universe" ', ' "have confidence in man" ' and those 'fixed princi-ples' of human nature which the narrator of that book rejects (CM, 290, 367, 110). But for the empiricist, the relation between consecutive events, between cause and effect, motive, or inten-tion, and act − the existence, that is, of a story − is unverifiable. For Locke, causality and identity are ideas of relation, and no episode of experience necessarily implies another. 'However baby man may brag of his science and skill', Ishmael warns, 'and however much, in a flattering future, that science and skill may augment; yet for ever and for ever, to the crack of dawn, the sea will insult and murder him, and pulverize the stateliest, stiffest frigate he can make' (235). Without the support of a possible story, the explanation supplied by motive, interest is voyeuristic, unjusti-fied, without alibi − the plea of having been elsewhere when something is done: on the contrary, the voyeur is unmitigatedly present.

That the story of *Moby-Dick*, which is held together by Ahab's insane belief in intention and the causal nexus, breaks into the unconnected episodes and styles of Ishmael's account, is a major preoccupation of Melville's critics. Robert Zoellner argues against the 'Traditional opinion. . . that the Ishmaelian, first-person point of view "breaks down", the collapse getting under way in Chapter 29, where Stubb and Ahab have a conversation which Ishmael could not possibly hear, and becoming unmistakable in Chapter 37, where Ahab, alone in his cabin, delivers a brooding monologue which Ishmael could report to us only if he were hidden under

Ahab's cabin-table', by pointing out that 'Chapter 46. . . is a
sustained mass of *surmises* (the title of the chapter), by means of
which Ishmael deals in the most explicit and detailed way with
his Captain's inner thoughts, motives and plans', so that 'if Ishmael
can give us conjectural material in expository form, he can also
give us conjectural material in dramatic form'.[4] Glauco Cambon
regards the shifts from past-tense narration to present-tense
dramatic monologue and dialogue as 'a rhetorical device very
common in the classical poets and historians. . . the *historical
present*, whereby the author who is telling his story of past events
suddenly adopts the present tense to bring home to his audience
the poignancy of some particular experience relived now',[5] And
H.L. Golemba sees no essential narrative discontinuity, for 'Ahab
is never completely alone. In his "monologue" in 37, Melville is
careful to station him near the window; in 44 he rushes from his
room. Ishmael's rich imagination, prodded by Elijah's dark hints
and fed by the ship's effective grapevine, sufficiently explains the
narrator's "omniscience" '.[6] But such syntheses presuppose that
symmetrically consistent model of self which is the maniacal
insistence of Ahab rather than the form of Ishmael's experience.
' "In the midst of the personified impersonal" ', declares Ahab,
' "a personality stands here. Though but a point at best. . . yet
while I earthly live, the queenly personality lives in me, and feels
her rights" ' (417). Ishmael's participation in an enthusiastic hunt
for a monster, his vision of peace at the heart of the whale colony
and the ghostly vision which overtakes him as he stares into the
try-works exemplify the variety of his unconnected postures
relative to the fact of the whale, just as he represents Ahab both as
woven in 'tragic graces' and 'in all his Nantucket grimness and
shagginess . . . a poor old whale-hunter' (104, 130). If the business
of dealing with a slain whale involves a chaotic 'running back and
forth among the crew' and 'no staying in any one place. . . . it is
much the same with him who endeavors the description of the
scene' (270).

THIS IS MY BODY: THE SELF-REFLEXIVE TEXT

Ishmael's narrative self varies as and is not abstractable from the
grammar and style that is employed at any point. Whereas Ahab

insists upon demonstrative proof of his personal sovereignty, the working out of a reality analogous to what he feels to be a spiritual truth, Ishmael's style of challenge involves letting go rather than making fast, a willingness to criticize any of his postures. He speaks of the soul as an 'insular Tahiti, full of peace and joy, but encompassed by all the horrors of the half known life. God keep thee! Push not off from that isle, thou canst never return! ' (236): Ishmael continually pushes off, self-destructs, just as first-person self-reference ceases at the confrontation with Moby Dick , only to reformulate in the epilogue. Likewise, Pip's glimpse of the weaver-god source of things, his speaking a truth alien to 'mortal reason', involves the destruction of his conscious identity — 'The intense concentration of self in the middle of such heartless immensity, my God! who can tell it? ' — so that he, like Ishmael in the final chapter, thenceforward speaks of himself in the third person: 'and in the sequel of the narrative, it will be seen what like abandonment befel myself' (348).

If the serenity at the center of the whale school reminds Ishmael of the verbally unamenable 'mute calm' at the centre of 'the tornadoed Atlantic of my being', then that serenity is ruptured (as is the pattern in *Moby-Dick*) by the runaway whale who slaughters his fellows with the careening cuttingspade (327). Unlike Ahab, that is, who commands the whale head to ' "tell us the secret thing that is in thee" ', Ishmael does not try to establish that which is but a point at best on a fixed basis of analogy (264). The sense of self, moreover, is always accompanied by 'sleep', 'dream', 'unconscious reverie', as when the sailor dreams in the masthead, or when each of the idle sailors seems 'resolved into his own invisible self'; it is at odds both with being awake and with seeing, that illustration of attention recurrent among the empiricists, for 'no man can ever feel his identity aright except his eyes be closed' (140, 185, 55). Melville speaks of the state of reverie in a letter to Hawthorne, in which he abominates Goethe's notion of 'the *all* feeling' of oneness with nature, though it has some validity when one is lying in the grass on a warm day: 'what plays the mischief with the truth is that men will insist upon the universal application of a temporary feeling or opinion'. And a few months later he writes Hawthorne that if the latter answers his letter 'and direct it to Herman Melville, you will missend it - for the very fingers that now guide this pen are not precisely the same that just took it up and put it on this paper. Lord, when shall we be done changing? ' (LHM, 131,143).

Locke's position of a universal liability to change, and his definition of self as that consciousness which accompanies thinking, are for Melville a textual concern addressed in the self-reflexive act of writing, as when Ishmael declares that the nature of the spout has remained problematic 'down to this blessed minute (fifteen and a quarter minutes past one o'clock P.M. of this sixteenth day of December, A.D. 1851)' (310): similarly in *White-Jacket*, 'I owe this right hand, that is at this moment flying over my sheet, and all my present being to Mad Jack' – 112). The text records the precise location of the self, is both what the self is not and what it does not transcend. For Locke, personal self is definable by memory only: 'if Socrates and the present mayor of Quinborough agree, they are the same person: if the same Socrates waking and sleeping do not partake of the same consciousness, Socrates waking and sleeping is not the same person' (*Essay*, II, xxvii, 19). Similarly for Melville, self is a narrative device, whether intra- or extratextual, whereby experience is organized (ideas related) and presented to the understanding, and which, as in Locke, cannot be perfectly consistent with substance, '*what is*'. Personal identity exists, as Locke says, 'not in the identity of substance, but... in the identity of consciousness' (II, xxvii, 19): just as in Hitchcock's *Psycho*, for example, two personalities are encoded on the same body, various personae – styles, grammars – are encoded on the text called Ishmael. 'Who but a fool', asks the Maltese sailor, 'would take his left hand by his right, and say to himself, how d'ye do? ' (148). The same situation occurs in *Naked Lunch*: 'Last night I woke up with someone squeezing my hand. It was my other hand' (NL, 66).

A text which attempts to report the facts breaks down into inconsistent and limited fragments; the first words of *Moby-Dick* speak of the consumptive usher to a grammar school and 'his old lexicons and grammars. . . . mockingly embellished with all the gay flags of all the known nations of the world. He loved to dust his old grammars; it somehow reminded him of his mortality' (MD, 1). Vocabulary and grammar are limited and limiting; Ishmael's fragmented and voyeuristic subjectivity is so limited, as Pip's conjugation suggests: 'I look, you look, he looks; we look, ye look, they look' (362). Point of view is grammar. Thus the sub-title of *White-Jacket or The World in a Man-of-War* suggests both an allegorical, microcosm-macrocosm significance and the account of a literal and linguistic *World* of 'established laws and usages' (WJ, 1), such as is indicated in Peleg's comment: 'Marchant service be damned. Talk not that lingo to me' (MD, 68). *Moby-Dick* is itself a lexicon, glossing whale- and sea-terms and Quee-queg's language, defining the terms of cetology ('The classification of the constituents of a chaos, nothing less is here essayed' [116]), producing statistics, quoting and questioning other sources, as in the comment on the 'elegant language' of an ancient account of the Right Whale's whiskers, and supplying an etymology, a survey of all known writings and a catalogue of experiences pertinent to whales (380, 283): an exhaustive consideration of vocabulary. If LUNPFM includes photographs, Ishmael describes Leviathan's 'pre-adamite traces in the stereotype plates of nature' (380), criticizes painted and carved representations and notes that the Sperm Whale, 'scientific or poetic, lives not complete in any literature', that completeness itself is 'faulty'; he is both the sub-sub-librarian's 'commentator', criticizing the gathered extracts, and a purveyor of his own 'researches': he regards his subject, as he does the whale's possible extinction, 'in every possible light' (383). In his strenuous attempt to clarify the meaning of the language of whaling, he is frequently in the critical posture of pointing out what it does not mean, of rejecting inadequate terms and descriptions. Pip suggests ' "Murray's Grammar" ' (362); the Pequod identifies herself to other vessels by means of reference to a signal book (269); Ishmael staggers 'under the weightiest words' of Johnson's dictionary, his chirography expanding to 'placard capitals' in his vain attempt to comprehend the whale (379). His world is bound by codes of vocabulary and grammar. While he covers all recorded time and space (his thoughts stretch 'as if to include the whole circle of the sciences, and all the generations of whales, and men, and mastodons, past, present, and to come' – 379) and himself reduces a living whale to clear oil, his knowledge remains superficial, confined to ideas derived from experience and related in a text – lexicographical, grammatical and mortal.

Melville elsewhere suggests the textual nature of 'self' or 'experience': Babbalanja speaks of ' "a new leaf in my experience" '; Lemsford remarks to a more fortunate sailor, ' "you have peace-

ful times; you never opened the book I read in" ' (WJ, 397);
Pierre dies proclaiming ' "Life's last chapter well stitched into the
middle" ' (a suggestion of the textual scrambling that interests
Agee and Burroughs), Lucy shrinking at his feet 'like a scroll'.[7]
The implications are more fully worked out in *Moby-Dick*. Ishmael has the dimensions of the whale's skeleton tatooed on his
right arm, exclusive of the odd inches 'as I was crowded for
space and wished the other parts of my body to remain a blank
page for a poem I was then composing – at least, what untattooed
parts might remain' (376): he is, his joke suggests, a walking
text. Queequeg too is a 'living parchment', 'in his own proper
person... a riddle to unfold; a wondrous work in one volume'
which cannot be read, even by himself (399). A text has the status
of a record, is itself evidential, so that Ishmael puts the oral story
of the Town-Ho 'on lasting record' (208); his censorship of Ahab's
urgent words to his boat crew and deigning only to hint at the
groin injury (192-193, 385) reflect a sense of delicacy about
what is committed to record, as does the narrator's refusal in
'The encantadas', regarding Hunilla's mishap, 'to file this thing
complete for scoffing souls to quote, and call it firm proof upon
their side' (GSW, 133). Ahab's injury renders him such a record,
for if he will ' "Clap eye on Captain Ahab" ', Peleg says, Ishmael
will find out what whaling is (MD, 69). And the whale too is a
textual record, with 'hieroglyphical' marks visible through the
isinglass surface, which also bears 'numerous rude scratches'
marking 'hostile contact with other whales' (260); one carries
embedded in its flesh a prehistoric 'lance-head of stone' (302);
whales are divided into 'three primary BOOKS (sub-divided into
Chapters)', folio, octavo and duodecimo (120); 'Leviathan'. as
Ishmael says, 'is the text' upon which he comments (378).

A text is the apparent form or soma (Ishmael calls his fictitious
classical writer 'old black-letter' – 19) on which is encoded understanding, the consciousness that accompanies thinking. Referring
to the doubloon as a book, Stubb remarks, 'The fact is, you
books must know your places. You'll do to give us the bare words
and facts, but we come in to supply the thoughts' (360): but as
Locke's example of the amputated finger (*Essay*, II, xxvii, 17)
and Ahab's discussion of his missing leg show, no precise correlation can be made on that basis. The quest for the white whale is
a search for the substance (for Locke it is moot whether that

substance is 'spiritual or material, simple or compound' — *Essay*, II, xxvii, 17) that underlies understanding. Ahab seeks to restore the symmetry of his former self, to confront the intention behind the act which has outraged him, and sees Moby Dick as the mirror image at which he grasps like Narcissus. Ishmael, absorbed by no such anthropomorphism, confronting a faceless whale and able to make no correlation between self and reflected image, describes the whale in detail, and finds his experience, his text, as anatomized and remote from life as is the boiled-down whale from the living fish. And just as understanding is itself unknowable, 'For whatever is truly wondrous and fearful in man, never yet was put into words or books' (396), so the life of the whale, which may or may not be analogous to that of man, is unamenable to any text: 'Only in the heart of quickest perils... can the fully invested whale be truly and livingly found out' (378).

The text may be regarded as a kind of map, for Chapter 45, 'The chart', is 'as important a one as will be found in this volume' concerning 'what there may be of a narrative in this book': Ahab's chart is a two-dimensional analog which pretends to correspond to the precise movements of Moby Dick, to reach below the ocean surface, just as his markings on it correspond to 'some invisible pencil... also tracing lines and courses upon the deeply marked chart of his forehead' (175, 171). But 'true places', as Ishmael says of Queequeg's home, are never 'down on any map' (56); and so for the text, for like his cetological definitions, 'This whole book is but a draught — nay, but a draught of a draught' (128), schematic, incomplete and arbitrary. Words are marks on the textual map: the whale is arbitrarily denominated a fish, its isinglass surface 'the skin' (299); Peleg insists that Queequeg is "Quohog" (84); the funeral ship is 'most miserably misnamed the Delight' (441); an etymological study of the term 'Specksynder' shows how far 'usage' strays from original meaning (128); and 'wild rumours' abound with only a modicum of 'reality for them to cling to' (156). Words, as Locke says, hold ideas together, just as the text forms them into propositions which, whether true or false, can be understood; they give that symmetrical shape to the world which is understanding, yet should the world, as Stubb speculates, be ' "anchored anywhere. . . she swings with an uncommon long cable" ' (420). If tragedy is an event in language, the breakdown of the symmetry of fixed verbal meanings, then

Ahab's tragic trappings are appropriate to his mission, for he goes forward 'to lay the world's grievances before that bar' from which he never returns (108); he is quite literally out of joint, but since he finally does penetrate the verbal mask of the text, it remains questionable whether he has put things right.

As in Locke's *Essay*, experience is the only teacher of verbal meaning: Starbuck is reputed one of the most ' "careful" ' men in the fishery, but the experience of rowing backward ' "into death's jaws" ' teaches Ishmael 'what that word "careful" precisely means when used' by a whale hunter (103, 196). Experience of the whale is experience which renders impossible (or for Ahab, defies) symmetrical formulation as self, or text; the organization of ideas derived from experience into a comprehensible, if fragmented, relation or pattern, operates as a veil covering an incomprehensible substance. The veil is a frequent metaphor. Ishmael quotes John Hunter on the ' "Impenetrable veil covering our knowledge of cetacea' ", and describes an engraving which depicts 'one single incomputable flash of time' during a Sperm Whale's tantrum, at which an oarsman appears 'half shrouded by the intense boiling spout... in the act of leaping, as if from a precipice' (117, 229). Radney too is ' "for an instant... dimly seen through that veil, wildly seeking to remove himself from the eye of Moby Dick" ' (222), who makes his final appearance 'Shrouded in a thick drooping veil of mist' (464). The image of the White Whale is associated with that of a veil or shroud through which can be glimpsed the panic-stricken gestures of threatened survival, Locke's single source of the certain knowledge of substance: the skeptic who wishes a glimpse through the veil may position himself in the vicinity of an angry Sperm Whale and observe the rapidity of his own movements.

A parallel incident is related in 'The two temples': the narrator is a tourist who has entered by stealth the tower of a modern church, 'a gorgeous dungeon' which allegorizes the subjective bubble, equipped with bells for communicating with the outside ('Some undreamed-of mechanism') and admitting only colored light through 'richly died glass' ('Though an insider in one respect, yet I am but an outsider in another'). He scratches 'a minute opening' to peer through and catches a glimpse of the man who has refused him entrance, and who eventually seizes and delivers him to the police: 'how could I help trembling at the apprehension of his discovering a rebellious caitiff like me peering down on him . . .? ' (GSW, 153, 157). What his white-light glimpse through the colored veil shows him, that is, is the precariousness of his subjective situation. Ahab would strike through the veil and do face-to-face battle with the author of that precariousness: rebuking it for the limited vision it affords, he dashes his quadrant, 'furnished with colored glasses', to the deck and tramples on it (MD, 411-412).

The specific relevance of Ahab's attitude to the fact of the text is suggested by his declaration that he 'never thinks; he only feels, feels; *that's* tingling enough for mortal man! to think's audacity. God only has that right and privilege' (460). But a text encodes the movement of thought (in *Science and Poetry*, Richards defines it as 'a machine for thinking'), arranging feelings (impressions) into sense or order, thereby exhibiting their habitual configuration in patterns of expectation. In the 'six-inch chapter' which is 'the stoneless grave of Bulkington' Ishmael offers the reader a glimpse of 'that mortally intollerable truth; that all deep earnest thinking is but the intrepid effort of the soul to keep the open independence of her sea' and avoid 'the treacherous slavish shore', the 'safety, comfort' and 'hospitality' of the port; Bulkington, like Ishmael, must always 'unrestingly push off' (97). If Ahab challenges the survival imperative in order to return the blow on behalf of his insulted feelings, Ishmael clings unfailingly to no such formulation. The only real certainty about his report is its contingency upon the reporter's survival.

THE LANGUAGE OF EMPIRICISM

The influence of Locke and his followers is evident in Melville's work, not only in terms of overall strategies and the shapes of particular episodes, but also in more specific allusions. The narrator of *Mardi* compares Jarl, in his practical attitude toward what he considers a phantom ship, to 'my Right Reverend friend, Bishop Berkeley — truly one of your lords spiritual — who metaphysically speaking, holding all objects to be mere optical delusions, was, notwithstanding, extremely matter-of-fact in all matters touching matter itself' (MI, 157). Berkeley is the source of Babbalanja's argument that ' "during my absence, my wife would have more reason to conclude that I was not living, than that I was . . . . To me it is not, except when I am there. If it be, prove it. To prove it, you carry me thither; but you only prove that to its substantive existence, as cognisant to me, my presence is indispensable" ' (M, II, 145). Babbalanja also quotes a Mardiian philosopher who, somewhat like Hume, maintains that ' "We are bundles of comical sensations' ", argues against the illusion of free will and the supremacy of any ' "moral sense" ' over circumstances, and poses the limits of empirical investigation regarding personal identity:

'What art thou, mortal?'
'My worshipful lord, a man.'
'And what is a man?'
'My lord, before thee is a specimen.' (M,II, 119, 116, 96)

White-Jacket, who echoes Locke's critique of 'what is called glory' (*Essay*, III, x, 3) and his position on the relativity of good and evil (II, xxi, 43) – 'in other planets, perhaps, what we deem wrong, may there be deemed right; even as some substances, without undergoing any mutations in themselves, utterly change their color, according to the light thrown upon them' – notes that 'Locke's *Essays* – incomparable essays, everybody knows, but miserable reading at sea', are part of the ship's library (WJ, 118, 194, 175), and attacks the chaplain (who 'drank at the mystic fountain of Plato; his head had been turned by the Germans'), for prancing 'on Coleridge's *High German horse*' rather than addressing the day-to-day state of affairs on the man-of-war (62-63, 174). White-Jacket protests against flogging as 'religiously, morally, and immutably *wrong*', but is 'ready to come down from the lofty mast-head of an external principle' and argue on the basis of experience that flogging is a substitute for leadership: 'I myself, in several instances, *know* to have been the case. . .' (152-154).

Pierre reade in Plotinus Plinlimmon's pamphlet a tirade against those who pretend to have found the 'Talismanic Secret' of reconciliation with the world: 'Plato, and Spinoza, and Goethe, and many more belong to this guild of self-impostors, with a preposterous rabble of Muggletonian Scots and Yankees, whose vile brogue still the more bespeaks the stripedness of their Greek or German Neoplatonical originals' (P, 290). Pierre is repeatedly in the position of contemplating paintings, so that when he visits the gallery with Lucy and Isabel he reflects that 'All the walls of the world seemed thickly hung with the empty and impotent scope of pictures' (487). In the first chapter of Book XXV, Lucy sits drawing at her easel in a closed room in which 'one window had been considerably elevated, while by a singular arrangement of the interior shutters, the light could in any direction be thrown about at will'; Isabel, jealous of his attention to Lucy, solicits a display of Pierre's affection and 'at the instant of his embrace' contrives to open the door to the studio; 'Before the eyes of seated Lucy, Pierre and Isabel stood locked; Pierre's lips on her cheek': as in Locke's *Essay*, the mind is represented as a *camera obscura* in which replicas are made of inwardly impelled images. But there is no conscious coming to terms with the incestuous nature of that image, for Pierre knows Lucy's 'expertness in catching likenesses, and judiciously and truthfully beautifying them; not by altering the features so much, as by steeping them in a beautifying atmosphere' (459-465). The atmosphere and habitual postures of romance are similarly proof against Pierre's awareness. Isabel has described to Pierre the series of subjective impressions that is the history of her childhood, and he suddenly wonders whether the story 'might have been. . . forged for her. . . and craftily impressed upon her youthful mind', for 'Tested by anything real, practical, and reasonable', her lack of knowledge that the sea is salt belies her recollection of an early ocean crossing. His original conviction is based on Isabel's resemblance to a portrait of his father (which is painted on the sly, by a singularly voyeuristic image-thief), but he now sees a similar resemblance in the portrait of a foreigner, one which is 'just as strong an evidence as the other', and for which there is 'perhaps. . . no original at all': the pictures hung in the subjective gallery have no necessary connection with the reality beyond. With the two women 'bodily touching his sides as he walked', Pierre turns over the empirical question: 'coming to the plain, palpable facts, — how did he *know* that Isabel was his sister? ' Unfortunately for the aroused lover, corroboration comes with experience: their ferry ride carries them over waves that roll in from the Atlantic and Isabel convulsively affirms, ' "I feel it! I feel it! It is! It is! " ' Knowledge is the agreement or disagreement of ideas; if the existence of the paintings is a mere ' "coincidence" ', then, says Isabel, ' "by that word. . . we but vainly seek to explain the inexplicable" ' (491-194).

The narrator of 'Bartleby' also experiences an undermining of his 'authority', finds his every assumption about Bartleby's behavior negated by his ambiguous substantial presence ('In the legitimate carrying out of this assumption, I might enter my office in a great hurry, and pretending not to see Bartleby at all, walk straight against him as if he were air'), and resorts to '*Edwards on the Will*, and *Priestly on Necessity*' in order to obtain a short-lived and similarly ousted comfort with Bartleby's persistence behind his screen (PM, 497-501). Like the White Whale, Bartleby represents the intractable substance behind appearances and out of reach of the understanding. The corresponding illustration in 'The encantadas' is that of the tortoises, whose chief impression on the narrator is 'that of age: – dateless indefinite endurance': his description of their first appearance on the deck – 'They seemed newly crawled forth from beneath the foundations of the world. Yea, they seemed the identical tortoises whereon the Hindoo plants his total sphere' (GSW, 104-105) – echoes Locke's comparisons of the notion of substance to the Indian philosopher's tortoise (*Essay* II, xiii, 19; xxiii, 2). The description of Amassa Delano's experience in 'Benito Cereno' questions the authority of any subjective account of appearances, and is repeatedly conceived in the terms of 'thought train' and 'association' (GSW, 298, 266, 271, 289); appearances, as Cereno points out, are always misleading, and what lies behind them, like the souls of Bartleby and Pierre (' "All's o'er" ', gasps Isabel, ' "and ye know him not" ' –P, 505), out of reach. Part of Delano's problem is his unwavering confidence in 'the ever-watchful Providence above' (GSW, 293): his point of view, like Pierre's, is limited by the rigidity of its grammar. While there are instances of Locke's terminology in *The Confidence Man* (a shoemaker's calling 'is to defend the understandings of men from naked contact with the substance of things'), more central is the critique of the 'doctrine of analogies. . . . Fallacious enough doctrine when wielded against one's prejudices, but in corroboration of cherished suspicions not without likelihood': 'analogy" ', one of the wiser marks points out, is not ' "argument" ', and he accuses the confidence man of punning ' "with ideas as another man may with words" '. Like

Ishmael, this man names himself: 'my name is Pitch; I stick to what I say'; though just as Ishmael is hypnotized by Ahab, Pitch is temporarily pried loose (CM, 315, 200, 189).

Locke's *Essay* contributes to *Moby-Dick* the model of the mind as mediator between corporeal and spiritual substances, and the appropriate terms. Ahab identifies with the whale 'not only all his bodily woes, but all his intellectual and spiritual exasperations'. His 'intellect', which had been an 'agent' is now an 'instrument' of his madness, though to describe a mental faculty is to speak in metaphor: 'If such a furious trope may stand, his special lunacy stormed his general sanity, and carried it, and turned all its concentrated cannon on its own mad mark' (*Essay*, II, xxi, 19; MD, 159-161). Starbuck, whose 'stubbornness of life' is continually asserting itself against Ahab, is not proof against him, but while Ahab dominates Starbuck's body and intellect, 'the chief mate, in his soul, abhorred his captain's quest' (183). Ahab confuses Starbuck's objections by invoking the doctrine of analogies, the existence of the little lower layer: like Dimmesdale, Ahab is powerfully eloquent and spurred by his own secret agony; Ishmael, on the other hand, remarks of the customary calculation of the Right Whale's age by counting the markings on certain bones, that 'the certainty of this criterion is far from demonstrable, yet has the savor of analogical probability' (282). Ahab's insistence that words have meaning – 'I like to feel something in this slippery world that can hold' (MD, 390) – that substance, physical or spiritual, conform to intellectual design, is a corollary of the manic activity of his 'characterizing mind', which 'does not exist unless leagued with the soul' (MD, 175): told of Fedallah's death he exclaims, ' "Gone? – gone? What means that little word? " ' (458). Ahab and Fedallah, in fact, are silent together 'as one man', gaze at each other 'as if in the Parsee Ahab saw his forethrown shadow, in Ahab the Parsee his abandoned substance' (411, 439); Fedallah is repeatedly a 'shadow' rather than 'mortal substance', and Ahab deplores his inability to transcend his vulnerable physical condition, referring to his ' "body" ' as his ' "craven mate" ', for 'be this Parsee what he may, all rib and keel was solid Ahab' (438, 458-460). He employs dualistic terms, opposes ' "man's old age' " to ' "matter's" ' (462), and is obsessed with an inscrutable intelligence behind and distinct from intractable appearances: ' "all the things that most exasperate and outrage mortal man, all

these things are bodiless, but only bodiless as objects, not as a-
gents. There's a most special, a most cunning, oh, a most malicious
difference" ' (461).

In Ishmael we have the mediating intellect, the encoded presence of understanding which attains to no unambiguous knowledge of substances, doubts all things earthly and intuits some
things heavenly, and 'regards them both with equal eye' (314);
'hell', he tells Queequeg, 'is an idea first born on an undigested
apple-dumpling' (63). If Ishmael would throw both Kant and
Locke overboard in order to float light and right, he, like Starbuck,
is 'held to knowledge', and he employs the vocabulary of the
empiricists in setting forth what he knows: 'there is no quality in
the world that is not what it is merely by contrast. Nothing
exists in itself' (148, 55). He echoes Locke and Berkeley in his
discussion of vision, noting its passivity and delineating the
problem of attention:

So long as a man's eyes are open in the light, the act of seeing is involuntary;
that is, he cannot then help mechanically seeing whatever objects are before
him. Nevertheless, any one's experience will teach him, that though he can
take in an undiscriminating sweep of things at one glance, it is quite impossible
for him, attentively, and completely, to examine any two things — however
large or however small — at one and the same instant of time; never mind if
they lie side by side and touch each other. But if you now come to separate
these two objects, and surround each by a circle of profound darkness; then,
in order to see one of them, in such a manner as to bring your mind to bear
on it, the other will be utterly excluded from your contemporary consciou-
ness. How is it, then, with the whale? True, both his eyes, in themselves, must
simultaneously act; but is his brain so much more comprehensive, combining,
and subtle than man's that he can at the same moment of time attentively
examine two distinct prospects, one on one side of him, and the other in an
exactly opposite direction? If he can, then is it as marvellous a thing in him,
as if a man were able simultaneously to go through the demonstrations of
two distinct problems in Euclid. Nor, strictly investigated, is there any incon-
gruity in this comparison. (279-80)

The association of ideas derived from experience accounts for
attitudes: Steelkilt is 'nurtured by... agrarian free-booting impressions' (209); 'by the continual repetition of... impressions' of the
sea's power, 'man has lost the sense of the full awfulness' (235).
Ahab lowers for the squid, perhaps, because 'he has now prepared
to connect the ideas of mildness and repose with the first sight of
the particular whale he pursued' (236-237). And his symbolizing
imagination combines arbitrary associations, as when he transfers

'the idea' of the Christian formulation of evil 'to the abhorred White Whale', or when, watching the homewardbound Bachelor, he holds a vial of sand, and 'looking from the ship to the vial seemed thereby bringing two remote associations together, for that vial was filled with Nantucket soundings' (160. 408). Whereas Ahab resents ' "The dead blind wall [that] butts all inquiring heads at last" ' (427), Ishmael investigates the wall; he insists that experience is the source of all ideas ('the only way in which you can derive even a tolerable idea of his living contour, is by going a whaling yourself' [228]), refers to what 'has been proved by experiment', checks his opinion concerning the whale's skin with 'experienced whalemen afloat and learned naturalists ashore', though 'it is only an opinion' (259-261), and distinguishes the 'anatomical fact' of the whale's breathing apparatus, which is 'indisputable', from 'the supposition founded upon it', which may be 'reasonable and true' (311). His scholarship is likewise tentative, the organization of data into a probable picture, for if 'you properly put these statements together, and reason upon them a bit, you will clearly perceive that... Procopius' sea-monster... must in all probability have been a Sperm Whale' (182). He finds insoluble the problem whether the 'mystifying' spout is water or vapour, for the substance dissolves human skin ('The wisest thing the investigator can do then... is to let this deadly spout alone'), though he puts forth the unsubstantiated 'hypothesis... that the spout is nothing but mist' (310, 313-314). It 'hypothetically' occurs to him that the 'lung-celled honeycombs' in the whale's head serve for buoyancy (289); hypothesis is the recurrent condition of the human mind, which develops towards 'manhood's pondering response of If' only to give way again to faith, skepticism and disbelief (406); Peleg fishes for Ishmael's interest with an hypothesis – ' "Supposing it be the Captain of the Pequod, what doest thou want of him? " ' (68) – and Ahab sneers at the carpenter, 'pudding-heads should never grant premises' (391): to grant a premise is to suspend disbelief, to accept and pursue the consequences of what might be true – a task, Ahab implies, appropriate to those of exceptional stature.

Ishmael's humbler approach is to insist upon his experience, however ambiguous: he offers 'something like the form of the whale as he actually appears to the eye' (224), is a 'veritable witness' who records the circumstances of his 'exact knowledge'

(373), and will himself only accept the evidence of a witness: 'Here, then, from three impartial witnesses, I had a deliberate statement of the entire case' (196). He refers to 'well-authenticated instances (207), points out that 'there are skeleton authorities you can refer to, to test my accuracy' (375), supplies excerpts from ' "testimony entirely independent of my own" ' (178), and jokingly remarks of Scoresby's facsimiles of Arctic snow crystals the 'over-sight not to have procured for every crystal a sworn affidavit' (231). Authenticity is an empirical issue. Ishmael's final recourse against his report's being received as fable or allegory is his word, that which he has given to Ahab and not kept, and which, as his self-introduction indicates, he regards as arbitrary: 'Such things may seem incredible; but however wondrous, they are true'; 'take my word for it' (177, 267). And in 'The affadavit' he repeats, 'I have personally known three instances . . . . I say I, myself, have known . . . . Here are three instances, then, which I personally know the truth of' (175-176); when his hearers demand to know if the Town-Ho's story ' "is in substance really true" ', Ishmael sends out for the largest available bible on which to swear that it ' "is in substance and its great items true. . . . I have seen and talked with Steelkilt since the death of Radney" ' (224).   The uncertainty of Ishmael's credibility has to do with the empirical critique of language and its relation to substance: Agee qualifies his record so strenuously 'only because I am reluctant to entirely lie' (LUNPFM, 134); even to speak, Burroughs says, is to lie (J, 199). The narrator of 'Bartleby' cannot guess the reliability of the 'report' he hears about the scrivener's identity (PM, 511); as Vere knows, to pronounce sentence is to employ an arbitrary code.

In his inconsistency, Ishmael does not present his proofs 'methodically', but is 'content to produce the desired impression by separate citations of items practically or reliably known to me as a whaleman, and from these citations, I take it — the conclusion aimed at will naturally follow of itself' (175): this is how Agee defines his effort in human actuality, his setting forth of discontinuous fragments and leaving their realization to the reader. Realization, or understanding, is as unspeakable and as self-interrogating as the notion of substance, and is to the text what the living whale is to its analysis. The reader must assume a critical attitude, must constantly consider the question, 'how do you know . . .? '

which occurs three times in the discussion of the substantial nature of the spout (313). Unlike Starbuck, who prays, ' "Let faith oust fact; let fancy oust memory" ', Ishmael insists upon his critical freedom, rails against 'precedents... traditions... old beliefs never bottomed on earth, and now not even hovering in the air. . .[and] orthodoxy', declares himself 'a savage, owing no allegiance but to the King of the Cannibals; and ready at any moment to rebel against him' (262, 232). And since 'all men's minds and opinions [and] . . . the thoughts of thinkers' are Loose-Fish, apt to be captured by 'ostentatious smuggling verbalists', the reader, who is both 'a Loose-Fish and a Fast-Fish, too', must also beware of being captured by any particular formulation (334).

This is consonant with Ishmael's allegorical mode, as opposed to Ahab's symbolism. Ishmael frequently ends a description by giving his material an allegorical signification, as he converts whales' heads to Kant and Locke, or to 'Plato's honey head' (291). While, with reference to the 'presumed congeneality' between the dense elastic head of the beached sturgeon and that of the English king to whom the law awards it, Ishmael uses the words 'allegorical' and 'symbolically' as if they were interchangeable (336), he elsewhere uses 'symbol' in a more specialized sense: symbols are the means of communication, such as perhaps are the gestures of the tail, which some say are 'akin to Freemason signs and symbols; that the whale indeed, by these methods, intelligently conversed with the world' (317); they generalize a particular situation, as Queequeg holding aloft the light of the swamped boat is both 'the sign and symbol of a man without faith, hopelessly holding up hope in the midst of despair' (195); and they suggest a transcendent reality, so that the wind seems 'the symbol of that unseen agency which so enslaved them to the race' after Moby Dick(545). But whereas Ahab, for whom Moby Dick is a symbol, regards meaning as immanent and discoverable, for Ishmael it is delegated and casual, a passing and not necessarily related comment. Melville doubts, he writes Hawthorne, that symbols have any meaning beyond themselves: 'We incline to think that the Problem of the Universe is like the Feeemason's mighty secret, so terrible to all children. It turns out. . . to consist in a triangle, a mallet, and an apron, − nothing more! ' Even within the depths of symbolization, that is, there are only constituent signs; and the understanding, which works against synthesis and ultimate significance, proceeds by negation: 'all men who say *yes*, lie; and all men who say *no* – why, they are in the happy condition of judicious, unencumbered travellers in Europe; they cross the frontiers into Eternity with nothing but a carpet-bag – that is to say, the Ego' (LHM, 125).

In the absence of symbolic purchase, the text itself is as liable to rupture as the Pequod, the serial situations of *Typee*, and the disconnected grammatical stances of Agee and Burroughs, and abounds with situations of poised suspense and surprise: before he dies, Starbuck is ' "deadly calm, yet expectant, – fixed at the top of a shudder" ' (463); the great squid disrupts a 'profound hush', just as Moby Dick at last 'bodily burst into view' (236, 455); the Wordsworthian 'dreamy quietude' which converts waves to rolling hills, so that 'fact and fancy, half-way meeting, interpenetrate and form one seamless whole', is a calm to be disrupted, for there is 'a storm for every calm' (406); and just as 'the profound calm which only apparently precedes and prophesies of the storm, is perhaps more awful than the storm itself', so the gracefully serpentine whale line, before it is in 'actual play', is the most terrible aspect of the hunt, suggesting the line around all men's necks: 'but it is only when caught in the swift, sudden turn of death, that mortals realize the silent, subtle, ever-present perils of life', a terror felt as intensely by the philosopher at his fireside as by the men in the whaleboat (241).

That the negation of pattern is the only pattern Ishmael finds useful illuminates his notion of metempsychosis. Hardly has the crew stowed down and cleared up after processing one whale, and hardly has a man 'learned to live in the clean tabernacles of the soul... when – *There she blows!* – the ghost is spouted up and away we sail to fight some other world' (357-358). Death (' "explosive death" ', as Benito Cereno calls it – GSW, 313) is defined negatively as a rupture of context, and is thus comparable to whaling, for 'not the dead man's ghost encountering the first unknown phantom in the other world... can feel stranger and stronger emotions than that man does, who for the first time finds himself pulling into the charmed, churned circle of the hunted Sperm Whale' (MD, 193). Locke regards the supposition of metempsychosis as having 'no apparent absurdity in it', pointing out that, since 'those who place thought in a purely material, animal constitution, void of an immaterial substance', must conceive of personal identity as 'preserved in something else than identity of substance', for the particles of the organism are always changing, it is conceivable that it be 'preserved in the change of immaterial substance'; and since 'the word *I*' refers to the identity of the same '*man*', and it is 'possible for the same man to have a distinct in- communicable consciousness at different times, it is past doubt the same man would at different times make different persons' (*Essay*, II, xxvii, 12-14, 20). The notion of metempsychosis, that is, has implications for the inconsistencies of Ishmael's narrative, which encodes or interweaves the thousand voices which can only be heard when the loom is escaped (374-375). ' "In one lifetime we live a hundred lives" ', says Babbalanja: ' "By the incompre- hensible stranger in me, I say this body of mine has been rented out scores of times, though always one dark chamber in me is retained by the old mystery" ' (M, II, 116). White-Jacket's specu- lation as to whether we think in words or thoughts is interesting in this regard: Agee speaks of the psychoanalytic function of sleep, in which some 'talk of themselves to themselves in silence, and may sometimes profit of it, and may sometimes break the paraly- sis of their parentage' (LUNPFM, 223). Again, just as in Hitch- cock's *Psycho*, more than one voice is encoded on a single larynx, each voice programming the behavior of the subject, so more than one voice is encoded in the text called Ishmael — discrete, not necessarily related personae whose worlds are the shapes of the episodes narrated. Brion Gysin, the originator of Burroughs' cutup method and collaborator with him in *Minutes to Go*, speaks of the various contradictory 'voices' or grammars that make up any text or subjective consciousness, and argues with other voices in his text: 'Just talk to yourself for a minute. You hear that little voice? Well, now argue with yourself: take two sides of a question. . . . I hesitate to advise, because I know only for me, that something pretty saucy will often get you a sharp answer. Realize it is an answer when you hear it and not just you. . . . This ain't no monopoly, lady. Shove off, you! Well, as I was saying before I was so brashly interrupted. . . . Stop and Listen'.[8] Attention itself is a submissive and salutary tool, and metempsychotic notions provide no explanatory myths that guarantee its security or vali- dity: the dissolution of verbal context provides the subject with knowledge by negation, of what he is not but does not transcend.

DUMB BLANKNESS: *MOBY-DICK* AND "THE TARTARUS OF MAIDS."

Melville's use of Locke's *Essay* is most clearly evident in his treatment of whiteness, the dumb blankness full of meaning which stabs from behind with the thought of annihilation, which stands for Locke's unknowable substance, and of which the White Whale is, in the most empirical sense of the word (that is, insofar as it is an idea representing a context of ideas of whiteness), the symbol. It is Ishmael's fear of the future, his concern for survival, that informs his prolonged meditation on the whale's whiteness: the whale leaves such a wake, according to *Job*, ' "One would think the deep to be hoary" ' (MD, 2). Moby Dick is an 'object remote and blank in the pursuit' (183), an absence or negativity — a 'broad white shadow' rising from the sea — rather than a positive presence, who presents his negating 'blank forehead' to the ship he is about to smash (268, 466). He is the possible manifestation of the 'big white God aloft there somewhere' to whom Pip prays (155). That Moby Dick's whiteness is associated with spiritual as well as corporeal substance is indicated by the initial reference to him as a 'grand hooded phantom, like a snow hill in the air' (16). The spout, the substantial nature of which is an insoluble mystery, is not only a manifestation of whiteness — Ishmael lodges under a sign 'with a white painting upon it, faintly representing a tall straight jet of misty spray, and these words underneath — 'The Spouter Inn: — Peter Coffin" ' (18) — but also an allegorical representation of the soul (death occurs when the ghost is spouted up'; Stubb declares himself ' "as good a fellow as ever spouted up his ghost" ' [358, 467]) which in Ahab is 'a ray of living light . . . but without an object to color, and therefore a blankness in itself' (175). And death, as Coffin's name suggests, is also connected with whiteness, the dead whale turning up 'the white secrets of his belly', the dying Queequeg preparing to sail 'the white breakers of the milky way' (301, 396). The uncolored substantial world wears a 'white shroud' (170), which is finally penetrated by Ahab and the Pequod (just as Radney approaches Moby Dick 'through a blinding foam that blent two whitenesses together [222]), 'a sullen white surf' beating the side of the gulf until 'the great white shroud of the sea rolled on as it rolled five thousand years ago' (469), a shroud which covers prenatal, postmortal, extra-experiential reality.

Whiteness has a similar function in *Mardi*: Yillah, whose 'snow-white skin' sets her apart from the Polynesians among whom she is found, is, like Moby Dick, an elusive and veiled dream apparition — 'hence the impulse which had sent me roving after the substance of this spiritual image' (M, I, 125, 145). White-Jacket's jacket is his name and identity, 'an outlandish garment of my own devising', the 'storehouse' of his possessions, a 'burden' to him when wet and very nearly his 'shroud'; it also suggests the text, for its material is slit in the making 'much as you would cut a leaf in the last new novel', and by means of it the narrator becomes 'a universal absorber' (WJ, 3-4, 40); when he falls from the mast into the sea ('the feeling of death crept over me with the billows') he arrives at a 'life-and-death poise', and discards the jacket which drags him down — the substance upon which his identity is encoded — and is reborn, whereupon the jacket is harpooned by his comrades, who take it for a ' "white shark" ' (WJ, 414-415). Pierre, upon recognizing that he has ' "no paternity and no past" ', speaks of the future as ' "one blank to all" ' (P, 277). And Babo regards Don Alexandro's skeleton, mounted on a 'bleached hull as a chaulky comment on the chaulked words below, *"Follow your leader"* ', as a 'whiteness' which is common to both caucasian and Negro (GSW, 296, 304-305).

The most complete treatment is in 'The Tartarus of maids', an allegory of the mechanism of birth. The narrator, a seed salesman, journeys to a papermill to contract for the production of envelopes for the dissemination of his seeds; the 'whitewashed' mill stands near the bottom of a hollow through which runs a 'brick-coloured stream' called 'Blood River', and which leads through 'Black Notch' into 'Mad Maid's Bellows-pipe'; the whole uterine setup faces west. He sets out in January and finds frosty 'white vapours' curling up from the 'white-wooded top' of Woedolor Mountain; his horse 'Black' is 'Flaked all over with frozen sweat, white as a milky ram'; in the 'white' hollow and amid buildings with a 'cheap, blank air' — a 'snow-white hamlet amidst the snows' — the narrator has difficulty seeing the mill. The associations are both of birth and of death, for the forests groan with 'the same all-stiffening influence' and the mountains are 'pinned in shrouds — a pass of Alpine corpses'; moreover, the rocky nature of the ground forbids 'all method in [the buildings'] relative arrangement', so that the narrator is entering a region which is allegorically both pre- and postconscious, outside methodical arrangement. Inside the 'intollerably lighted' factory, 'At rows of blank-looking counters sat rows of blank-looking girls, with blank, white folders in their blank hands, all blankly folding blank paper'. Since the human voice is 'banished' by the hum of the machinery, 'Not a syllable' is spoken: the extraexperiential is extralinguistic. The two men in the mill are 'dark-complexioned' and 'red-cheeked', the former attending to 'Two white spots' of frostbite on the narrator's cheeks; and the power that runs it comes from a 'dark, colossal water-wheel, grim with one immutable purpose'. But the women who process rags 'washed white' for conversion into paper are all 'pale' with labor. Guided by red-cheeked 'Cupid', the attendant of the machines, the narrator follows the course of some 'white pulp' into a room 'stifling with a strange, blood-like abdominal heat, as if here, true enough, were being finally developed the germinous particles', and on to its completion as paper (usually ' "foolscap" ', but sometimes ' "finer stuff" '), a process which takes ' "Nine minutes to a second" ', rather than nine months; it is 'delivered into' the hands of a former nurse. The machinery, ' "a miracle of inscrutable intricacy" ', is compared, not to Leviathan, but to 'some living, panting Behemoth', though it operates with the Sperm Whale's 'metallic necessity. . .[and] unbudging finality': it ' "*must* go. . . . just that very way, and at that very pace you there plainly *see* it go" ' and the pulp, passively maneuvered by the machine, ' "can't help going" ' (GSW, 210-222). The birth that eventuates, of course, is Locke's 'white paper, void of all characters, without any ideas' (*Essay*, II, i, 2): whiteness is that which substantiates the text, just as Ishmael speaks of the untatooed parts of his body as 'a blank page' (MD, 429); and the narrator's reflections on the textual nature of consciousness suggest the 'pallid hopelessness' engendered in Bartleby by his work in the dead-letter office (PM, 512):

Looking at that blank paper continually dropping, dropping, dropping, my mind ran on in wonderings of those strange uses to which those thousand sheets eventually would be put. All sorts of writings would be writ on those now vacant things — sermons, lawyers' briefs, physicians' prescriptions, love-letters, marriage certificates, bills of divorce, registers of births, death-warrants, and so on, without end. Then, recurring back to them as they here lay all blank, I could not but bethink me of that celebrated comparison of John Locke, who, in demonstration of his theory that man had no innate ideas, compared the human mind at birth to a sheet of blank paper; something destined to be scribbled on, but what sort of characters no soul might tell. (GSW, 220-221)

MOTIVE AND INTENTION: *BILLY BUDD* AND *MOBY-DICK*

Substance, or context, is finally the problem of motive and intention: what lies behind language? Where am I and how did I get here? what do 'I' mean? The hunt for Moby Dick is a projection of intention and a search for motive, for the hidden source both of the images that appear on the walls of the subjective jar, and of the language that relates them. In *Typee*, not only is Tommo frequently ignorant of the 'cause' of a whole gamut of phenomena, but also his accounts of his own motives are in terms of the empirical distinction between a reason and a cause. While the 'intention' of Tommo's captors is frequently a matter of 'supposition', their 'bloodthirsty disposition... is mainly to be ascribed to the influence of [European] examples' (T, 27) – that is, to a model or plan, Just so, Tommo's making up his mind to jump ship is a taking stock of 'circumstances' (23) and formulating an appropriate plan or intention, which is nevertheless confuted at every step; his movements are the consequences of having 'little choice', ' "no other alternative" ' (51, 63), and his intention to leave the island is as circumstantial as that to leave the ship: 'There was no one with whom I could freely converse; no one to whom I could communicate my thoughts; no one who could sympathize with my suffering' (231). The narrator of *Mardi* gives a similar reason for quitting his ship – 'There was no soul a magnet to mine; none with whom to mingle sympathies' – and, like Tommo (20), charges his captain with 'contravention of the agreement between us' (M, I, 3-5). These are circumstances which point those who live them in a certain direction, but do not necessarily lead to the actions taken, actions which, as the title, 'The watery world is all before them', suggests, constitute a kind of death and rebirth, the foresaking of a predictable context for the instability of chance. Taji's assertion that 'Those who boldly launch cast off all cables. . . . Hug the shore naught new is seen' (I, 27), suggests that the new is visible only with the breaking up of old habits of thought: Babo's substitution of a skeleton for the image of Columbus aligns with Taji's statement that the 'new world here sought. . . . is the world of the mind; wherein wanderers may gaze around with more of wonder than Balboa's band' (II, 207). For Taji, however, who does not name himself, discovery becomes a compulsive quest for paradise rather than a letting go: with Taji's reception of his name, Ishmael becomes Ahab, and the book changes direction. In *Naked Lunch*, a book about literary and linguistic as well as heroin habits, Burroughs refers to being 'Obsessed with codes. . . . Man contracts a series of diseases which spell out a code message'; Agee also speaks of the 'disease' of 'symmetry' present in 'the deity the race has erected to sheild it from the horror of the heavens, in the pressed wall of a small Greek restaurant where some of the Greek disease persists through the persistence of a Renaissance disease' (LUNPFM, 229-230): 'Cure', Burroughs says, 'is always: Let go! Jump! ' (NL, 66, 222).

A code is an analog device: to let go is to test it, to bring into play an unaccountable, unsupported, discontinuous and digital awareness; the difference is between Ahab's map, his imposition of a story with a symmetrical plot, his demand for justice and the restoration of symmetry, and Ishmael's counting up the pieces of evidence. Letting go is associated in Melville with the westerly direction in which the machinery of birth faces in 'The Tartarus of maids' and towards which move the frontier explorers of *The Confidence Man* and the Pequod, the symbol of civilization; Jarl and the narrator of *Mardi* set off on a 'western voyage', for 'Though America be discovered, the Cathays of the deep are unknown' (I, 24, 35); and Ishmael speaks of the Pacific as 'un-civilized' (MD, 155), as 'terra incognita' (235), as a graveyard and finally as the home of Moby Dick (399-400). While for Ahab it is a direction towards, for Ishmael it is a direction away, allegorizing the movement of the intellect away from an implicit acceptance of codes.

Babbalanja's formulation sums up the problem of motive: ' "I am a blind man pushed from behind; in vain I turn about to see what propels me" '; he seems, he says, " 'not so much to live of myself, as to be a mere apprehension of the unaccountable being that is in me. Yet all the time this being is I myself" ' (M, II, 114-116). White-Jacket, who like Ishmael must 'surmise' the motive of his captain (WJ, 117), likewise speaks of men as 'sailing with sealed orders... the repositories of a secret packet, whose mysterious contents we long to learn. . . . but let us not give ear to the superstitious, gundeck gossip about whither we may be gliding, for, as yet, not a soul on board of us knows — not even the commodore himself; assuredly not the Chaplain; even our professor's scientific surmisings are in vain' (419); his protest against flogging is a critique of habitual rationalization, a suggestion that depravity among the men is, 'in a large degree, the effect, and not the cause and justification of oppression' (148). The narrator of *Pierre* remarks that 'In their precise tracings out and subtle causations, the strangest and fiercest emotions of life defy all analytical insight. We see the cloud and feel its bolt; but meteorology only idly essays a critical scrutiny as to how that cloud became charged, and how this bolt so stuns' (92). And Bartleby simply appears on the scene without story or context: ' "And what is the reason? " ' demands the narrator; ' "Do you not see the reason for yourself? " he indifferently replied' , an answer which his employer proceeds to misconstrue (PM, 429); like Locke, Bartleby points to the presence of the self-evident, the futility of explanation. This is precisely the narrator's problem, in 'The two temples', concerning his furtive point of view: 'Explanation will be in vain. Circumstances are against me' (GSW, 157). In 'Benito Cereno', Delano regards a series of gestures, at first 'Thinking he divined the cause' (GSW, 254), and then becoming progressively less certain about the motive or intention indicated: 'suddenly he thought that one or two of them returned the glance with a sort of meaning (265); 'the idea flashed across him, that possibly master and man, for some unknown purpose, were acting out, both in word and deed, nay, to the very tremor of Don Benito's limbs, some juggling play before him' (282). He becomes aware, that is, that his ideas occur in 'coincidence' (261), that their meaning ('What meant this? . . . had some random unintentional motion... been mistaken for a significant beckoning? ' [269]) is ambiguous, that causality, intention and motive are neither abstractable from nor necessarily inherent in them; 'Absurd then, to suppose that [Cereno's] questions had been prompted by evil designs' (263). The narrator, who pieces the story together from the court records, must similarly use words like 'perhaps' and 'possibly' (288-289) when speculating about Delano. Realizing that he has been taken in by the Confidence

Man, Pitch likewise 'revolves, but cannot comprehend, the operation, still less the operator. . . . Two or three dollars the motive
to so many nice wiles? ' (CM, 199-200). Like the reader, who
constructs a continuity out of the episodic textual information
and assumes a single actor or causal agent behind the mask (though
the final chapter implies that he is legion), Pitch seeks the explanatory motive, and is thereby duped.

Billy Budd, finally, is a study in the nature of judgment. Billy's
bidding good-bye to the *Rights-of-Man*, his spilling soup in Claggart's path (' "Handsomely done. . . . And handsome is as handsome did it too! " ' [BB,72]), and the blow with which he kills
Claggart, followed by his 'impassioned disclaimer of mutinous
intent' (106), are all pointed instances of the ambiguity and possible misconstruction of 'intention' (49), as, at the moment of
Billy's crime, are Vere's words which, 'contrary to the effect
intended. . .prompted yet more violent efforts at utterance';
the ensuing blow, 'Whether intentionally or but owing to the
young athlete's superior height', strikes Claggart's forehead and
kills him (99). Like Bartleby, Billy simply appears, is 'dropped
into a world' dangerous to his innocence, without explanation:
' "Don't you know where you were born? – Who was your
father? " ' ' "God knows, Sir" ' (70, 51). So does Claggart simply
appear, concerning whom, in 'the dearth of exact knowledge',
the crew circulates reports which 'nobody could substantiate',
for 'About as much was known... of the Master-at-Arms' career
before entering the service as an astronomer knows about a
comet's travels prior to its first observable appearance in the sky'
(65-67). Romance, as is implied by the crew's aptness 'to exag-
gerate or romance it' (67) concerning Claggart's origin, invokes
an explanatory context or nexus, but Billy is not the 'conventional
hero' of a 'romance' (53); and the narrator refuses 'to invent
something [which] might avail . . . to account for whatever enigma may appear to lurk in the case' of Claggart's 'spontaneous
and profound' antipathy toward Billy, 'the cause' of his being
'*down* on him', which is 'in its very realism as much charged with
the prime element of Radcliffian romance, *the mysterious*... as
any that the ingenuity of [that] author. . . could devise' (73-74).

There is no clearing up this mystery. In the ensuing discussion
of motive the narrator quotes an old scholar, who is neither
religious nor committed to any philosophical system, and who

has nevertheless advised him that experience can supply ' "but a superficial knowledge" ' of the workings of human nature, and that ' "for anything deeper" ' something else is required, 'that fine spiritual insight' whereby a young girl, for example, has been known to get the better of an old lawyer; since 'that lexicon which is based on Holy Writ' has fallen into disfavor (again, the problem is of vocabulary and grammar), the narrator applies Plato's definition of ' "Natural Depravity" ', the phrase which critics invariably emphasize, to Claggart's peculiar 'mania' (74-76). Precisely as Ahab is drawn to Moby Dick, feeling him ' "all a magnet" ' (MD, 368), Claggart 'magnetically' feels the 'ineffability' which is 'the spirit lodged within Billy', is left 'apprehending the good, but powerless to be it'; and if Ahab is fated to live out the implications of a name he did not give himself, Claggart's nature also exemplifies a words-before-things situation, must, 'like the scorpion for which the Creator alone is responsible, act out to the end the part allotted to it', since he is incapable of not identifying with his own designs (BB, 78).

But the narrator's recourse to Plato, like his comments on the decreasing confidence in the Bible (they occur twice and without qualification of tone   [75, 76]   and are comparable to that of the eavesdropper, ' "Awake in his sleep" ', who, when the Confidence Man describes the gospel as ' "good news" ', mutters ' "Too good to be true! " '   [CM, 366-367]), is ironic. In 'Hawthorne and his mosses', Melville states the wish to glorify excellent books 'without including their ostensible authors', for 'the names of all fine authors are fictitious ones'; the problem of authority so put is to be connected with Melville's refusal to mythologize Shakespeare into one of the 'Anglo-Saxon superstitions' (PM, 400, 409), with Ishmael's savagely rebellious critical stance, with attempts to resist the Confidence Man, and with Vere's awareness of the arbitrary nature of authority; it is also to be connected with the final source of error with which Locke deals in the *Essay*, that of authority, whether of 'friends or party, neighbourhood or country', or of 'reverend antiquity', for 'All men are liable to error, and most men are in many points, by passion or interest, under temptation to it' (*Essay*, IV, xx, 17). Since ˏ'one must turn to some authority', says the narrator of *Billy Budd* (thereby summarizing the argument of the novel), he will refer to 'the authentic' translation of Plato (BB, 75); but he notes, in Melville's marginal additon to the text, that in more usual cases neither lawyers nor 'remunerated medical experts' can agree on questions of moral responsibility; nor, were they asked, could 'clerical proficients'.[9] The ship's surgeon has the last disdainful word on classical authority, with reference to Billy's final motive: ' "Euthanasia, Mr. Purser, is something like your *will-power*; I doubt its authenticity as a scientific term. . . . It is at once imaginative and metaphysical, – in short, Greek! " ' (BB, 125). Claggart's 'nature', despite the use of Plato's lexicon, remains hidden, the narrator tentatively referring to his 'monomania. . . if that indeed it were' (90); Vere, moreover, answers on Billy's behalf the question, 'unintentionally touching on a spiritual sphere wholly obscure to Billy's thoughts', what could have motivated Claggart's making a fase charge:

'The question you put to him comes naturally enough. But how can he rightly answer it? or anybody else? unless indeed it be he who lies within there', designating the compartment where lay the corpse. 'But the prone one there will not rise to our summons. In effect though, as it seems to me, the point you make is hardly material. Quite aside from any conceivable motive actuating the Master-at-Arms, and irrespective of the provocation to the blow, a martial court must needs in the present case confine its attention to the blow's consequence, which consequence justly is to be deemed not otherwise than as the striker's deed.' (107)

Just as Claggart's 'motive' cannot be considered, neither can the intention behind the ' "prisoner's deed" ', for 'War looks but to the frontage, the appearance' (here might be recalled Moby Dick's unreadable brow, and Claggart's stricken forehead): 'Budd's intent is nothing to the purpose' (108, 112). Like Ishmael, and like the narrator of *Billy Budd*, Vere operates within the confines of a conventional code, cannot strike through the mask as Claggart pretends to: the latter's 'conscience being but the lawyer to his will' builds a 'strong case' on the basis of 'the motive imputed to Billy in spilling the soup' (80); he argues to Vere that Billy is ' "a deep one" ' and offers to produce ' "substantiating proof" ', which is but his own fiction (94, 96). It is for Vere to judge Claggart's ' "foggy" ' tale: a Fairfax, he must do fairly; a Vere, he must seek truth, as he insists that the doctor ' "verify" ' that Claggart is dead (100). Aware that he is 'not authorized' to act in any way but according to the martial code, and being 'no lover of authority for authority's sake' (103-104), Vere knows that the implications of his name are arbitrary, that there is no Justice beyond codified

law, no Truth beyond ' "facts" ' (111). ' "Who's to doom" ',
demands Ahab, ' "when the judge himself is dragged to the bar? " '
(MD 445); Burroughs is more cheerful: 'As one judge said to the
other: "Be just and if you can't be just, be arbitrary" ' (NL, 4).
It is in the adherence to an arbitrary code, in fact, that Vere's
situation is comparable to that of Melville's cousin, who pressed
for conviction, though in quite different circumstances, under
'Articles modeled on the English Mutiny Act': motive again is
irrelevant, for 'the urgency felt, well-warranted or otherwise, was
much the same' (113). Officers, says Vere, like impressed men, are
not ' "natural free agents" '; the code must be enforced because
the sailors, ' "long moulded by arbitrary discipline' ", will, however they feel about Billy, expect such enforcement of efficient
commanders (110, 112): the only justification for any course of
action consists in habitual patterns of association and expectation
– the basis, for Locke, of language and thought. The official
' "code" ', of course, is digital: ' "We must do; and one of two
things we must do – condemn or let go" '; this is not the 'letting
go' equated with cure by Burroughs, whose prescription more
aptly paraphrases Vere's argument against the claims of ' "the
heart" ' and of ' "the private conscience" ' (111). The code
having been followed, the ship's company echoes Billy's blessing
of Vere 'Without volition as it were' (123), murmuring something
'inarticulate... dubious in significance' after his death, but eventually 'yielding to the mechanism of discipline' (126). The awesome Symbolism of Billy's ascension at sunrise is undercut by
the intrusion at that moment, again, in a fashion that anticipates
the textual scrambling and fondness for anticlimax of Agee and
Burroughs, of a later comic scene in which the Purser attributes
the remarkable motionlessness of Billy's body to ' "the force
lodged in will power" ', and is rudely contradicted by the surgeon's denial that the absence of ' "mechanical spasm in the mus-
cular system" ' is attributable to ' "will power, a term" ', he says,
' "not yet included in the lexicon of science' ":

'You admit then that the absence of spasmodic movement was phenomenal.'
'It was phenomenal, Mr. Purser, in the sense that it was an appearance the
cause of which is not immediately to be assigned.' (125)

Ishmael's status as a record of empirical data makes sense of the fact that he spends the first chapter of *Moby-Dick* — 'Loomings', or indistinct appearances — trying to formulate his motive for going to sea, which is 'a way I have of driving off the spleen and regulating the circulation'; he lists four 'whenever' conditions — symptoms like grimness about the mouth, dreary weather in the soul, funeral attendance, the urge to knock hats off — of which the sequel is, 'then, I account it high time to get to sea as soon as I can': 'whenever' I see the alphabet written up to K, 'then' I know that L comes next. Ishmael, that is, is 'in the habit of going to sea'; arbitrary habit is his, as it is Vere's, sole explanation: 'With a philosophical flourish Cato throws himself upon his sword; I quietly take to the ship'. There is evidence in Manhattan that things are set up that way, where 'Right and left, the streets take you waterward'; and one must explain why so many people stand gazing out to sea ('What do they here? '), why a walk in the country invariably leads to water, why a landscape painting is incomplete without it, 'Why' poets place the sea above practical needs, 'Why' the Greeks deified it with the brother of Jove, if one is to explain Ishmael's motive (MD, 13-14). Later on Peleg demands that explanation of Ishmael, who answers that he wants ' "to see what whaling is. . . . to see the world" '; for the former, says Peleg, it is necessary only to clap eye on Ahab; for the latter, ' "just step forward there, and take a peep over the weather bow" ': Ishmael is forced to acknowledge that he does in fact see the world — ' "Well, what's the report? " ' — and cannot explain why he wants to see more of it; 'I was a little staggered, but go a-whaling I must and I would' (70). His list of reasons for going as a 'simple sailor' rather than as a passenger or as an officer reinforces his wise-guy personality, are witty rationalizations, that is, of a situation over which he has no control, and emphasize his consenting passivity before the universal thump. But he cannot explain why he goes as a whaleman rather than a merchant sailor, and parodies the notion of a program drawn up by the Fates, wedging 'WHALING VOYAGE BY ONE ISHMAEL' between a presidential election and a battle in Afghanistan. While he 'cannot tell why it was exactly', his recollection of 'all the circumstances' affords him a limited and retrospective glimpse into the then 'cunningly' disguised 'springs and motives' of his becoming a whaleman, which not only direct him but cajole him 'into the delusion that it was a choice resulting from my own unbiased free will and discriminating judgment': these are the desire to witness 'a thousand Patagonian sights and sounds' and the lure of danger and of the sea, but 'Chief among these motives was the overwhelming idea of the whale himself', dominated in turn by, of all whales, 'one grand hooded phantom, like a snow hill in the air'.

The formula, 'whale, especially Moby Dick, equals motive', sets up the empirical boundary of investigation: if the Narcissus story of 'the image of the ungraspable phantom of life' is 'the key to it all' (14-16), then Ishmael, whose questioning of his own motive leads him to envision the White Whale, joins the search for it in order to find out what, finally, can be known of motive. Whales are ostensive motives to action, whale hunts providing oil 'for almost all the tapers, lamps, and candles that burn round the globe', though it is ironic that the pitiful old whale must cruelly 'be murdered... to illuminate the solemn churches that preach unconditional inoffensiveness by all to all' (99, 301). And Ahab identifies his tenacity – ' "Ahab's hawser tows his purpose yet" ' (459) – with the motive force of harpooned Sperm Whales, which tow boats at terrifying speed: ' "Here we go like three tin kettles at the tail of a mad cougar! . . . this is the way a fellow feels when he's going to Davy Jones" ' (299). Ishmael's investigation of what moves Ahab, the crew and himself is his investigation of what moves the whale, a search for the substance behind appearances; 'there is death in this business of whaling', he says, but perhaps 'we have largely mistaken this matter of Life and Death': banishing his morbid thoughts in the chapel, he opines that his 'true substance' hearkens to 'Delightful inducements to embark', for death is an event of the body which, like the text, can neither be transcended nor identified with; 'take it I say, it is not me' (41).

Although Ishmael gives us a chapter of surmises on Ahab's motives for continuing to lower for whales while hunting Moby Dick, all he can certainly report – 'Be all this as it may. . .' – are Ahab's orders for vigilance (185); whether he follows an associative pattern or whether simply 'betrayed' by his eagerness, 'whichever way it might have been', what Ahab perceptibly does is lower for the squid (237); as to his conciliating gesture to Starbuck, 'It were perhaps vain to surmise exactly why it was that . . . Ahab thus acted', whether out of 'honesty' or 'mere prudential policy': 'However it was, his orders were executed' (394). Compulsively identifying himself with the design which, except when he rushes from his state room, is all-consuming, Ahab helplessly acknowledges that 'all my means are sane, my motive mad'; his actions from the loss of his leg forward are a successful but unwilling 'dissembling' his mad motive, so that the 'report of his undeniable delirium' on the return voyage and his subsequent 'moodiness' are mistakenly 'ascribed to a kindred cause', natural grief at his casualty (161-162): Ishmael can only guess at what might be behind Ahab's gestures as he carries on according to normal 'forms and usages...incidentally making use of them for other and more private ends than they were legitimately intended to subserve' (129). At the first appearance of Fedallah and his crew, the men, owing to Archy's having overheard them, are 'for the time freed from superstitious surmisings; though the affair still left an abundant room for all manner of conjectures as to dark Ahab's precise agency in the matter from the beginning': Stubb's comment that ' "The White Whale's at the bottom of it" ' (189) suggests the limit of understanding on that score. Ishmael is equally in the dark as to 'with what intent' Elijah might be following him, as he seems to be, after their interview (88); and what 'possessed Radney to meddle with such a man in that corporeally exasperated state, I know not; but so it happened' (212); nor can he guess the content of the threat which stays the captain's hand from Steelkilt, and gives even Radney pause (219). He merely speculates as to the owners' motives for sending Ahab back to sea (again, 'be all this as it may...'), and renounces any knowledge of what motivates the crew, including himself, to chase Ahab's whale: 'all this to explain, would be to dive deeper than Ishmael can go. The subterranean miner that works in us all, how can one tell whither leads his shaft by the even shifting, muffled noise of his pick? . . . What skiff in tow of a seventy-four can stand still? For one, I gave myself up to the abandonment of the time and the place; but while yet all rush to encounter the whale, could see naught in that brute but the deadliest ill' (162-163).

Disencumbered of the illusion of free will, Ishmael remains a witness. While Ahab, who posits a world of metaphor and linked analogies, identifies with his will and insists upon its integrity — 'What I've dared, I've willed; and what I've willed I'll do! ' (147) —Ishmael remarks of his position at the end of the monkey rope that 'my free will had received a mortal wound', and moreover that 'this situation of mine was the precise situation of every man that breathes' (271). In the chapter immediately following his surmises of Ahab's motives, Ishmael sits weaving a mat, threading the shuttle of free will among the fixed threads of necessity, stretched on the 'Loom of Time', Queequeg's careless manipulation of his sword functioning as chance, which 'has the last featuring blow at events'; chance, free will and necessity are neither incompatible nor abstractable one from another: but at the moment that Tashtego sings out at the sight of the first Sperm Whale of the voyage — 'you would have thought him some prophet or seer beholding the shadows of Fate' — Ishmael leaps to his feet and 'the ball of free will dropped from my hand'. The Sperm Whale pre-empts notions of free will; like the threads of necessity, 'subject to but one single, ever returning, unchanging vibration', and like the Behemoth machinery of birth in 'The Tartarus of maids', the 'Sperm Whale blows as a clock ticks, with the same undeviating and reliable uniformity' (85-86): whether that necessity assumes the anthropomorphic proportions of 'Fate' appropriate to Ahab's tragic stature, or does not transcend the observation of constant conjunction, as in Locke and Hume, is a central question in *Moby-Dick.*

The idea of weaving is recurrent: when Stubb abandons Pip ('he did not mean to') at mid-ocean, the latter sees 'strange shapes of the unwarped primal world... the multitudinous, God-omnipresent coral insects, that out of the firmament of waters heaved the colossal orbs. He saw God's foot upon the treadle of the loom, and spoke it; and therefore his shipmates called him mad' (347). The 'weaver-god' is again linked with the Sperm Whale when Ishmael measures the skeleton: 'as the ever-woven verdant warp and woof intermixed and hummed around him, the mighty idler seemed the cunning weaver; himself all woven over with vines'. Ishmael's threading his way among the bones of the overgrown skeleton, marking his path by unravelling a ball of twine, makes him a weaver, or rather a shuttle in search of the weaver, just as the whale is both 'weaver' and 'woven'. Examining the whale from head to tail — here, as throughout the book — he searches in vain among the anatomized fragments for the ungraspable phantom of life: 'I saw no living thing within; naught was there but bones.' Empirical investigation becomes a thoroughly self-reflexive interrogation of subjectivity; 'only when we escape' the deafening hum of the loom 'shall we hear the thousand voices that speak through it' (374-375): Ishmael does not escape, is a text which encodes and interweaves many voices, just as he weaves 'tragic graces' around his characters (104). The word, 'text', appropriately enough, is derived from the Latin for 'that which is woven': Ishmael, a text without a context, is, like the whale, both weaver and woven.

His later reference to 'the mingled, mingling threads of life. . . woven on warp and woof' reinforces this self-reflexiveness, the inseparability of weaver and woven, intention and gesture, motive and act; as does Ahab's reflection, with the school of whales among whom 'Moby Dick himself' might swim before him, and Malay pirates behind, that he is 'both chasing and being chased to his deadly end' (406, 321): but Ahab will not accept that what is before his eyes is the limit of what can be known about what is behind them. Ishmael describes the Sperm Whale as 'a mass of tremendous life. . . and all obedient to one volition, as the smallest insect' (285), though he repeatedly wonders that whales 'can possibly be instinct, in all parts, with the same sort of life that lives in a dog or a horse' (234); 'Think you not that brains, like yoked cattle, should be put to this Leviathan. . .?' (376). He notes that 'his tail is the sole means of propulsion', theorizes, but 'cannot demonstrate', that 'the sense of touch is concentrated in the tail', and doubts that 'any sensation lurks' in the head (316, 285). He is barred, that is, from the whale's subjectivity, 'his incommunicable contemplations' (314) and the possible symbolism of his tail gestures: 'But if I know not even the tail of this whale, how understand his head?' (318). ' "Think" ', says Stubb, ' "of having half an acre of stomach-ache!" ' (296).

Just as Ishmael does not know the cause of Tashtego's falling into the Sperm Whale's head, so that it throbs 'as if that moment seized with some momentous idea' (288), or whether ambergris is the 'cause' or the 'effect' of the whale's dyspepsia (342), he does not know to what degree the whale is an intelligent agent capable of intention: the 'resemblance' of his skull to a human's is sufficiently close that, 'scaled down. . . among a plate of human skulls. . . you would involuntarily confound it with them', though neither its shape nor its size gives any indication of 'his true brain'. The puzzle of what motivates the whale — 'I put that brow before you. Read it if you can' (293) — is the puzzle of Ishmael's own motive: the whale is spoken of in the Shaster as the avatar of 'Vishnoo', and in Stubb's song as 'a joker' (306, 413); it is rumored by 'the superstitiously inclined... that Moby Dick was ubiquitous; that he had actually been encountered in opposite latitudes at one and the same instant of time' (158); he is characterized as an ' "immortal" ' tool of fate (221), as a dream apparition (223-224), as 'the Shaker God incarnate' (267) and as 'the old great-grandfather' (365). If death is 'speechlessly quick' (41), approaching with 'a last revelation, which only an author from the dead could adequately tell' (396)–in *Mardi* it is 'voiceless as a calm' (I, 217); in 'Benito Cereno', a 'voiceless end' (GSW, 35)–the whale also 'has no voice. . . . But then again, what has the whale to say? Seldom have I known any profound being that had anything to say to this world' (312). Death, which might be a slumbering dream (399) or an 'eternal unstirring paralysis, and deadly, hopeless trance' (41), is an 'endless end' (395) and cannot be witnessed (Ahab is 'voicelessly . . . shot out of the boat, ere the crew knew he was gone' [468]), is observably only an inanimate gesture, Tashtego's hammer 'frozen' to the mast as the skyhawk is dragged down (496). And just as Ahab's brow is dented with 'the foot-prints of his one unsleeping, ever-pacing thought', and the 'shades' of thought sweep over Queequeg's face, so the birds are 'the gentle thoughts' of the air, and whales, swordfish and sharks 'the strong, troubled, murderous thinkings' of the sea (140, 442). But the intention behind these visible manifestations cannot be deduced, for the calm swelling of the sea is both the lulling of 'the seductive god... Pan' (400) and a treacherous surface hiding 'the tiger's heart that pants beneath it' (405): Queequeg's remark that ' "de god wat made shark must be one dam ingin" ' (257) epitomizes Ishmael's puzzlement as to the motive source of things.

Locke writes that the problem of cosmic causality is subordinate to the more obvious one of the subjective phenomenon of will: 'my thought only changing, the right hand rests, and the left hand moves . . . explain this and make it intelligible, and then the next step will be to understand creation' (*Essay*, IV, x, 19). Ahab too focuses on the problem of voluntary action: ' "What is it, what nameless, inscrutable, unearthly thing is it; what cozzening, hidden lord and master, and cruel remorseless emperor commands me. . . . Is Ahab, Ahab? Is it I, God, or who, that lifts this arm? " ' (445). But unlike Locke, he insists upon a continuous and consistent identity, and regards necessity as something more than the observed conjunction of ideas: ' "Ahab is forever Ahab, man. This whole act's immutably decreed. 'Twas rehearsed by thee and me a billion years before this ocean rolled. Fool! I am the   Fates' lieutenant; I act under orders" ' (459). His personification of necessity as Fate invests every event with intention, so that his groin injury is 'but the direct issue of another woe' (385); words come before things: the causal nexus has the force of a predetermined gesture.

'But in each event — in the living act, the undoubted deed — there, some unknown but still reasoning thing puts forth the mouldings of its features from behind the unreasoning mask. If man will strike, strike through the mask! How can the prisoner reach outside except by thrusting through the wall? To me, the white whale is that wall, shoved near to me. Sometimes I think there's naught beyond. But 'tis enough. He tasks me; he heaps me; I see in him outrageous strength, with an inscrutable malice sinewing it. That inscrutable thing is chiefly what I hate; and be the white whale agent or be the white whale principal, I will wreak that hate upon him.' (144)

A prisoner, like Ishmael, of his subjectivity, Ahab regards his uniqueness as a punishment or exile, and thrusts through the wall of experience by projecting his compulsively autonomous sense of purpose or intention ('Swerve me? The path to my fixed purpose is laid with iron rails, whereon my soul is grooved to run' [148]) onto the empirical appearance of things, investing them with the depth of fixed significance: for him Moby Dick's assault is a rational and intentional gesture. Nor, Ishmael points out, is this belief an anomaly: maritime rumors incorporate 'all manner of morbid hints, and half-formed foetal suggestions of supernatural agencies, which eventually invested Moby Dick with new terrors unborrowed from anything that visibly appears' (156). While accidents in the fishery are frequent, 'such seemed the White Whale's infernal aforethought of ferocity that every dismembering or death that he caused was not wholly regarded as having been inflicted by an unintelligent agent' (159). When Ishmael demonstrates that 'the most marvellous event in this book is corroborated by plain facts of the present day' by citing Owen Chace's 'plain and faithful narrative' of his ship's having been rammed and sunk by a Sperm Whale, he notes Chace's mention that ' "Every fact seemed to warrant me in concluding that it was anything but chance which directed his operations . . . . He came. . . as if fired with revenge. . . producing. . . impressions in my mind of decided, calculating mischief, on the part of the whale" ' (179-180). Ishmael himself expects the reader to renounce 'all ignorant incredulity' regarding some of the Sperm Whale's 'more inconsiderable braining feats' (285).

However, whereas Ahab seeks a showdown with Moby Dick, that 'set time or place. . . when all possibilities would become probabilities, and, as Ahab fondly thought, every possibility the next thing to a certainty' (173), Ishmael's vision is obviated by the blank brow. Narcissistic Ahab sees to the exclusion of all else his own image in the depth of the pool, but Ishmael, who does not identify with — know the meaning of — his own image, is left on the surface of rumor and report, the text, just as his knowledge of the whale is irremediably superficial: 'Dissect him how I may, then, I but go skin deep; I know him not and never will' (318). Despite Ahab's being told by the surgeon of the Samuel Enderby that ' "what you take for the White Whale's malice is only his awkwardness" ' (368), despite Starbuck's outrage at the blasphemy of ' "Vengeance on a dumb brute. . . that simply smote thee from blindest instinct" ' (144), and despite his insistence, as the whale swims away, that ' "Moby Dick seeks thee not. It is thou, thou, that madly seekest him" ' (465), Ahab immovably believes in the whale's reputed 'intelligent malignity' (159). At his own coming into the presence of Moby Dick, Ishmael describes his movements in tentative, conditional terms: 'as if perceiving this strategem, Moby Dick, with that malicious intelligence ascribed to him. . .' (448); he 'seemed only intent on annihilating every separate plank' (456); 'whether fagged by three days' running chase. . . or whether it was some latent deceitfulness and malice in him: whichever was true. . .' (465); 'catching sight of the nearing black hull of the ship, seemingly seeing in it the source of all his persecutions; bethinking it — it may be — a larger and nobler foe. . .' (466); Ishmael simply doesn't know. Whether the 'Retribution, swift vengeance, eternal malice' in Moby Dick's 'whole aspect' as he charges the Pequod indicate the intentional gesture of a mirror-image intelligence, or are the figments of a limited, fictive vocabulary, remains moot (468); there is finally no ground for an anthropomorphic vision, or for the possibility

of making things amenable to words: symbols are without ultimate purchase.

Unlike Billy Budd, Ahab is the hero of a romance, but Ishmael's
curtain speech prevents *Moby-Dick* from being a romance, works
against the symmetrical resolution towards which a story presided
over by Fate should proceed, and questions the inevitability of the
redemptive pattern thereby suggested. In his episodic narration,
his taking things apart for close investigation rather than drawing
them towards the hub of a single comprehensive point of view,
Ishmael does the opposite of the narrator of *The Scarlet Letter*
— turns a romance, that is, into a digital, discontinuous record:
whereas that book tells of the working out of the redemptive plan,
the final realization of divine intention, Ishmael's experience is
of what he politely and ironically calls an 'interregnum in Providence' (MD, 271). The fulfillment of Ahab's romantic promise to
break through the empirical surface remains immanent, but, like
Ishmael, we are left floating on it.

According to Tommo, 'As wise a man as Shakespeare has said,
that the bearer of evil tidings hath but a losing office' (198); like
the reporters who return to Job, Ishmael brings bad news, for no
news is good news. Chillingworth-style, he has watched and listened, but his very presence, his commission of what Agee describes
as the *faux pas* of anticlimax, testifies that he had not been absorbed into the ritual last act: 'The Drama's done. Why then does
one step forth? ' Like David Locke, he has left his tape recorder
running, and replays it — retells the event — for our consideration.
But there are things that the text will not compute — 'awe', for
example (78, 395-396); and if there is 'an aesthetic', it is 'in all
things' (238): in the course of the ongoing translation that we
witness, what does not compute is lost, for 'however peculiar . . .
any chance whale may be, they soon put an end to his peculiarities by killing him, and boiling him down into a peculiarly valuable
oil' (176). Given all the possible co-ordinates, the knowledge of
what a whale is, or of who Ishmeal is, is unavailable; 'though of
real knowledge there be little, yet of books there are a plenty'
(117). There is a message in evidence, but there is no empirically
detectable sender or receiver: it is the Confidence Man who deals
in ' "communication" ' (CM, 367). The shape of the story of
Moby-Dick is finally a joke, the mad gesture of a transcendental
symbolist, for the critique of metaphysics and the anthropomor-

phic vision leave the reader in a voyeuristic situation, observing (literally, adhering to) without alibi, data without context.

It is possible, *Moby-Dick* suggests, to escape one's habitual terms only by means of a kind of violence, so that the White Whale smashes the romantic shape of the text by smashing the Pequod, leaving a baseless and unlikely postscript. As the quotation heading that postscript implies, the reader is finally in the position of Job, to whom messengers report the news that everything has been destroyed: 'But where shall wisdom be found? and where is the place of the understanding? . . . The depth saith, It is not in me: and the sea saith, It is not with me' (*Job* 28: 12-14). God's chastisement of Job — 'Where wast thou when I laid the foundations of the earth? declare if thou hast understanding' (38: 4) — does not clear up the mystery, but compounds it with a catalogue of inexplicable wonders: 'Canst thou draw out Leviathan with an hook? . . . Will he make a covenant with thee? . . . Who can open the doors of his face? ' (41: 4, 14). Words do not grasp the ungraspable phantom of life — neither the understanding, nor what is understood. 'A word', says Godard's voice-over in *La Chinoise*, 'is what remains unsaid'.

NOTES

1. Herman Melville, *Mardi and A Voyage Thither*, volume I. London, Chapman and Dodd, 1923: 132. Subsequent references are noted in the text (M,I; M,II).
2. Herman Melville, *White-Jacket or The World in a Man-of-War*, ed. by A.R. Humphreys. Oxford University Press, 1966: 51, 373. Subsequent references are noted in the text (WJ).
3. Herman Melville, 'Bartleby', in *The Portable Melville*, ed. by Jay Leyda. New York, Viking, 1974: 466. Subsequent references are noted in the text (PM).
4. Robert Zoellner, *The Salt-Sea Mastodon: A Reading of Moby-Dick*. Berkeley, University of California Press, 1972: xi.
5. Glauco Cambon, 'Ishmael and the problem of formal discontinuities in *Moby Dick*', *Modern Language Notes* 76, 1961: 522.
6. H.L. Golemba, 'The shape of *Moby-Dick*', *Studies in the Novel*, 5, (2) 1973: 210.
7. Herman Melville, *Pierre or, The Ambiguities*. New York, Grove, 1957: 502-503. Subsequent references are noted in the text (P).
8. Byron Gysin, 'Cut me up', in *Minutes to Go*. San Francisco, City Lights, 1968: 43-44. Subsequent references are noted in the text (MG).
9. F. Barron Freeman, editor,'Billy Budd, foretopman', in *Melville's Billy Budd*. Harvard University Press, 1948: 188-189.

5

The Print and the Paupers: Narcissism as Nostalgia in *Let Us Now Praise Famous Men*

"Look here, this is a book he had when he was a boy. It just shows you." He opened it at the back cover and turned it around for me to see. On the last fly-leaf was printed the word SCHEDULE, and the date September 12, 1906. And underneath:

Rise from bed . . . . 6.00   A.M.
Dumbell exercise and wall-scaling . 6.15-6.30 A.M.
Study electricity, etc. . . . . 7.15-8.15 A.M.
Work . . . . 8.30-4.30 P.M.
Baseball and sports . . . . 4.30-5.00 P.M.
Practice elocution, poise and how
   to attain it . . . . 5.00-6.00 P.M.
Study needed inventions . . . . . . 7.00-9.00 P.M.

GENERAL RESOLVES

No wasting time at Shafters or [a name, indecipherable]
No more smoking or chewing
Bath every other day
Read one improving book or magazine per week
Save $5.00 [crossed out] $3.00 per week
Be better to parents.

"I come across this book by accident," siad the old man, "It just shows you, don't it?" "It just shows you."

F. Scott Fitzgerald
The Great Gatsby

SCOPOPHILIAC SHUDDERS

Following the extensive preliminaries, James Agee begins Book

Two of *Let Us Now Praise Famous Men* by questioning the motives and intentions of the project as set up by *Fortune* magazine:

'I spoke of this piece of work we were doing as "curious" '. I had better amplify this.
   It seems to me curious, not to say obscene and thoroughly terrifying, that it could occur to an association of human beings drawn together through need and chance and for profit into a company, an organ of journalism, to pry intimately into the lives of an undefended and appallingly damaged group of human beings, an ignorant and helpless rural family, for the purpose of parading the nakedness, disadvantage and humiliation of these lives before another group of human beings, in the name of science, of "honest journalism" (whatever that paradox may mean), of humanity, of social fearlessness, for money, and for a reputation for crusading and for unbias which, when skillfully enough qualified, is exchangeable at any bank for money (and in politics, for votes, job patronage, abelincolnism, etc.[1] [[1]money]); and that these people could be capable of meditating this prospect without the slightest doubt of their qualification to do an "honest" piece of work, and with a conscience better than clear, and in the virtual certitude of almost unanimous public approval.

That Agee and Evans have 'so extremely different a form of respect for the subject and responsibility towards it' (LUNPFM, 7) mitigates neither their involvement in this exposure nor their hope their publishers will recover their investment and 'a little of your money might fall to poor little us' (LUNPFM, 15). The passage sets up the self-interrogative themes of the prose, for without recourse to the excuse of respectable motives and intentions the book is an act of unredeemed voyeurism. Agee describes it to Father Flye, in fact, as a 'piece of spiritual burglary', 'a sinful book at least in all degrees of "falling short of the mark" and I think in more corrupt ways as well' (LFF, 117, 135).
   The status of the witness as voyeur is a major issue throughout Agee's work. The early story, 'Death in the desert', offers the image, mediated by a car window, of a marooned and desperate Negro gesturing wildly for help on a desert highway — 'For some shameful reason the effect was grotesquely funny, if indeed there was any effect' (CSP, 80) — who is abandoned; the narrator, by definition a teller of stories, and a liar even to those with whom he collaborates by his silence, finishes by struggling to arrange his thoughts into a credible order, a story by which that collusion might be extenuated. The narrator of 'They that sow in sorrow shall reap', who gives the Richardsian meditation on epistemology

quoted earlier, regards himself as 'a horrible failure' at carrying any 'one idea through', getting 'at the bottom of anything': at writing a coherent story. His fellow lodgers, like him 'myopic' in their limited points of view, are unaware of his taking note of their mundane attitudes: 'when, caught in these flimsy inescapable cogs, they are contemplated in their unrealized relation to the timeless severence of the vast radiance of life, and the enormous shadow of death, they become magnificent, and tragic, and beautiful' (CSP, 96-98). '1928 story' describes the tentative recollection of a phase of his youth by a middle-aged writer, who feels that his reconstruction is 'Very likely... completely subjective'; this self-examination unfolds like a telescope, for this early phase is itself given over to intense self-contemplation; fascinated, at that time, by the image of a girl he has seen only once, he seeks her family's cottage at dusk and watches through the window:

Taking care to stay out of the light, he came closer. She read in a way that fascinated and satisfied him, detachedly, yet in complete absorption. Each time she turned a page, it was like watching someone take another mouthful of food, with perfect elegance. Then, with the same elegance, she put her finger tip into one nostril, and worked, patiently, without interrupting her reading, until she had extracted the annoyance. Still reading she rolled it between the tips of her forefinger and thumb, until it was dry, smelled of it, and flicked it to the jute carpet. God, Irvine thought: she's wonderful! He felt ashamed of himself; for now he waited, hoping that she would do this or something like it again; and when he became sufficiently aware of his shame, he withdrew, to past the rear of the cottage. There on the line, he could see bathing suits. He struck a match so that he might enjoy the cedar color. Suddenly we [sic] wanted to smell the suit. What sort of a Peeping Tom am I, he said to himself, touched it – it was a fine silk-wool – and walked away.[1]

'A mother's tale' describes a cow's relation to an audience of calves of the apocryphal story (' "It was my great-grandmother who told me. . . She was told by *her* great-grandmother, who claimed she saw it with her own eyes, though of course I can't vouch for that' ") of the one who came back from the stockyards bearing 'the mark of the Hammer... like the socket for a third eye', having been hung up and flayed before actually dead, inviting his hearers 'to examine his wounded heels... as closely as they pleased' (CSP, 255-256, 250), and telling of the fate that awaits all cattle: Ishmael, escaped alone to tell us; Christ as reporter.

Just as the prose in LUNPFM is Agee's investigation of his own memory images and states of emotional poise, *The Morning Watch* and *A Death in the Family* are progressive extensions into and researches of his more remote subjective past, much as is suggested by Irvine's meditation in '1928 story': Father Flye remarks of *A Death in the Family* that, with a few modifications, the circumstances of Agee's father's death and the portraits of the characters involved 'are just taken literally from fact; that is, they're practically photographic'.[2] In 1937 Agee proposed to the Guggenheim foundation the writing of an autobiographical novel of which 'Only relatively small portions would be fiction (though the techniques of fiction might be used); and these would be subjected to nonfictional analysis ('Plans for work', CSP, 165); and he later wrote, 'I find that I value my childhood and my father as they were, as well and as exactly as I can remember and represent them, far beyond any transmutation of these matters . . . into poetry or fiction' ('Four fragments', CSP, 142).

The title, *The Morning Watch*, connects the idea of self-investigation with looking, and portrays the child's effort to fix his attention during the ritual vigil of Good Friday morning ('Could ye not watch with me one hour? ' 'Pay attention, he told himself. Mind your own business') as the vision of 'his mind's eye',[3] before which images appear against his volition: of Christ, in a maudlin portrait of affected passion (MW, 31); of Christ's wounds profanely compared, via the line, *'he saw more wounds then one'* in *Venus and Adonis*, with a 'rawly intimate glimpse' of a female playmate (56); and of his father's corpse (49), the same image which is the final meditation of *A Death in the Family*. Whereas Agee's act of devotion, his watching or concentration of attention, is to his minutely remembered past, Richard's memories are an impious interruption of his vigil. Richard himself is watched by God ('remembering Thou God seest me' [27]), by Father Whitman (' "Don't think I won't be watching for you" ' [25]), by the forest ('each separate blossom enlarging like an eye' [27]), by the locust shell ('the eyes looked into his' [130]), by the snake ('the eye seemed to meet Richard's' [144]), by his companions as they undress to swim, by Agee, and by the reader. His own coming to manhood is a movement away from his naive sense of piety and anxiety for precedent, and a defiance of watchful authority by an awakening attention that strains against the 'silly rules' of the school (40). Agee's idea of God, like Babbalanja's, requires that 'either he delivers autonomy to all his creation and creatures and in compassion and ultimate confidence watches and awaits the results, or he is a second-rate God, a sort of celestial back-seat driver' (LFF, 180); in *A Death in the Family*, Rufus struggles with the idea that ' "God wants us to make up our own minds" ': ' "Even to do bad things right under his nose? " ' [4]

To watch and wait is to endure the ambiguous without the guarantee of precedent, as Richard does when he overstays his watch and goes truant from school, an act which affords him his unprecedented vision of a brilliantly colored snake: 'for a few seconds he saw perfected before him, royally dangerous and to be adored and to be feared, all that is alien in nature and in beauty: and stood becharmed' (MW, 141). Whereas Richard's attention ought to be an agent of discipline ('you just watch your mouth' [44]), it is sacrilegious in its uncontrolled wandering, furtively deployed in a giddy, unsteady freedom: with his companions, 'their six eyes emphatic in the sleepless light', he admires senior students at work, whose eyes are 'fixed in the profound attentiveness of great scientists' (36-37), and particularly relishes 'this surprising chance to be so near [the athlete Willard] and to watch him so closely', especially the hump between his shoulders, which Richard 'had never yet had the chance to examine so privately' (41, 42). Later he eavesdrops as these seniors discuss him, becoming suddenly 'frightened because he was spying' (101). His attention is limited by, but not to be identified with, the position of his eyes, which can disguise his inspections: 'along the side of his eye Jimmy advanced' (51); 'he opened his eyes. . . and without turning his head glanced narrowly around him through his lashes' (78). When he surveys the apparently empty mannerisms of Claude, he feels it 'as shameful to be watching him this way, so unaware that he was being watched, or that he might look in the least silly, so defenseless, as it would be to peer at him through a keyhole' (81). Meditating Christ's sufferings at the hands of the soldiers, Richard 'can see him only as if he spied down on what was happening through a cellar window', a point of view comparable to that of Peter the Betrayer, 'hiding on the outskirts, spying through the window. He was afraid to show himself and he couldn't stand to go away' (113-114). Just as Peter strikes an ear from the servant of the serpentine Judas (22), Richard strikes the head of a potentially venomous snake; a

contrite voyeur, he too confronts his terrifying solitude, intensified both for Richard and for the narrator by the lack of unambiguous connection between the subjective image and 'reality'
('he began to wonder whether these tricks of visualization were
not mere tricks and temptations of emptiness' [105]), by the
sense of having 'failed' in the meditative quest for knowledge,
respectively, of God ('make me to know thy suffering' [23]),
and of self, the nature of attention. 'My cup runneth over, something whispered within him, yet what he saw in his mind's eye
was a dry chalice, an empty Grail' (119).

'Dream sequence', unpublished until 1968 and apparently
written as an introduction to *A Death in the Family*, is set in
Knoxville, Tennessee, Agee's home town. A frightened dreamer
awakens in doubt 'that the meaning of any dream could ever
be known', but 'sure that that was where the dream indicated he
should go. He should go back into those years. As far as he could
remember; and everything he could remember... nothing except
... what he had seen with his own eyes and supposed with his
own mind'. As for trying to 'understand' the experience, he will
'make the journey, as he had dreamed the dream, for its own
sake, without trying to interpret'. Suddenly he is aware of his
father's presence in the room, a witness 'who also knew the
dream, and no more knew or hoped ever to know its meaning
than the son', a ghost similar to one of Hitchcock's, whose function, like that of the camera, is to look on. Comforted by the presence of his father – 'God keep you. Or whatever it is that keeps
you'[5] – the dreamer takes up the third-person narration of the
events surrounding the death of Rufus Follet's father, including
such scenes as are built around words and noises heard by Rufus
in the night through sleep, and so forgotten 'that years later, when
he remembered them, he could never be sure that he was not
making them up' (DF, 29).

The empirical problem of distinguishing dream from reality is
identified, again as so often in Hitchcock, as a problem of reconstruction, as is illustrated by the long family argument over
whether or not it has been visited by Jay Follet's ghost (76-85).
The existence of ghosts is problematic for Rufus, who cannot
sleep for fear of a darkness which is alternately gentle, 'hollowed,
all one taking ear', 'all one guardian eye', and protective of a
menacing and abysmal 'creature... which watched him' (82, 84).

Like Richard, Rufus feels spied upon, ashamed of his inappropriate behavior before the ghost of his father: 'But if his father's soul was around, always, watching over them, then he knew. And that was worst of anything because there was no way to hide from a soul, and no way to talk to it, either. He just knows, and it couldn't say anything to him either, but it could sit and look at him and be ashamed of him' (264-265). Rufus himself is an indefinable attention, struggling with the meanings of words and of his father's death: the narrator of 'Knoxville: summer, 1915', speaks of 'the time when I lived there so successfully disguised to myself as a child', and of the sound of the blood 'which you realize you are hearing only when you catch yourself listening' (11, 13); there is a painfully hilarious scene of panic when Rufus and his sister are almost caught eavesdropping on their Mother's conversation with the minister (281); and in that view of his father's body which climaxes the book — given in a series of descriptions beginning 'He could see. . .' 'He watched. . .' 'He watched. . .' 'He gazed. . .' — the body is 'actual' as is nothing else in the room, and Rufus is able, in his hushed wonder, to see him 'much more clearly than he had ever seen him before' (290-291).

W.M. Frohock has pointed out that Agee brings to *A Death in the Family* the techniques of script writing, moving his narrative vision over the details he describes like the view finder of a camera[6]; we are notified of this method, in fact, in the description in chapter one of Rufus and his father sitting twice through a William S. Hart movie, the sequence of scenes connected only by a recurrent 'and then', and the dynamized rectangle viewed as if by a detached analyst, so that 'the great country rode away behind [Hart] as wide as the world': the appearance of Charlie Chaplin, hooking a woman's skirt up with his cane and 'looking very eagerly at her legs' (19-20), suggests the nature of that watching. Agee's screenplays consistently portray the camera as interloper and spy, entering and exploring a Victorian house so that the 'whole quality of emotion should be that of a microscopic slide drawn into razor focus and from now on totally at the mercy of the lens', and pausing to look 'at itself close and hard in the mirror' ('The house', CSP, 184, 187). The camera in 'Man's fate' is regarded by a Chinese soldier 'sternly, and with a kind of cold tragic scorn, as if into the leaning and questioning eyes of a likewise doomed comrade who does not fully understand the situation' (CSP, 233); in 'Noa Noa', which makes repeated use of Gauguin's painting, 'The spirit of the dead watches', it advances with other onlookers to gaze at Gauguin's corpse, reads his mail over his shoulder, is caught intruding on his privacy — 'Then for a moment he seems to catch sight of us, staring at us' — and receives the resentful glances of a half-dressed model.[7] In his 'introduction' to a series of photographs taken by Walker Evans with a concealed camera on the New York subway, Agee speaks of them as privileged moments comparable to that which ends *City Lights*, at which the subject's guard is down: 'The simplest or the strongest of these beings has been so designed upon by his experience that he has a wound and nakedness to conceal, and guards and disguises by which he conceals it'[8]; the series is rhythmically punctuated, in fact, by the startled glares of those who catch the camera at work.

As a film critic, Agee praises a wartime report composed of captured film for presenting 'an image of a world, a phase, which we shall never see by any other means, since it will be wholly altered by the mere presence of our fighters, cameramen, and observers, once they get there', and recommends it 'to anyone who would like to be walking in Europe, invisibly, today'.[9] And scenes in Rossellini's *Open City* are 'as shatteringly uninvented-looking as if they had been shot by invisible newsreel cameras' (AF, I, 195). Some scenes in the war-record film *Attack!* are of such power as to have 'made me doubt my right to be aware of the beauty at all', and Agee recommends, for the 'communicating' rather than just the 'recording' of war, 'a still more intrusive use of the camera in places where cameras are most unwelcome... since the reaction of those who resent the prying would react in turn upon the consciousness and conscience of the audience' (99-100). He likes *The Raider*, played by sailors re-enacting actual experiences, for its realization that 'you have no right to record the sufferings and honor the fortitude of men exposed in a life-boat unless you make those sufferings at least real enough in swollen features and livid coloring, feebleness of motion and obvious crushing headache, to hurt an audience and hurt it badly' (224); and he qualifies his praise for two editions, by Paramount and by Fox, of film recording the Battle of Iwo Jima:

Very uneasily, I am beginning to believe that, for all that may be said in

favor of our seeing those terrible records of war, we have no business seeing
this sort of experience except through our presence and participation. I have
neither space nor mind yet, to try to explain why I believe this is so but. . .
I cannot avoid mentioning my perplexity. . . . If at an incurable distance from
participation, hopelessly incapable of reactions adequate to the event, we
watch men killing each other, we may be quite as profoundly degrading ourselves and, in the process, betraying and separating ourselves the farther from
those we are trying to identify ourselves with; none the less because we tell
ourselves sincerely that we sit in comfort and watch carnage in order to
nurture our patriotism, our conscience, our understanding, and our sympathies.
(152)

Motive and declared intention do not mitigate the vicarious nature
of the voyeuristic experience.

   This is the central anxiety addressed in LUNPFM. Agee is a
'northern investigator' in depression Alabama, 'a spy, travelling as
a journalist'; and Evans is 'a counter-spy, travelling as a photographer' (LUNPFM, 377, xxii). Agee regards 'aspects of a young
couple which are less easily seen. . . when one's own eyes and face
and the eyes and face of another are mutually visible and apprais-
ing'; Agee and Evans are, 'in spite of our knowledge of our own
meanings, ashamed and insecure in our wish to break into' and
examine a church; and Agee agonizes over his unworthiness of
Emma Wood's declaration, 'we don't have to act any different
from what it comes natural to act, and we don't have to worry
what you're thinking about us, it's just like you was our own
people' (40, 64). In all such situations he plays his 'part through',
rehearses and re-rehearses 'my demeanors and my words', is
'unable to communicate to them at all what my feelings were'
(31, 32, 37); yet he takes every opportunity to observe – 'While
we talked I was looking around slowly' – and finds 'even the light-
est betrayal of our full reactions unwise' (431, 470).

   It is 'most important of all', he says, to realize that those of
whom he writes are actual human beings, 'living in their world,
innocent of such twistings as these which are taking place over
their heads. . . who were dwelt among, investigated, spied upon,
revered, and loved, by still others, still more alien; and. . . are now
being looked into by still others, who have picked up their living
as casually as if it were a book' (13). The prose in LUNPFM is a
verbal transcript, 'simply an effort to use words in such a way that
they will tell as much as I want to and can make them tell of a
thing which happened and which, of course, you have no other

way of knowing', and as such is comparable to the war-record film he later reviews for its implication of the reader in his voyeurism: 'Who are you who will read these words and study these photographs, and by what right do you qualify to. . .? ' (246, 9). The presence of the reader's attention, emphasized by Agee's use of the first person plural as he explores the deserted Gudger house (137, 171), is of questionable motive, 'actuated toward this reading by various possible reflexes of sympathy, curiosity, idleness, et cetera, and almost certainly in a lack of consciousness, and conscience, remotely appropriate to the enormity of what [he is] doing' (13). Involved in his perception of the beauty of the tenants' world, 'best discernible to those who by economic advantages of training have only a shameful and a thief's right to it', is the interrogation of the ' "sense of beauty" ', of his own perspective: 'but by what chance have I this "opinion" or "perception" or, I might say, "knowledge"? ' (203, 314). Agee is fiercely defensive against his own and his reader's prying, and celebrative of that about the tenants which cannot be described, their own condition as crippled and deprived witnesses or subjective 'centers'. His 'effort', he says, 'is to recognize the stature of a portion of unimagined existence, and to contrive techniques proper to its recording, communication, analysis and defense. More essentially, this is an independent inquiry into certain normal predicaments of human divinity' (xiv). He defines this divinity, and his own attention, empirically — that is, by negation — dealing only with recorded data and its mode of availability: the record. He self-reflexively addresses the medium of this exposure, the word and the photographic and mnemonic image: his subject, like Ishmael's, is himself, who 'must mediate, must attempt to record, your warm weird human lives' (99): 'The immediate instruments are two: the motionless camera and the printed word. The governing instrument — which is also one of the centers of the subject — is individual, anti-authoritative human consciousness' (xiv).

Like *The Morning Watch*, LUNPFM abounds in images of eyes and watching: a sky which 'held herself away from us and watched us' (21); Negro workers 'watching carefully to catch the landowner's eyes, should they be glanced after' (27); a child's 'repeated witness' of his parents' intercourse, which 'he lifts his head and hears and sees and fears and is torn open by' (109); the knee-high details of 'the earliest and profoundest absorptions of a very young child' (149); the freshness of light in a shuttered room 'as if the objects were blinking or had been surprised in secret acts' (157-158); the floors, roof, walls and furniture of a room as 'all watch upon one hollow center' (220); the 'wild blind eyes of the cotton staring in twilight' as the work day ends, and surveying 'like the eyes of an overseer' the daily picking (344, 327); Ricketts compulsively talking and laughing 'while, out of the back of his eyes, he watched me' (388); and the tenant women undressing, 'turning part away from each other and careful not to look' (71). Most disturbing are 'the eyes of the streets' of the Alabama town (9), '(eyes, eyes on us, of men, from beneath hat brims)' (67), of people who 'slowed as they passed and lingered their eyes upon us', and of people on farmhouse porches, visible in the rearview as the car passes (25, 32). Agee deals with the eyes of bystanders in 'They that sow in sorrow shall reap' and in two fragments describing mobs who witness gory deaths and respond with 'the craziest, gayest sort of laughter' (CSP, 137-140); and the Knoxville townspeople of 'Dream sequence' exhibit an impassive 'interest... strangely out of ratio to the thing they were looking at'.[10] But the 'following, the swerving, of the slow blue dangerous and secret small-town eyes' in Alabama (373), with which he must cope at his first meeting with the tenant farmers, is that of the potential southern mob salient in the American imagination from *Huckleberry Finn* to *Easy Rider*, 'mean white faces that turned slowly after me watching me and wishing to God I would do something that would give them the excuse' (362, 377).

An equally dangerous and impersonal kind of watching is that of the camera, 'an ice-cold, some ways limited, some ways more capable eye' (234), the danger of which is the 'so nearly universal a corruption of sight' resulting from its misuse' (11). Appended to LUNPFM is a New York *Post* interview with Margaret Bourke-White about her collaboration with Erskine Caldwell on *You Have Seen Their Faces* (1937), another photo-prose coverage of impoverished farmers: her statement that 'One photograph might lie, but a group of pictures can't' (453), is at odds with Agee's, in his introduction to Helen Levitt's *A Way of Seeing*, that ' "The camera never lies" is a foolish   saying. . . . The camera is just a machine, which records with impressive and as a rule very cruel faithfulness precisely what is in the eye, mind, spirit, and skill of its operators to make it record.'[11] In this sense, as an instrument of subjectivity sharply limited in its relation to any exterior 'reality', the camera, 'handled cleanly and literally in its own terms. . . is, like the phonograph record and like scientific instruments and unlike any other leverage of art, incapable of recording anything but absolute, dry truth' (LUNPFM, 234). And Agee regards as central to his 'sense of the importance and dignity of actuality and the attempt to reproduce and analyze the actual. . . a sense of "reality" and of "values" held by more and more people, and the beginnings of somewhat new forms of, call it art if you must, of which the still and moving cameras are the strongest instruments and symbols' (245).

Thus, much of the description in LUNPFM is in terms proper to the camera: the quality of withdrawal in the dead of night is compared to 'the lifted foot arrested in stopshot' before completing its step (52); details of the countryside emerge at dawn 'like a print in a tank' (87); light in a dark-walled room is 'restricted, fragile and chemical like that of a flash bulb' (198); leaves twitter in heavy rain 'as under the scathe of machinegun fire, or alternate frames cut from a stretch of film' (394); the erosive action of a river is conceived as if 'by sped up use of the moving camera' (251); the geometry of furniture legs and the grains and scars of a bare wood floor are such as 'a moving camera might know' (149); and the various gestures of work are seen as 'the grave mutations of a dance whose business is the genius of a moving camera, and which it is not my hope ever to record' (324). The image of Mrs. Gudger and her family as they diminish in the distance and disappear over the horizon is set up as a lingering shot in a filmic memory, and dissolves into the present tense – 'They are gone' – with Agee alone in their undefended house: 'upon this house the whole of heaven is drawn into one lens; and this house itself, in each of its objects, it, too, is one lens'. Agee's clandestine exploration of the dwelling, his 'being made witness to matters no human being may see' (135-136), his thorough itemization and description of its contents and their arrangements, his 'knowledge of those hidden places. . . those griefs, beauties, those garments whom I took out, held to my lips, took odor of, and folded and restored so orderly' (188), his activity as a 'cold-laboring spy' (134), is paralleled by the 'cold absorption' of the camera, 'a witchcraft. . . colder than keenest ice', used secretly and repeatedly under the guise of 'testing around' or 'using the angle finder':

'(you never caught on; I notice how much slower white people are to catch on than negroes, who understand the meaning of a camera, a weapon, a stealer of images and souls, a gun, an evil eye.)' (362-365). Among the objects Agee examines is a photograph of Annie Mae's mother, the face faded 'as if in her death and by some secret touching the image itself of the fine head. . . had softly withered, which even while they stood there had begun its blossoming inheritance in the young daughter at her side' (164): death at work.

THE STATUS OF THE RECORD: A CRITIQUE OF REALISM

The photograph, which records the 'triple convergence' of sun, object and lens (39), is a two-dimensional grid or map describing one aspect of an arrangement. The book is a series of such maps, like the cartographical representations of non-Euclidian space called for by the Theory of Relativity – a series of notes, plans and tangential comments on a loose skeletal structure. For Agee 'a contour map is at least as considerably an image of absolute "beauty" as the counterpoints of Bach which it happens to resemble' (233). He supplies a precise floor plan of the Gudger house (138), speaks of 'having examined scientifically or as if by blueprint how such a house is made from the ground up' (184), finds maps in wood grain (142), in rain-shaped ground (406) and in the surrounding landscape (111), and recommends 'Road maps and contour maps of the middle south' as supplements to his study (449). A map is a descriptive record in terms of given co-ordinates, is the limit, within these terms, of what can be known; so that 'a new suit of overalls has among its beauties those of a blueprint: and they are the map of a working man' (266).

Mechanisms and instruments are related concerns: leaves tremble 'as delicately as that needle which records a minute disturbance on the far side of the thick planet' (85); the tenant families, their cotton 'de-personalized forever' by the monstrous gin, are 'sown once more at large upon the slow breadths of their country, in the precision of some mechanic and superhuman hand' (347); flexing the hand as it is flexed in picking cotton will demonstrate 'how this can very quickly tire, cramp and deteriorate the whole instrument' (399). Just as, in 'They that sow',

the eight roomers are 'endowed with as many different machines
for attacking existence, and defending themselves against it'
(CSP, 97), subjectivity is described in LUNPFM as mechanism,
the carried child's head swiveling 'mildly upon the world's globe,
a periscope' (135): while the senses can be assisted 'by dream, by
reason, and by those strictures of diamond glass and light whereby
we punch steep holes in the bowels of the gliding heavens... and
step measurements upon the grand estate of being', the tenant
child is deprived of 'instruments' whereby even to recognize
complex moral issues, for 'the lenses of these are smashed in his
infancy, the adjustment screws are blocked' (105, 108). The
universe can be seen in the Blakian grain of sand, 'as good a lens
as any and a much more practicable one than the universe',
though Agee declines its use (242); words are the 'instruments'
of the writer's art (236). In '1928 story', as in *The Passenger*,
memory is connected with the replaying of a phonograph record;
in LUNPFM it is connected with all recording devices, but chiefly
with the camera: 'the child, the photographic plate receiving:
These are women, I am a woman. . . this is how women are, and
how they talk' (72). Such comparisons emphasize the passivity of
the witness before his experience, the impossibility of abstracting
himself from it, and of any exhaustive, self-consistent mode of
representing it. The 'taking' of the senses

is titantic beyond exhaustion of count or valuation, and is all but infinitely
populous beyond the knowledge of each moment or a lifetime: and that
which we receive yet do not recognize, nor hold in the moment's focus, is
nevertheless and continuously and strengthfully planted upon our brains,
upon our blood: it holds: it holds: each cuts its little mark: each blown leaf
of a woodland a quarter-mile distant while I am absorbed in some close
exactitude: each of these registers, cuts his mark: not one of these is negli-
gible. (105-106)

Agee refers to this vast and cumulative transcript as the 'record
in the body' (10): like Gauguin, whose corpse is found 'savagely
paintmarked' (AF, II, 145), and like Ishmael, Agee's body is a
text, a record or piece of exposed film. And he insists upon a
maximum exposure: to hear Beethoven's Seventh or Schubert's
C-Major Symphony, you must turn the sound up and 'get down
on the floor and jam your ear as close to the loudspeaker as you
can get it and stay there, breathing as lightly as possible. . . . As
near as you will ever get you are inside the music; not only inside

it, you are it; your body is no longer your shape and substance, it is the shape and substance of the music' (15-16). He becomes 'entirely focused' (49) on an object he describes, defines himself as a focus unabstractable from what is observed. A detailed present-tense description of Ivy Woods' clothing, as she waits under the stares of some town men to see a doctor, finishes with the observation that 'her dark sweated nipples are stuck to the material and show through, and it is at her nipples, mainly, that the men keep looking' (285); 'Two images' also comprises detailed present-tense descriptions, one of Squinchy Gudger being breast-fed, centered upon his partly erect penis, the other of Ellen Woods asleep under a flour sack, a celebration of her vulva (441-442): each description holds in focus and explores an image, and each excludes mention of the watcher, who stares at Mrs. Woods as surely as do the Cookstown men. Agee's contempt for himself as a voyeur and his reverence for his victims involve him in a problematic self-negation which aligns with the implications of his epistemology:

If I were not here; and I am alien: a bodyless eye; this would never have existence in human perception.
    It has none. I do not make myself welcome here. My whole flesh; my whole being; is withdrawn upon nothingness. . . . What is taking place here, and it happens daily in this silence, is intimately transacted between this home and eternal space; and consciousness has no residence in nor pertinence to it save only that, privileged by stealth to behold, we fear this legend: withdraw; bow down; nor dare the pride to seek to decipher it.

The wasp who cruises the roof, on the other hand, 'is not unwelcome here: he is a builder; a tenant. He does not notice; he is no reader of signs' (187-188). More positively, watching is a metaphor for attention, alert and joyfully participating in the actual, 'the whole realm of what our bodies lay in and our minds in silence wandered, walked in, swam in, watched upon', the body 'inseparable from the mind, identical with it': 'at such time we have knowledge that we are witnessing, taking part in, being, a phenomenon analogous to that shrewd complex of the equations of infinite chance which became, on this early earth, out of lifelessness, life'. To watch, to be conscious and know it, is literally wonderful, but wonder is perhaps, like beauty, merely a linguistic 'sense', part of a provincial and transient vocabulary:

the difference between a conjunction of time, place and unconscious consciousness and a conjunction of time, place and conscious consciousness is,
so far as we are concerned, the difference between joy and truth and the
lack of joy and truth. Unless wonder is nothing in itself, but only a moon
which glows only in the mercy of a sense of wonder, and unless the sense of
wonder is peculiar to consciousness and is moreover an emotion which, as
it matures, consciousness will learn the juvenility of, and discard, or only
gratefully refresh itself under the power of as under the power of sleep and
the healing vitality of dreams, and all this seems a little more likely than not,
the materials which people any intersection of time and place are at all times
marvelous, regardless of consciousness. (225-227)

The question, as always, is whether we may project past the data
of experience.

Like Antonioni's camera within a camera, Agee's bodiless eye
is inexpressible except by invalid analogy; similarly, what it regards can be described only in tentative, subjective terms, for there
is no striking through the mask of appearances to an unambiguous
hold on reality: as for the narrator of 'They that sow', it is impossible to get at the bottom of anything. In *The Morning Watch*,
Richard prays in his Dedalus-like fervor to 'know' Christ's suffering, pictures himself crucified with a reporter's flash bulb pop-
ping in his face, and tries 'to imagine how it would feel to be
scourged... and to wear a crown of thorns' (MW, 75, 152). His
attempts to communicate with Christ, to realize his suffering, are
guided by the liturgical forms which control and limit experience:
it is sinful 'to be so unaware of where you were that... a thought
could occur spontaneously' (50). Time is 'a power of measure
upon the darkness' (87), and Richard tries to reach Christ in a
way analogous to that in which he alters his visual focus to eliminate the hands and numbers of a clock, the face appearing as 'the
great Host in a monstrance' (87). But like Wittgenstein and Godard,
Richard finds that he cannot take another's place, experiences
Christ as an absence, for there is 'Nothing at all' on the altar
during this 'dead time between' (46, 116), and contemplates the
words, 'God: Death; so that the two were one' (48). His own
hooky-playing hiatus, his solitary death, rebirth and defeat of the
serpent, are meaningful only to Richard, though their shape is
liturgically derived. His acceptance of the failure of communication reduces the mythic power of those events over him: 'Bet
it doesn't hurt any worse than that', he says of the locust's struggle with its shell, 'to be crucified' (131). Similarly, in *A Death in*

the Family, a realistic epistemology is portrayed as something to be outgrown. Mary Follet spends all her time trying to make her thoughts appropriate — to her father-in-law's illness, to her husband's lack of religious faith, and chiefly to the possibility of the latter's death, during an anxiously ambiguous time between. She prays that God will make her right (DF, 57), and is shocked when Rufus' elders tease him with untruths (232). Her aunt suspects 'something mistaken, unbearably piteous, infinitely malign' about her faith (129); and her father comments on the naivety of her care to learn every detail of Jay's death, and her summing it up in a terse epitaph: 'So you feel you've got some control over the death, you *own* it, you choose a name for it. The same with wanting to know all you can about how it happened. And trying to imagine it as Mary was'. Such knowledge is finally a 'subterfuge' (166).

Commenters have chiefly found in Agee's film criticism a 'realist' aesthetic,[12] although Edward Murray alone troubles over the meaning of the term, deciding that Agee uses it too variously to make precise definition possible.[13] While 'realism' in the philosophic sense, one which informs Agee's aesthetic requirements, is built into the empiricism he derives from Richards, it is a realism which presumes an unknowable world of substantial things, unamenable to comprehensive formulation, knowable only in terms of the language with which it is explored. While he opposes images to spoken or written words, especially in his recurrent defense of silent comedy, he refers to its 'language', 'vocabulary' and 'idiom' (AF, I, 3), to Harold Lloyd's 'thesaurus of smiles' (10), to Chaplin's 'lexicon' of emotions (13), and to 'the basic vocabulary of conventional movies', 'the movie alphabet' and 'the documentary manner' (263, 266); a 'situation' is a 'logic' which can be incredibly extended by a comic genius — indeed, all humor is ruthlessly logical (11, 18); a captured German film 'moves... in resonant sentences, which construct irreducible paragraphs', becoming at times 'small fine poems' (34); certain shots are 'basic to decent film grammar' (79). 'Realism' is an aspect of this grammar, ' "reality" in its conventional camera sense' (191), the rules of which may be violated by Mack Sennett, and less happily by Hollywood's use of professional actors to portray ' "real" people' (31, 129), and by attempts to represent the speech of peasant farmers: 'I think that finding a diction proper to so-called simple folk is one of the most embarrassing, not to say hopeless, literary problems we have set ourselves' (109). Agee manipulates these rules himself when he calls, in 'Noah Noah', for ' "documentary" noonday sunlight', in 'The blue hotel', for a shot 'heightened above realism' by the use of every third frame and simulation on the soundtrack (AF, II, 146, 464), and, in 'Man's fate', for film that is 'grainy, hard black and white, flat focus, the stock and tone of film in war newsreels. . . . It should not seem to be fiction' (CSP, 244). And he admires *Open City* and *The Raider*, 'not *because* they use non-actors, or are semi-documentary, or are "realistic" ', but for their 'aesthetic and moral respect for reality — which "realism" can as readily smother as liberate'; 'most documentaries', in fact, 'are as dismally hostile to reality as most fiction films' (AF, I, 237): *The Raider* succeeds by virtue of an understanding 'of what, artistically, is more "real" than the actual and what is less real' (233).

The camera is uniquely able to 'record unaltered reality' (296), and Agee is interested in an alert use of details, 'little things which brilliantly lock men and their efforts and feelings into the exact real place and time of day' (240), in films which have 'approached and honored rather than flouted and improved on reality' (127). In Helen Levitt's still photography, 'the actual world constantly brings to the surface its own signals and mysteries'; the strenuous perception of actuality involves resisting the impingement of habitual grammars, for 'The mind and the spirit are constantly formed by, and as constantly form, the senses'.[14] If, as Richards says, our hold on reality consists in patterns of expectation, Agee disparages film sets which 'seem over-prepared, with nothing left to chance' (174), 'the utterly controlled and utterly worthless effect' (137), the stultifications of *'rigor artis'* (66) and the timid use, in 'straight record films', of the idiom of 'American commercial romanticism, as taught, for example, by the *Life* school' (65). He praises a concern with 'what happens inside real and particular people among real and particular objects' (118), and the feeling, in da Sica's *Shoeshine*, 'that almost anything could happen, and that the reasons why any given thing happens are exceedingly complex and constantly shifting their weight' (208). The intricately detailed sets of *A Tree Grows in Brooklyn* prove 'that the best you can do in that way is as dead as an inch-by-inch description or a perfectly naturalistic painting, compared with accepting instead the still scarcely imagined difficulties and the enormous advantage of submerging your actors in the real thing, full of its irreducible present tense and its unpredictable proliferations of energy and beauty'; the makers miss the chance to move a subjective camera through the streets of New York, 'the free-gliding, picaresque, and perfect eye for a Saturday school-child's cruising of the city' (142) − precisely what Agee gives us in the script for *The Quiet One*.

The subjective camera is repeatedly recommended (174, 184), and Hitchcock is a frequently cited standard: Walsh's *Background to Danger* illustrates 'the unconquerable differences between a good job by Hitchcock and a good job of the Hitchcock type' (49); he is adept at 'establishers of casual reality, and oblique cutting edges of ironic or sensous detail' (150), at 'communicating the exact place, weather and time of day' (214), and is 'abreast of all but the few best writers of his time' (73); among his excellences is the fact that he is 'nearly the only living man I can think of who knows just when and how' to use the subjective camera (214). It has recently been pointed out that the kidnapping sequence in Hitchcock's *Family Plot*, a rapid series of images of motion, takes place in a much shorter time on the screen than it possibly could in reality, and is true to our dislocated sense of time, to our unquestioning acceptance of things that happen in a flash[15]; Agee similarly commends the 'timing' of several shots in Vincente Minelli's *The Clock* as 'boldly and successfully unrealistic' (AF, I, 166-167), remarks of *The Lost Weekend* that a few deft signals of a subjectively experienced hangover state 'might have told the audience as much in an instant as an hour of pure objectivity could' (184), and condemns *An Ideal Husband* as 'too slow and realistic' (294). He advocates, that is, a subjectivistic rather than a realistic handling of materials. LUNPFM incorporates the 'forms... of motion pictures' (LUNPFM, 244), particularly those recommendations Agee makes for record films − 'Stop-shots, slow-motion repetitions, and blow-ups... unrehearsed interviews... intensive use' of the 'unwelcome' camera (AF, I, 99-100) − which we recognize as the methods of *cinema vérité*. The book aims at an empirical subjectivism of this sort, though Agee has yet, he says, 'to attempt proper treatment':

It seemes likely at this stage that the truest way to treat a piece of the past is as such: as if it were no longer the present. In other words, the 'truest' thing about the experience is now neither that it was from hour to hour thus and so; nor is it my fairly accurate 'memory' of how it was from hour to hour in chronological progression; but is rather as it turns up in recall, in no such order, casting its lights and associations forward and backward upon the then past and the then future, across that expanse of experience. (LUNPFM, 243-244)

This subjective mode of presentation is musical rather than narrative, he says, and is not ' "naturalism", "realism" ', though this is a 'slippery watershed': the 'straight "naturalist" ' shows little understanding of 'music and poetry', and his best work is 'never much more than documentary'; naturalistic description 'sags with... length and weight', is remote 'from what you have seen, from the fact itself'; the 'language of "reality" ' is 'the heaviest of all languages', incapable of imparting 'the deftness, keenness, immediacy, speed and subtlety of the "reality" it tries to reproduce' (235-237). Whereas American naturalistic writing shares with philosophical Pragmatism its dependence upon Darwin's hypothesis, is concerned, that is, with the destruction of illusion, usually through an evolution or development in character, and arrival at an alignment of thought appropriate to the movement of natural forces in the causal continuum, Agee despairs of any such ultimate propriety of form and attitude. And he rejects the realism of dialect and vernacular idiom, the 'professional-Americanism' of Twain and the ' "talk-American" ' writing of Steinbeck.[16] He incorporates tenant dialect rarely, and unquoted, into his description: 'Clair Bell sprints in affrighted: that her father has left for work without kissing her good-bye. They take her on their laps assuring her that he would never do no such a thang' (89). In 1935, Agee proposed a style of writing which would mix the idioms and jargons conventionally thought of as special to particular groups, and thus liberate writer and reader from the ' "anthropological" correctness' and 'scientific-journalistic-scrupulousness' of contemporary naturalism (LFF, 77).

Like Tommo on the Typees, Ishmael on whales and Burroughs on drug addiction, Agee is exhaustive on the food, shelter and clothing of the tenants (classifications derived from Louise Gudger's third-grade geography text, and to that degree their own terms), and the work by which they have them; but like Tommo, Ishmael and Burroughs, he repeatedly sets up, reflects upon and undercuts a limited point of view. Gudger is a 'real' human being rather than a fictional character, living in a world 'irrelevant to imagination' and works of art:

But obviously, in the effort to tell of him (by example) as truthfully as I can, I am limited. I know him only so far as I know him, and only in those terms in which I know him; and all of that depends as fully on who I am as on who he is.
   I am confident of being able to get at a certain form of the truth about him, *only if* I am as faithful as possible to Gudger as I know him, to Gudger as, in his actual flesh and life (but there again always in my mind's and memory's eye) he is. But of course it will be only a relative truth.
   Name me one truth within human range that is not relative and I will feel a shade more apologetic of that. (LUNPFM, 233, 239)

Empirical analysis in no way transcends the subjective viewpoint to become 'realism', though the aspiration to an unambiguous hold on reality is indefatigable: 'Human beings may be more and more aware of being awake, but they are still incapable of not dreaming'; that is, the attempt to 'embody' or become identical with the truth is 'one of the strongest laws of language', despite the fact that 'Words cannot embody; they can only describe' (237-239). Agee's task is to examine the forms of his linguistic exertion.

AGEE'S SEMIOTIC: ANALYSIS AND THE SELF-REFLEXIVE TEXT

He often refers, in fact, to his role as analyst and 'skeptic' (one of his frequent words). In his Guggenheim application he speaks of LUNPFM as a 'record' which is 'not journalistic; nor on the other hand is any of it to be invented. It can perhaps most nearly be described as "scientific", but not in a sense acceptable to scientists, only in the sense that it is ultimately skeptical and analytic' (CSP, 149-150). He also plans to compile a dictionary of key words to be 'examined skeptically', along the lines of one that I.A. Richards was compiling, with which Agee's would not 'be at all in conflict'; speaks of a 'Non-supernatural, non-exaggerative' story (twenty years before Robbe-Grillet) about 'the horror that can come of objects and of their relationships, and of tones of voice', concentrating 'on what the senses receive and the memory and context does with it'; of 'Analyses of the "unreality" of

"realistic" color photography', of contemporary communist
literature, of the corruption and miscommunication of ideas
('In one strong sense ideas rule all conduct and experience'), of
myths of sexual love ('tentative, questioning and destructive of
crystallized ideas and attitudes'), and of images that have never
been experienced in "reality": 'In these terms, Buenos Aires itself is neither more nor less actual than my, or your, careful
imagination of it told as pure imaginative fact' (CSP, 154-157,
164, 161). 'Actuality' has no necessary relation to a 'reality'
external to the subject: in '1928 story', Irvine contemplates 'a
distinct image of a place he had never known. When he tried to
take the image apart he realized that nothing much like it was. . .
likely to exist', though he later decides that 'of course it did exist,
and so did ten thousand other things. . . in just such music'.[17]
Agee also speaks of the word-by-word analysis of personal letters,
which are 'in every word and phrase immediate to and revealing of,
in precision and complex detail, the sender and receiver and the
whole world and context each is of'; the analysis should 'help to
shift and destroy various habits and certitudes of the "creative"
and of the "reading", and so of the daily "functioning" mind'
(CSP, 151, 153).

He is an early enthusiast for home-mode photography, and suggests
that 'Some of the best photographs we are ever likely to see are
innocent domestic snapshots, city postcards, and news and scientific photographs'.[18] As a film critic, he frequently operates in the
capacity of 'diagnostician' (AF, I, 53): 'every piece of entertainment, like every political speech or swatch of advertising copy,
has nightmarish accuracy as a triple-distilled image of a collective
dream, habit, or desire', and *Stage Door Canteen* 'is a gold mine
for those who are willing to go to it in the wrong spirit' (41-42);
Frenchman's Creek is 'masturbation fantasy. . . infallible as any
real-life dream and as viciously fascinating as reading such a dream
over the terrible dreamer's shoulder' (120); *Hail the Conquering
Hero* is an 'elaborately counterpointed image' of the American
'neurosis' (117); *The Birth of a Nation* is 'a perfect realization of a
collective dream of what the Civil Was was like' (313). The image
has meaning, not in itself, but in context or use, so that to regard
the criticism of films which incorporate superb records of war
as 'vulgar, small and irrelevant. . . . is like being moved by words
like love, death, blood, sweat, tears, regardless of how well or ill

they are used' (51). And just as Bogart's slaughter of helpless German airmen in *Passage to Marseilles* is dangerous to that uncritical 'majority who will accordingly accept advice on what to do with Germany' (80), advertising is 'a kind of bourgeois folk-art' to which, nevertheless, all classes are 'vulnerable'.[19] Agee planned a magazine which would treat all aspects of popular culture in an effort 'to undeceive readers of their own — and the editors' — conditioned reflexes'.[20] In LUNPFM, he emphasizes that in an important sense nothing is untrue, for 'A falsehood is entirely true to those derangements which produced it and which made it impossible that it should emerge in truth; and an examination of it may reveal more of the "true" "truth" than any more direct attempt upon the "true" "truth" itself'; so that while journalism is merely 'a broad and successful form of lying', and no part of Agee's method, 'a page of newspaper can have all the wealth of a sheet of fossils, or a painting' (LUNPFM, 230, 234). The task of education, he writes Father Flye, is to be 'medical and surgical of mental habits, inherited prejudices, lacks of questioning'; and he proposes 'a whole method and science of mere skepticism', epitomized by his own aspiration to 'the coolness and truth of the camera's... eye' (LFF, 111-112, 134).

LUNPFM, he says, 'is perhaps chiefly a skeptical study of the nature of reality and of the false nature of recreation and communication', (CSP, 151). Since Agee can report about the tenants 'only what I saw, only so accurately as in my terms I know how' (LUNPFM, 12), the book addresses the limitations of the subjective point of view and the written word. Agee portrays himself as a recording device, 'searching out and registering in myself all the lines, planes, stresses of relationship' in a country church, or running a fingertip along the grain of a wood floor (39). He is restricted to and preoccupied by 'surfaces' — another recurrent word: 'What is the use? . . . Let me just try a few surfaces instead' (147) — of his body, so that for a while he judges a bed-bug attack to be 'my own nerve-ends' (425); of other people, Mrs. Gudger 'smiling sleepily and sadly in a way I cannot deduce' (419); and of things, such as the odor and feel of the moisture covering the outer surfaces of a lamp: 'I do not understand nor try to deduce this, but I like it' (50). His memory preserves images removed from their context — 'All that I see now is this picture. . .' (398) — and perceived 'distinctly, yet coldly as through reversed field-glasses', no longer 'at least immediate in my senses', so that he must ' "describe" what I would like to "describe", as a second remove, and that poorly' (403): as in the description of the movie screen which opens *A Death in the Family*, we see, not ' through ' the image, but the image itself – in terms, as Godard says, not of what it signifies, but of what signifies it.

The text, given Agee's lack of 'warmth or traction or faith in words' (LUNPFM, 403), is to be regarded likewise skeptically, for 'if, antiartistically, you desire not only to present but to talk about what you present and how you try to present it', you must continually make your failure to represent reality clear (238). Agee does, and indicates in his account of the four planes from which he handles the experience – recall and contemplation *in medias res* ('On the porch'), ' "As it happened" ', 'recall and memory from the present' and 'As I try to write it: problems of recording' (243) – that the self-reflexive is a major aspect of the work. [21] He describes himself 'working out my notes' (63) and quotes them verbatim (422), shifts time and tense 'to a thing which is to happen, or which happened, the next morning (you musn't be puzzled by this, I'm writing in a continuum)', and back again (62, 69), uses phrases in the text to mark his place and re-vise his effort (372), and shifts planes suddenly: '(It occurs to me now as I write...)' (368). While he permits himself 'imagination' on the third plane, he scrupulously footnotes its use: 'Invention here: I did not make inventory, there was more than I could rem-ember'; 'These are in part by memory, in part composited out of other memory, in part improvised' (133, 201). He reiterates that LUNPFM is not 'Art', does not require 'the killing insult of "suspension of disbelief" ' (240), and discusses at length his 'antagonism towards art', based on his belief that its 'clarifying' power is so frequently accompanied by its 'muddying' power 'that we may suspect a law in ambush' (245, 232).

The skeptically, reflexively treated concerns of self and text merge in the act of writing. While, in Richards' terms, mental reference is not necessarily linguistic, thinking is: one might watch the changes of pine boards in sunlight for 'speechless days on end merely for the variety and distinction of their beauty, without thought or any relative room for thinking' (131); but to think is to symbolize a reference by placing it in a context, a text. To write is to sort, and while words could 'be made to do

or tell anything within human conceit', they cannot 'communicate simultaneity with any immediacy' (236-237): Agee lists the
ingredients of an odor 'more subtle than it can seem in analysis'
(154). The wealth of detail which 'so intensely surrounds and takes
meaning from' any one subjective 'center... should be tested,
calculated, analyzed, conjectured upon, as if all in one sentence
and spread suspension and flight or fugue of music', a perfect
vehicle of simultaneity which Agee finds himself incapable of
sustaining, for 'one can write only one word at a time' (111).
Excerpts from Louise Gudger's school books, quotations of
Shakespeare and Marx, advertising slogans, a tenant sign reading
'PLEAS! be Quite! ' (197) and inscriptions in the Gudger bible
are presented as vehicles, manipulative and symptomatic, of verbal
meaning. A scissored piece of newsprint lining a drawer is quoted
in full, including its fragments of words, sentences and photographs, and is held against the light so that 'the contents of both
sides of the paper are visible at once' (169): as in Burroughs'
cutup method, the attention is to the status of words and images
as sensory signs, the fragments of arbitrary symbols or conventions
of meaning. 'Sense' becomes self-interrogative. The formulation,

((?)   )   :)
How were we caught? (81),

diagrams the presence of a puzzled and possibly inquiring attention, bounded by marks of signification which it can neither
transcend nor identify with, the colon indicating impending
change in the form of elaboration, qualification or contradiction.
Understanding is limited by its form, and, in the absence of
ultimate context, involves obviation rather than insight. As he sits
writing by lamplight, Agee is a 'center' in the midst of a frightening darkness, at the edge, as it were, of his thinking:

so that I muse what not quite creatures and what not quite forms are suspended like bats above and behind my bent head; and how far down in their
clustered weight they are stealing while my eyes are on this writing; and how
skillfully swiftly they suck themselves back upward into the dark when I
turn my head: and above all, why they should be so coy, with one slather of
cold membranes drooping, could slap out light and have me: and who own
me since all time's beginning. Yet this mere fact of thinking holds them at
distance, as crucifixes demons, so lightly and well that I am almost persuaded
of being merely fanciful; in which exercise I would be theirs most profound-

ly beyond rescue, not knowing, and not fearing, I am theirs.

As he expands his meditation to the infinite and impersonal darkness far beyond the ceiling, in which 'no one so much as laughs at us', he questions, 'do we really exist at all? ' (52-53). The text itself, the ongoing arrangement of words which encodes his questioning, is the only evidence.

THE DISEASE OF SYMMETRY: MOTIVE

Like Ishmael, Agee uses the metaphor of weaving to describe the matrix or nexus of events: the tenant child is 'brought forth on a chain of weaving, a texture of sorrowful and demented flesh' (102); rather than resort to narrative fictions, Agee wishes to represent the 'texture' or 'chain of truths [which] did actually weave itself and run through' (240). The history of a family is a series of drawings together — under shelter, on a bed — and being held by the 'magnetic center' of the economic unit (55-56); that of an individual unfolds as the crucifixions of personal existence, of sexual love, of egg and sperm (100, 102-103); the section 'Recessional and vortex' describes spatial arrangement, each family a center 'drawn-round with animals', each animal a different kind of 'center and leverage', and lists the rings of animal, vegetable and mineral existence and the surrounding geography, in the middle of which 'the floor, the roof, the opposed walls, the furniture... all watch upon one hollow center' (212-220): all these 'flexions' have the form of musical theme and variation, and 'are the classical patterns, and this is the weaving, of human living' (56). The matrix involves necessity, 'the plainest cruelties and needs of human existence in this uncured time' (134), but only in the limited sense that there is nothing particularly necessary about human existence itself, 'that life and consciousness are only the special crutches of the living and the conscious' (226). It involves chance: like 'those subtlest of all chances' whereby the oak shapes itself out of the acorn, river systems, 'among whose spider lacings by chance we live', branch over the planet and human dwellings alter the chance pattern of the landscape 'by chance' (252, 147). And it involves will: while 'it is our own consciousness alone, in the end, that we have to thank' for the joy of actuality, it is 'almost purely a matter of chance', a 'lucky situation' which Agee and Evans could not 'for an instant have escaped ... even if we had wished to' (225-228); Agee's scuttling the car ('I didn't know then, and don't know now... whether or not it was by my will'), donning sneakers ('there was no sense in this and I don't understand why') and 'passive waiting' before the Gudger house in hope 'that "something shall happen", as it "happened" that the car lost to the mud' (409-411), illustrate his skepticism as to the precise agency of will. The 'causes' of cruelty to Negroes and to animals can only be expressed as 'traits, needs, diseases, and above all mere natural habits differing from our own' (216-217); the 'sources' of economic disadvantage are 'psychological, semantic, traditional, perhaps glandular'; and the 'wrong assignment of causes', by indicting such oversimplifications as 'tenantry', is dangerously glib (207-208).

The nexus of events has for Agee the subtlety and 'symmetry of a disease: the literal symmetry of the literal disease of which they were literally so essential a part'; the sore and scab of this disease comprise 'all substance' and 'fill out... the most intangible reaches of thought, deduction and imagination' (229). This symmetry is visible in tenant-farm dwellings, which exhibit a 'classicism created of economic need, of local availability, and of local-primitive tradition' (203); in clothing which, with the exception of overalls, 'a relatively new and local garment', is probably indistinguishable from peasant clothing in ancient Greece (265, 277); and 'in everything within and probably in anything outside human conception' (203). Symmetry is this disease, a spare and stingy classicism, complicated and subtlized in its pliancy before the irregularities 'of chance (all of which proceeded inevitably out of chances which were inevitable)': chance and necessity complement and undercut each other, are inextricably interwoven. Symmetry, as Richards points out, is perceptibility, and is ultimately linguistic, as is the 'language' in which 'the name and destiny of water' is written on the earth's surface. Conscious consciousness is being awake to what we are present before, and thus to the form by which it is present, 'hearing... a complex music in every effect and in causes of every effect and in the effects of which this effect will be part cause', which ' "gets" us perhaps nowhere' simply because we are, in fact, 'already there'. The irregular syncopations of chance which issue in the various and impermanent phases of symmetry are imagined as 'complex equations' (230-231, 252): marriage and conception occur 'in obedience to... pressures' of economy (103), as a wall in the Ricketts house is decorated 'in obedience of [particular] equations' (199) and nailheads are arranged in wood 'according to geometric need' (143). LUNPFM is written in the conviction that nothing is 'more moving, significant or true' than that 'every force and hidden chance in the universe has so combined that a certain thing was the way it was' (241), and derives its truth from its status as evidence rather than the success of Agee's attempts 'to take what hold I can of any reality', which attempts 'cannot be otherwise than true to their conditions' (10).

Agee's assertion that 'the unimagined world is in its own terms an artist'[22] is consistent with Richards' notion of the inextricability of self and environment, and renders irrelevant the idea of intention: to the question whether things are ' "beautiful" which are not intended as such, but which are created in convergences of chance, need, innocence or ignorance', Agee answers,

first, that intended beauty is far more a matter of chance and need than the power of intention, and that 'chance' beauty of 'irrelevances' is deeply formed by instincts and needs popularly held to be the property of 'art' alone: second, that matters of 'chance' and 'nonintention' can be and are 'beautiful' and are a whole universe to themselves. Or: the Beethoven piano concerto #4 IS importantly, among other things, a 'blind' work of 'nature', of the world and of the human race; and the partition wall of the Gudger's front bedroom IS importantly, among other things, a great tragic poem. (203-204)

INTENTION AND FAILURE

Intention is a recurrent issue in Agee's work: the narrator of 'They that sow', who muses, 'to some extent we guide our lives, to some extent are guided by them' (CSP, 97), is concerned with the degree of his agency in a disastrous event. Richard struggles both to bring his thoughts into line with a hopelessly corrupt and elusive intention, and against the vanity of his devotion (' "not that you *mean* it of course" '); and he defends the rashness of a companion with: ' "he just wasn't thinking".... "He didn't mean anything" ' (MW, 66, 44). *A Death in the Family* is filled with instances of misinterpreted intention and questions of meaning, both among the adults ('She was never to realize his intention. . .'

[DF, 53]), and between adults and children: ' "You mean so well, but the child may just turn out to hate it" '.[23] While, as Michael Sragow points out, Agee never indulges in 'trade secrets or "creative intentions" ' in his film criticism,[24] he does frequently cite what he gathers to be the 'sober' or 'decent' or 'general' intention of a film, usually to mitigate utter rejection: of the makers of *Sunday Dinner for a Soldier*, 'The confused but genuine sweetness of their intention is as visible through all the mawkish formulas, and as disturbing, as a drowned corpse, never quite surfacing' (AF, I, 140). But intention has no such necessary relation to final product as those who defy the dictum of Beardsley and Wimsatt must assume; Agee's status as an amateur critic serves him well, he says, since he needs 'feel no apology for what my eyes tell me as I watch any given screen, where the proof is caught irrelevant to excuse, and available in proportion to the eye which sees it, and the mind which uses it' (AF,I, 23). In response to a newspaper account of his ' "intentionally clumsy, almost wild manner" ', Agee's Gauguin sneers, 'That's what I call an *intelligent* critic; he knows art is *intentional*' (AF, II, 99).

The failed intentions recorded in LUNPFM — 'tenderly intended' but destructive parental love (105), a piece of middle-class furniture which 'has picked up tenant-kitchen redolences for which it was never intended' (179), houses which look even ' "poorer"... than... by original design' (270), the failed 'intention' of teachers and school texts (294, 299), plans of action gone awry (374) — complement the repeated failed intentions to describe: 'But there must be an end to this... a new and more succinct beginning' (99); 'But somehow I have lost hold of the reality of all this' (414). With its various plans and descriptions of overall design, LUNPFM is a compilation of Agee's unrealized intentions, listed as casually as if by a conceptual artist: 'This volume is designed in two intentions: as the beginning of a larger piece of work, and to stand of itself'; 'Ultimately, it is intended that this record and analysis be exhaustive', but 'Of this ultimate intention the present volume is merely portent and fragment, experiment, dissonant prologue' (xv); 'The text was written with reading aloud in mind. That cannot be recommended'; 'It was intended also that the text be read continually, as music is listened to or film is watched' (xv); 'If I could do it, I'd do no writing at all here. It would be photographs... fragments of cloth, bits of cotton, lumps of earth, records of speech, pieces of wood and iron, phials of odors, plates of food and of excrement' (13);

> Let me say... how I wish this account might be constructed.
> I might suggest, its structure should be globular: or should be eighteen or twenty intersected spheres, the interlockings of bubbles on the face of a stream; one of these globes is each of you. (101)

Like *Naked Lunch*, LUNPFM is a blueprint, a how-to book. Finally, to allow description to sag into naturalism, which is 'at the opposite pole from your intentions, from what you have seen, from the fact itself', is to fail; but Agee can only say of the remedies he discusses that 'Failure... is almost as strongly an obligation as an inevitability, in such work: and therein sits the deadliest trap of the exhausted conscience' (236, 238). While he exalts and credits his 'best intention' he, like Ishmael, must acknowledge that 'Performance, in which the whole fate and terror rests, is another matter' (16).

In his concern for the 'cleansing and rectification of language' (237), Agee gives constant attention to the clarification of terms: 'The tenants' idiom has been used ad nauseam by the more unspeakable of the northern journalists but it happens to be accurate: that picking goes on each day from can to can't'(340). While he does not, like the naturalist, abjure metaphor, he comments on and undercuts it, reducing it, for example to the terms of physiology in his discussion of cotton farming:

> I can conceive of little else which could be so inevitably destructive of the appetite for living, of the spirit, of the being, or by whatever name the centers of individuals are to be called: and this very literally: for just as there are deep chemical or electrical changes in all the body under anger, or love, or fear, so there must certainly be at the center of these meanings and their directed emotions; perhaps most essentially, an incalculably somber and heavy weighted and dark knotted iron of sub-nausea at the peak of the diaphragm, darkening and weakening the whole body and being, the literal feeling by which the words a broken heart are no longer poetic, but are merely the most accurate possible description. (327)

This inability to name or define the centers of individuals is a central issue: 'What is it, profound behind the outward windows of each one of you, beneath touch even of your own suspecting, drawing tightly back at bay against the backward wall and blackness of its prison cave, so that the eyes alone shine of their own

angry glory, but the eyes of a trapped wild animal, or of a furious
angel nailed to the ground by his wings, or however else one may
faintly designate the human "soul" ' (99). Unable to establish its
origin and identity, subjectivity, like Ahab and Ishmael, is orphaned: in *A Death in the Family*, Rufus naively exults in his status as
an orphan, though the darkness has taunted him as he lies awake
(like the writer of LUNPFM, fighting off horrid imaginings),
'You hear the man you call your father: how can you ever fear? '
(DF, 294, 84); and Agee finishes 'Dream sequence' by acknowledging that his life 'had been shaped by his father and by his
father's absence'.[25] The woven chain of flesh does not imply an
unambiguous identity; in 'The house', Agee details a shot of
swastikaed uniformed midgets, their feet 'grinding faces of Negroes, Jews', and carrying the effigy of a crucified woman under
the legend, 'MOTHER', her head 'a schoolboy globe of the earth'
(CSP, 173): as in Burroughs' story, 'The coming of the purple
better one', the evolution myth is portrayed as a form of Nazism.

Agee's skepticism about myths of origin is clearest in his rejection of anthropomorphic description:

We bask in our lavish little sun as children in the protective sphere of their
parents: and perhaps can never outgrow, or can never dare afford to outgrow,
our delusions of his strength and wisdom and of our intelligence, compe-
tence and safety; and we carry over from him, like a green glow in the eye-
balls, these daytime delusions, so inescapably that we can not only never
detach ourselves from the earth, even in the perception of our minds, but
cannot even face the fact of nature without either stone blindness or sentimentality . . . .
   We have known, or have been told that we know, for some centuries
now that the sun does not 'set' or 'rise': the earth twists its surface into and
out of the light of the sun.
   In its twisting the earth also cradles back and forth, somewhat like a
bobbin, and leans through a very slightly eccentric course, and it is this re-
tirement out of and a return into a certain proximity to the sun which causes
the change of seasons. . . . Just how much poetry, or art, or plain human
consciousness, has taken this into account. You have only to look at all
the autumn art about death and at all the spring art about life to get an
idea . . . .
   No doubt we are sensible in giving names to places: Canada; the Argentine.
But we would also be sensible to remember that the land we have given these
names to, and all but the relatively very small human population, wear these
names lightly. (LUNPFM, 247-249)

He nevertheless frequently describes anthopomorphically, projects
what he calls 'local fact' (248) onto unknowable objects and land-

scapes, so that a silent glade 'seems to be conscious and to await the repetition of a signal' (130), and a hill under rain is trenched and seamed 'as if' it were an exposed human brain (139). However, the anthropomorphism is pointedly self-interrogative in such comparisons as of the earth to a sleeping human head, 'yielded over to the profound influences and memories. . . of its early childhood, before man became a part of its experience' (247). It is used, as the phrase 'as if' is often used, to isolate and clarify an image by vivid comparison, so that a roof beyond the 'bones of rafters' is 'a stomach sucked against the spine in fear' (52). Conditional similes introduced by 'as if' are tentative but sharply drawn comparisons, which tersely wrench an impression away from any necessary connection with its source into a jarring, unrelated but illustrative context – 'Miss-Molly, chopping wood as if in each blow of the axe she held captured in focus the vengeance of all time' (324), a deranged old man restrained 'as if he were a dog masturbating on a caller' (35): the precision of such renderings has to do, not with the object, but with its appearance, so that the symmetry of a wooden church is as strong 'as if it were an earnest description, better than the intended object' (38).

Descriptions are the forms and limits of understanding: 'The peace of God surpasses all understanding; Mrs. Ricketts and her youngest child do, too' (289). Although he prescribes exercises and gives extended descriptions of labor in the second person (339), like Godard, who has Jane Fonda and Yves Montand do actual work in a sausage factory in *Tout Va Bien*, the implication of Agee's skepticism is that no matter how much is known of a tenant woman's life, 'you cannot for one moment exchange places with her' (321). That skepticism assumes, at times, Berkeleyan proportions, as in recurrent allusions to the sounds of night, which 'have perhaps at no time ceased, but that will never surely be known. . . one hears them once again with a quiet sort of surprise, that only slowly becomes the realization, or near certainty, that they have been there all the while' (84). In his meditation on chance and necessity, Agee entertains 'the more than reasonable suspicion that there is at all times further music. . . beyond the simple equipment of our senses and their powers of reflection and deduction to apprehend' (231). And while he contemplates an event's 'ramified kinship and probable hidden identification with everything else', he can himself offer only 'a series of careful but tentative, rudely experimental, and fragmentary renderings of some of the salient aspects of a real experience' (245-246), cannot do 'better than blankly suggest, or lay down, a few possible laws' (105). Like the tenant child, 'this center, soul, nerve', Agee is the center of a subjective 'bubble and sutureless globe' (104), unable to penetrate the screen of his own experience.

RICHARDS AND THE SYMBOL

It is Richards' form of skepticism, the distinction between the 'what' and 'how' of events, that is chiefly exhibited in Agee's work: the distinction between use and intention in meaning; the concern to develop intellectual weapons against advertisement and propaganda (a drawback, Agee feels, in *Birth of a Nation* and *Open City*); the by-product account of a consciousness which is not a unique relation; the rejection of the evolutionary model of cognition and of the notion that a naturalistic (or any other) account can be a complete one; and the use, nevertheless, of causal language and a physiological hypothesis. Agee's plan for a multiple-definition dictionary complementary to Richards' (CSP, 154-155), his promotion of Basic English in *The Nation* (AF, I, 38) and his comparison of text to machine ('Screen comedies used... to be machines as delicately, annihilatingly designed for their purpose as any machines that have ever been constructed out of words or tones' [AF, I, 202]), are salient pointers to a more comprehensive influence. Agee too describes the experience of beauty and complex emotion in terms of an individual's 'fully "realizing" his potentialities' (LUNPFM, 307); Richards' notion of the fusion of clearly defined and more subtle reports of the senses 'with the whole mass of internal sensations to form the *coenesthesia*, the whole bodily consciousness' (PLC, 95), reappears in such descriptions as of 'a quality in the night itself not truly apparent to any one of the senses, yet, by some indirection, to every sense in one' (LUNPFM, 51), and in Agee's insistence upon realization, 'not merely with the counting mind, nor with the imagination of the eye, which is no realization at all, but with the whole of the body and being' (183). Like Richards, Agee distinguishes between 'meaning' and 'emotion' (236-237) in language use, between 'knowledge' and 'attitude', or objectless belief (293), and attends to 'variations of tone, pace, shape, and dynamics' as integral to and not to be abstracted from the 'meaning' of the text (xv): so that he describes the singing of three men in terms, not of the lyrics, but of the rhythmic and melodic interplay of voice (29-30), eavesdrops on talk that 'is not really talking, but another and profounder kind of communication, a rhythm to be completed by answer and made whole by silence, a lyric song' (71), and engages in conversation 'which means little in itself, but much in its inflections' (417).

While Agee does not reject the existence of evil,[26] he portrays the projection of an absolute separation of Good and Evil as a form of hypocrisy, as represented by the bishop in 'Noa Noa' (AF, II, 145), or of mania, as by the preacher in *The Night of the Hunter*, with 'LOVE' and 'HATE' tattooed on each fist: 'Shall I tell you the little story of Right-Hand-Left-Hand — the tale of Good and Evil? ' (280). Accordingly, a symbol does not embody a transcendent moral order but is an arbitrary substitution, meaning with a small 'm': a mule is badly treated 'because he is the immediate symbol of this work, and because by transference he is the farmer himself, and. . . is the one creature in front of this farmer' (LUNPFM, 216). Symbols are representative portions of larger contexts, so that there are complex 'symbolisms' of headgear among the men of the country (272), Ricketts' spectacles are 'symbolic' of his status as a reader in Church (261), cotton is the 'central leverage and symbol' of the tenants' 'privation' (326) and still and moving cameras are the 'instruments and symbols' of Agee's analytical style (245). As for Richards, symbolic Belief is connected with a relatively primitive state of consciousness — children, for example, 'like figures of speech or are, if you like, natural symbolists and poets' (300) — and Agee speaks of the tenants' 'propitiative prayer' before the elements (129), of the utter fear of storms 'which is apparently common to all primitve peoples' (336) and of their planting, 'like the most ancient peoples of the earth. . . in the unpitying pieties of the moon' (325). That thought, as Richards says, is metaphoric, and that perfect analogy is not possible (only 'adequate' references and symbols), imply not only that propriety of description and attitude is impossible, but that the requirement of symmetry or repeatability in the primitive mind, as exemplified by Gudger's attempt 'to create a saving rhythm against the unpredictable thunder' (398), is clutching at an illustory sense of control: Agee speaks repeatedly of 'unprecedented' beauty (253), of patterns of grain in wood which are 'unrepeatable from inch to inch', its variations in light and weather 'subtly unrepeatable and probably infinite' (146); experiences and those who witness are never 'quite to be duplicated, nor repeated, nor have they ever quite had precedent' (56); each person 'is not quite like any other', is a 'single, unrepeatable, holy individual' (321).

Meaning, or sense, depends upon context: context is symmetrical — based, that is, on the assumption of repeatability — and habitual: understanding, the grasp of context, is simultaneously 'the one weapon against the world's bombardment, the one medicine, the one instrument, by which liberty, health, and joy may be shaped or shaped toward', and 'its own, and hope's, most dangerous enemy' (289) by dint of being based upon, and thus subject to, habit. It is no exaggeration to say that Agee's major preoccupation is with overcoming the paralysis of habit, destroying the 'crystallized ideas and attitudes' which 'rule all conduct and experience' (CSP, 164); just as, in 'Dedication', he dismisses myths, or 'false and previous visions', of political and scientific progress and of 'love of the fatherland',[27] he attacks, in the film criticism, Negro stereotypes (AF, I, 80), nationalism (284), the Stalinist myth of the future, which involves 'contempt for present humanity' (286), Hollywood's 'cruel, fetid, criminal little myths about death' (92) and 'cherished pseudo-folk beliefs about bright-lipped youth, childhood sweethearts, Mister Right, and the glamor of war' (74). And habit is defined as central in LUNPFM: the tenants are 'saturated in harm and habit, unteachable beliefs' (LUNPFM, 102); 'the deepest and most honest and incontrovertible rationalization of the middle-class southerner is that the tenants are "used" to it' (210); children are born into a 'physical, sensual, emotional world whereof... not the least detail whose imposure and whose power to trench and habituate is not intense beyond calculation' (109); sexual freedom in all classes is stifled by 'the conditioned and inferior parts of each of our beings' (62); and as a reporter of experience Agee must call self-conscious attention to 'Every deadly habit in the use of the senses and of language; every "artistic" habit of distortion in the evaluation of experience' (241). Habit is challenged by change, the new, as when Richard confronts a snake 'more splendid than he

had ever seen before' (MW, 140), or when Rufus contemplates
his father's body: Gudger's 'emotions and his mind are slow to
catch up with any quick change in the actuality of a situation'
LUNPFM, 412); the joyful perception of actuality occurs 'in any
rare situation which breaks down our habitual impatience, superficial vitality, overeagerness to clinch conclusions, and laziness'
(228). Richards asserts that good poetry breaks up habitual patterns of response and promotes a readiness for action; Agee sub-
mits that 'any new light on anything, if the light has integrity, is
a revolution'.[28] The ear-to-speaker experience of Beethoven is as
'savage and dangerous and murderous to all equilibrium in human
life as human life is; and nothing can equal the rape it does on all
that death; nothing except anything, anything in existence or
dream, perceived anywhere remotely toward its true dimension'
(LUNPFM, 16).

In his resistance to habitual context, Agee insists that 'no picture needs or should have a caption' ('Plans for work', CSP, 159),
that photographs be examined 'without the interference of
words',[29] and that films be made without voice-over commentary
or music. The quotations of Shakespeare and Marx in LUNPFM
'mean, not what the reader may care to think they mean, but
what they say'; and the Lord's Prayer is recited, 'not by its captive
but by its utmost meanings' (LUNPFM, xix, 439). When he
examines the cluster of calendars and advertisements over the
Ricketts fireplace, Agee lists and describes the pictures exhaustive-
ly, and separately from his list of the political, commercial and
religious slogans which are their captions (199-201). He speaks of
himself as 'essentially an anarchist', a 'frenetic enemy against
authority and against obedience for obedience's sake' (LFF, 100,
105), admires the bravery of Huey Long's assassin and would
approve both an organization designed to eliminate 'the 300 key
sonsofbitches on the earth' and laws which 'interdicted the use of
all words to which the reader cannot give a referent' and 'disbarred
any lawyer or judge who made use of precedent' (LFF, 83-84,
106). Against the War Department's suppression of Huston's
Let There Be Light, 'if dynamite is required, then dynamite is
indicated' (AF, I, 200): like Melville, Burroughs, Antonioni and
Leone, Agee admires the potential of the explosion, and speaks,
despite his horror at its use against living creatures, of the atom
bomb's having split 'all thoughts and things', 'split open the

universe and revealed the prospect of the infinitely extra-ordinary'.[30]

On the individual level, this means that the understanding, the unknowable witness of experience, has no identity – cannot be identified, as Richards says, with subvocal speech, with the nervous system or with any context: as in Melville, birth and maturation is a process of letting go, or rejecting identity, so that Gauguin experiences 'a steady *stripping away*, like the taking apart of an onion to its center' ('Noa Noa', AF, II, 139), and the bull who returns from the slaughterhouse, his hide partially strip-ped, is no longer 'one with all his race', knows 'what it is to be himself alone, a creature separate and different from any other, who had never been before and would never be again' ('A mother's tale', CSP, 264). The Follet family, together for the first time after Catherine's birth, is similarly aware of itself: ' " Well, little Rufus... here we are" '[31]; the tenant child, naked of exper-ience, bursts into existence 'to find himself' (LUNPFM, 103); and in his truancy, Richard strips and dives to the bottom of a chilling lake, waiting past safety and endurance until he springs to the surface shouting within himself, '*Here I am!* ' (MW, 139). Here, but who? and where is here? 'Knoxville: summer, 1915' ends with the narrator being put to bed by beings 'who quietly treat me, as one familiar and well-beloved in that home: but will not, oh, will not, not now, not ever; but will not ever tell me who I am'; in the night, the darkness taunts Rufus: 'when in this meeting, child, where are we, who are you, child; are you? ' (DF, 15, 184). Gauguin's painting, 'Where do we come from? What are we? Where are we going? ' is a leading motif in 'Noa Noa' (AF, II, 111); the painter's struggle against convention, and especially his treatment of the Polynesian islanders as a subject of study, suggest Agee's defiance, in LUNPFM, of the 'safe world' of the accepted in literature, and his determination, with Evans, to treat their subject 'not as journalists, sociologists, politicians, entertainers, humanitarians, priests, or artists, but seriously' (LUNPFM, 16, xv). Safety, as defined by the elder cow in 'A mother's tale', is where 'we *know* what happens, and what's going to happen, and there's never any reason to doubt about it, never any reason to wonder' (CSP, 255). Agee expresses contempt both for 'any organization or Group or Movement or Affiliation' whereby his effort might be identified, and for any excuse for

writing extensive descriptive prose, which is 'chronically relegated
to a menial level of decoration or at best illumination, distortion,
apology': 'Cocteau... remarks that the subject is merely the excuse for the painting, and Picasso does away with the excuse'
(LUNPFM, 354, 239). Like Melville, Agee says no; like Richards,
he is without Beliefs. This mythless condition applies to existence,
the beginning of which is 'before stars' and 'no one knows where
it will end' (55); to the human situation, for 'we can no longer
with any certitude picture ourselves as an egregiously complicated
flurry and convolved cloud of chance sustained between two
simplicities' (231); and to his own predicament as an 'anomaly'
before the tenants: 'just say I am from Mars and let it go at that'
(412, 405). It is the sense of strain involved in this last implication that gives into the only story-shaped, conclusion-directed
episode in the book.

THE ROMANTIC EPISODE

'Part Three', entitled 'Inductions' and prefaced by the Introit of
the Mass — which is also quoted to preface the discussion, 'SHEL-
TER' (123), involving approaches to the '*altar*' of a table with
precisely arranged objects and its '*Tabernacle*', a drawer and its
contents — narrates the progression from a first meeting with the
three farmers in Cookstown to Agee's penetration of a center,
'Six sides of me all pine' (420), a room in the Gudger house in
which he reads and examines the family bible. The section, '*First*',
concerns their being taken to the Ricketts house to photograph
the three families and the anticlimax — 'which, you must understand, is just not quite nice. . . . this is just one of several reasons
why I don't care for art' (366) — wherein Agee falls in love with
Louise Gudger and conceives the aim of establishing 'ultimate
trust' and 'love' between the tenants and the reporters (370).
'*Second*' moves through '*Gradual*', arranging with Woods to stay
among the families, '*Reversion*', a shift back to the events leading
up to Agee's first night with the Gudgers, and '*Introit*', his entrance of the Gudger house during an afternoon storm. Having
retired to Birmingham for refreshment, Agee and Evans experience
themselves as tourists, consuming in detail the sights of the city,

and as voyeurs, watching an opposite window as 'a woman is shifting from nightgown through nakedness to day clothing but the sun is spread strongly enough on that tall windowed wall that we can scarcely see anything' (374). Agee takes the car, leaves without Evans and without specific destination, settling 'down into the driving as if into a hot bath', passively 'watching the road disinvolve itself from the concealing country and run under me' (375); it is as if the windshield were the dynamized rectangle of a movie screen, and with similar implications of peeping: 'Through windows could be seen details of rooms. . . and at the same time the window surfaces gave back pieces of street and patterns of leaves on light' (379).

Agee, that is, is behind the glass — the windshield, the camera lens, the sutureless subjective bubble — an impermeable surface which mediates all experience. When he compares his secret exploration of the Gudger house to his pubescent masturbation, he recalls having 'planted my obscenities in the cold hearts of every mirror in foreknowledge'; but as a voyeur rather than a narcissist, Ishmael rather than Ahab, his attention is to the naked body of the house, which is itself 'one lens', and computes surface rather than depth, the corrupted mirror 'rashed with gray, iridescent in parts, and in all its reflections a deeply sad zinc-to-platinum' (136-137, 161). Agee elsewhere uses the image of glass to illustrate the same point, speaking in 'Permit me voyage' of air that is 'passionless as glass'[32]; and the destruction in 'The house' is paralleled by the smashing of a fishbowl which leaves a goldfish gasping on the carpet (CSP, 192). The breaking of glass in some form, or the removal of spectacles (as when Degas examines Gaugin's painting in 'Noa Noa' [AF, II, 97]), so as to suggest penetration and contact, is a stock device in the vocabulary of the cinema, and frequently accompanies eye contact, as well as sexual or otherwise violent occurrences: when Agee slows his car — the speed of which 'had walled me away as though with the glass of a bathosphere from the reality of this heat; but now the glass was broken and... I was a part once more of the pace and nature of this country' (LUNPFM, 378) — he indicates the shape of this episode, its movement from seeing through a glass, darkly, to an attempt to see face to face.

Like Ahab, Agee is crippled, cut off from any sense of identity, and bent on some form of resolution: his sense of sexual urgency crystalizes as a fantasy, as he sits 'unable to move... looking out through the windshield', of an ideal girl with whom perfect communication might briefly be established, for which he ridicules himself as a 'fantast' (382-384). Since, despite the importance of breaking down the identification of word and thing, human beings are incapable of not dreaming, Agee has come in search of identity, of meaning; his period in the city has brought him 'terrible frustration, which had in its turn drawn me along these roads and to this place scarce knowing why I came, to the heart's blood and business of my need' (389). The voyeur has again become a narcissist: like Ahab, Agee raises his personal need for an identity — 'who am I, who in Jesus' name am I' (284) — to the status of a necessity. And it is satisfied, he says, 'twice over... two "dreams", "come true" ', which are compared in their fulfilling power, to an adolescent fantasy of love, this perfect sharing involving enthusiasm for a marching song of rescue, 'though our images were different', hers of World War I prisoners, his, via daguerrotypes and Brady photographs, of a Civil War prison camp and deserted loved ones. The comparison is not inappropriate, Agee says, since those of whom he writes are likewise 'imprisoned' and waiting, though he doubts whether rescue will come in the form of Russian Communism. He also compares his fulfillment to refreshment at a forest spring, 'so cold, so clear, so living, it breaks on the mouth like glass', and to drinking at a 'human' springhouse, staring into the 'broad affronted eyes' of a bullfrog (389-393).

The first dream come true comprises Agee's visit to the Gudgers, withdrawn into their darkened house in terror of a storm, a powerful experience of eye contact with Louise Gudger, and a movement out after the rain, which has ended a long drought and seems to Gudger 'sure enough to have been an answer to a prayer', into the communal work effort of mending damaged trees and sorting fruit, which brings Agee close to tears: 'and there was a movement and noise all round me where at length I found myself' (406-407). The *'Second introit'* involves his return, after his car has become stuck in the mud, to stand 'silently... vertical to the front center of the house' (411) — Ahab confronting his whale — until the Gudgers are awakened by their dog and take him in: as the Tennessee-born Agee sits talking and eating the meal Mrs. Gudger has prepared, the feeling increased itself upon me that at the end of a wandering and seeking, so long it had begun before I was born, I had apprehended and now sat at rest in my own home, between two who were my brother and sister, yet less that than something else; these, the wife my age exactly, the husband four years older, seemed not other than my own parents, in whose patience I was so different, so diverged, so strange as I was; and all that surrounded me, that silently strove in through my senses and stretched me full, was familiar and dear to me as nothing else on earth, and as if well known in a deep past and long years lost, so that I could wish that all my chance life was in truth the betrayal, the curable delusion, that it seemed, and that this was my right home, right earth, right blood, to which I would never have true right. For half my blood is just this; and half my right of speech; and by bland chance alone is my life so softened and sophisticated in the years of my defenselessness, and I am robbed of a royalty I can not only never claim, but never properly much desire or regret. And so in this quiet introit, and in all the time we have stayed in this house, and in all we have sought, and in each detail of it, there is so keen, sad, and precious a nostalgia as I can scarcely otherwise know; a knowledge of brief truancy into the sources of my life, whereto I have no rightful access, having paid no price beyond love and sorrow. (415)

Without transition he turns to an impersonal, unflattering listing and description of the foods and their tastes, and his efforts to keep it down and appear pleased by it, undercutting by anticlimax the most powerful passage of communication in the book. As in *Moby-Dick*, and throughout Agee's work, the struggle is between dreamer and cold critic. Agee is given a room, examines the record of marriage, births and death inscribed in the family bible, with its 'strong cold stench of human excrement' (424), and struggles to sleep in a vermin-ridden bed; the next morning the car is reclaimed and he drives Gudger to work, again experiencing the world through a windshield. The northern reporter on the tenant situation and harbinger of help, who advises Emma Woods and apostraphizes the Ricketts children '(Jesus, what could I ever do for you that would be enough)' (386), sits talking with Gudger in the car 'about what the tenant farmer could do to help himself out of the hole he is in', until Gudger gets out to go to work: 'I told him I sure was obliged to him for taking me in last night and he said he was glad to have holp me' (431-432). The communal experience is such that Gudger assumes his own role, is helper rather than helped; despite shared food and louse bites, and the most strenuous observation and description, he is unique, alien, ultimately unknowable: the White Whale disappears uncaptured, taking Ahab with him and leaving Ishmael afloat on the surface – ambiguous, unexplained, somewhat embarrassed

STARTING FROM WHERE YOU ARE: THE EMPIRICAL POINT OF VIEW

This is knowledge by negation, a rendering of Agee's attitudes or states of emotional equilibrium and upset before Gudger, and a description of the forms of Gudger's life, which never quite reach Gudger. ('*On the Porch: 3*', which ends the book, diagrams Agee's effort to perceive and communicate and bears out his declaration of respect for 'any experience whatever... because it turns out that going through, remembering, and trying to tell of anything is of itself... interesting and important to me' (244). At this time of night Agee and Evans usually 'compare and analyze' those 'reactions' which they must conceal by day; as they contemplate their surroundings, 'there now came a sound that was new to us', communicating to them 'a new opening of delight' – habit challenged by the unprecedented – and to which they give complete attention, engaging 'in mutual listening and in analysis of what we heard, so strongly, that in all the body and in the whole range of mind and memory, each of us became all one hollowed and listening ear'. The noise is 'most nearly like' that of hydrogen ignited in a test tube, 'soprano, with a strong alto illusion', but 'colder', running 'eight identical notes. . . in this rhythm and accent:

_____ : ____ : __ ____ :

Each note is precisely described; a paragraph is spent on its spacial location, so that 'after a little we got it in range within say twenty degrees of the ninety on the horizontal circle which at first it could have occupied any part of. . . . between an eighth and a quarter mile away'; they are assisted in their 'geometry' by the signal of a second caller, which also makes possible distinctions of 'personality', the 'illusion' of seeker and sought, identification with the seeker, the perception of call played against silence and of the mutual interenhancements of calls, and of calls and other night sounds 'which, now that we were listening so intently, became once more a part of the reality of hearing'. The calls proceed 'through any number of rhythmic-dramatic devices of delays in question and answer', like a vaudeville act repeating the same word in different tones, 'but at all times beyond even the illusion of full comprehension'; it is conjectured that they are fox calls, though 'we had no clue, no anchorage in knowledge' by which that might be verified. The calls are considered in terms of dramatic and musical structure; a call a fraction away from the pattern of expectation 'computed' by the ear breaks the listeners open into 'a laughter that destroyed and restored us', and which is connected with passages from Mozart and Shakespeare, and with a variety of personal experiences including that of the initial phase of romantic love, which is expounded at length.

A particular stable poise, that is, yields that pattern of associations with which it is alone possible to come to terms with the new. The experience of this sound derives its value from the maximal organization of Agee's impulses, a full coenesthetic response and readiness for action, with which it is met; description in no way reaches what it is, but records the play of interests in the perceiver. It is impossible to assign any change to the series of calls 'save through the changefulness and human sentimentality of us who were listening and making what we could of it'. And the communication gap, 'the frightening joy of hearing the world talk to itself, and the grief of incommunicability', is not only between sound and hearer, but between the describer's 'useless' and 'utterly hopeless effort' and the reader's understanding, for 'communication of such a thing is not only beyond possibility but irrelevant to it'. The book closes as Agee and Evans lay 'thinking, analyzing, remembering, in the human artist's sense praying... until at length we fell asleep' (463-471)': like the prose description of Melville and Burroughs, and like Antonioni's *Blow-Up*, LUNPFM addresses the simple and ambiguous fact of being awake.

HUMANISM AND HOW TO SAVE IT

Agee's empiricism consists in his holding to the spatial relationships of objects and to evidence which speaks for itself, in his conviction 'that much can be implied out of little: that everything to do with tenant education, for instance, is fairly indicated in the mere list of textbooks' (308), in his care in pointing out 'unsupported statements' (202), in his skepticism about the possibility of 'communication' (12) and in his attention to definition, and to the fact of the text itself; but it is counterbalanced by his ardent humanism, his location of the 'elementary beginnings of true reason. . . in the ability to recognize the ultimate absoluteness of responsibility of each human being' (AF, I, 278). The indefinable human core of the onion consistently, in Agee's work, synthesizes evidence to arrive at human recognition: the narrator of 'They that sow' recreates the life of his landlord in 'fragments, and by implication' (CSP, 95); 'Noa Noa' opens with a group of men in the dead Gauguin's house 'summing up a man's nature, through what he has left' (AF, II, 5), just as Rufus contemplates his dead father's chair, smells its surfaces, tastes the smudges in the ash tray (DF, 265); in an unfinished screenplay written for Chaplin, 'Scientists and tramps', Charlie appears after a nuclear explosion, 'wandering in a dead metropolis, examining a dead civilization'[33] ; one of the last shots in 'The blue hotel' is of the patterns of sand on the barroom floor which record the Swede's fight (Agee, of course, has made Crane's Easterner, the man whose prejudices have not kept him from seeing what happened, a reporter), similar to the 'changed surface' of Gudger's front yard, the only evidence of Agee's intense experience there (LUNPFM, 407). LUNPFM, too, is an evidential 'fragment' (xv) out of which much might be implied, displaying and listing unsynthesized socioeconomic details:

Granted — more, insisted upon — that it is in all these particularities that each of you is that which he is; that particularities, and matters ordinary and obvious, are exactly themselves beyond designation of words, are the members of your sum total most obligatory to the human searching of perception: nevertheless to name these things and fail to yield their stature, meaning, power of hurt, seems impious, seems criminal, seems impudent, seems traitorous in the deepest: and to do less badly seems impossible: yet in withholdings of specification I could but betray you still worse. (100-101)

A related consideration is Agee's use of more than one description to record a situation: if Richards calls for a General Theory of Critical Relativity, it is not inappropriate to borrow Niels Bohr's concept of complimentarity to describe the method of LUNPFM — the use, that is, of mutually exclusive and contradictory pictures of atomic systems, each legitimate in its place, logical contradiction being avoided by 'the uncertainty relation', the fact that incomplete knowledge of a system is an essential part of every quantum formulation. Just as, in *A Death in the Family*, several modes of interpreting facts are portrayed in interrelation, LUN-PFM consists not only of several forms — epistle, drama, verse, scripture, prayer, sentence, notes, appendices, 'forms... of music, of motion pictures, and of improvisations and recordings of states of emotion, and of belief' (LUNPFM, 244) – but of several styles and modes, what Agee calls 'art devices' (242). He speaks of 'every good artist' as 'usable' (353), and uses his models against one another: if 'we should dare to be "teaching" what Marx began to open... we should do so only in the light of the terrible researches of Kafka and in the opposed identities of Blake and Celine' (294). As he eavesdrops through the partition wall, Agee's listening assumes a Whitmanesque shape, 'as if I were in each one of these seven bodies, whose sleeping I can almost touch through this wall, and which in the darkness I so clearly see', only to be shattered into alien lucidity by the sudden 'Burt half-woke,whimpering before he was awake. . .' (57-58). Each situation is perceived as a convention of representation, the darkened, storm-beseiged house 'as "rembrandt", deeplighted in gold, in each integer colosally heavily planted', becoming in sunshine 'a photograph, a record in clean, staring, colorless light, almost without shadow' (404). As he drives through Alabama he indulges in Faulknerian renderings of hot Sunday paralysis: 'Not even a negress cook stole out delicately by the back way in her white slippers on the lawn and her hat and her white sunday dress. . .' (379). The absence of necessary relation among various aspects of the same event permits, and seems to demand, various attempts at rendition: Agee's refreshment by his experience with the Gudgers is 'as if' a personified sky rained on a thirsting man, and 'secondly, quite different', as if refreshed at a forest spring, 'or better', as if at a springhouse (392-393): the structure of the Gudger house is described at length in terms of its stark symmetries in sunlight, the record of its construction, 'Or by another saying', of its aesthetic simplicity, 'Or by a few further notes', of its Doric sobriety and evidence of manual talent, 'Or again by materials', a study of the geometry of wood grain, and 'By most brief suggestion' a list of salient colors under four varieties of light (142-146): these aspects overlap, repeat details in different contexts, and are mutually oblivious. '(*On the Porch*' functions as the 'center of action, in relation to which all other parts of this volume are intended as flashbacks, foretastes, illuminations and contradictions' (245); the four planes on which the book is written 'are in strong conflict. So is any piece of human experience. So, then, inevitably, is any partially accurate attempt to give any experience as a whole' (243).

The problem is to connect, to give human realization to the details of an experience recorded in a self-contradictory fashion. The deluded narrator of 'Death in the desert', for whom 'the ego is inconsequent manure', is bothered at first by his 'responsibility' for a stranded man — 'These thoughts, disconnected at first, in time took a substance and form' — but concludes in retrospect that 'I thought too much' (CSP, 83-85), whereas the teller of 'They that sow' tries, albeit in vain, 'to clarify his ideas, to give them some proper connection' (CSP, 97). Rufus' prudish mother does not explain her pregnancy to him because 'I just have a feeling he might m-make see-oh-en-en-ee-see-tee-eye-oh-en-ess, between — between one thing and another' (DF, 102); *A Death in the Family* is an account of his learning to think — 'Rufus began to see the connection between all this and the bath. . .' (266) — his becoming human, though there is pointedly no accounting for the acquisition of habits: ' "Some people just learn more slowly than others" ', his grandmother assures him over his bedwetting, though he knows the cautionary procedure his mother has taught him 'by heart and he knew there was no use in it'.[34] To be human is not only to connect, but to be aware of the arbitrary nature of connection, to embrace and hold in mutually oblivious suspension the disparate aspects of experience: democracy, Agee says in his column on the Hollywood ten, must be able to 'contain all its enemies' (AF, I, 285); *Monsieur Verdoux* is the supreme portrayal of one personality's, and modern civilization's, failure to keep its soul 'intact' by communicating honestly with both its best and worst elements, its living in a 'broken and segregated' condition, whereas, in *Lifeboat*, Hitchcock becomes 'so engrossed in the solution of pure problems of technique that he has lost some of his sensitiveness toward the purely human aspects of what he is doing' (AF, I, 257, 72). As a critic, Agee typically qualifies exhuberant praise, as for the film *New Orleans*, with statements like, 'All the same, the movie is a crime' (AF, I, 271), or finishes a point-by-point comparison of Faulkner with Shakespeare, in a review of *The*

Hamlet, with 'there is nevertheless not one sentence without its share of amateurishness, its stain of inexcusable cheapness'[35]: the human critic exhibits a versatility of attitude parallel to, and made possible by, his linguistic dexterity.

The mind, according to Richards, is a fiction, to be spoken of only as an inexplicable connecting organ; language, the ordering of references, is the mind itself at work, and the interdependencies of words are those of our being. But the adult cotton tenant 'is incapable of any save the manifest meanings of any but the simplest few hundred words and is all but totally incapable of absorbing, far less correlating, far less critically examining, any "ideas" whether true or false' (LUNPFM, 306), is restricted to an almost purely 'tactile... fragrant, visible, physical world' (108), and is all but excluded from the realm of the human (for human equality is a matter of 'potentiality' [LFF, 149]), as, for example, from an appreciation of beauty, out of 'habit. No basis of comparison. No "sophistication" (there can be a good meaning of the word)':

It is true that in what little they can obtain of them, they use and respect the rotted prettinesses of 'luckier' classes; in such naivety that these are given beauty: but by and large it seems fairly accurate to say that being so profoundly members in nature, among man-built things and functions which are almost as scarcely complicated 'beyond' nature as such things can be, and exist on a 'human' plane, they are little if at all more aware of 'beauty,' nor of themselves as 'beautiful,' than any other member in nature, any animal, anyhow. (314-315)

Agee's shame at his own privileged skills of perception is the ultimate self-interrogation of his point of view. Lacking a linguistic sophistication that would facilitate an efficient organization of impulses, the tenant cannot realize — relate, hold in value-suspended focus — as the reader must:

The most I can do — the most I can hope to do — is to make a number of physical entities as plain and vivid as possible, and to make a few guesses, a few conjectures; and to leave to you much of the burden of realizing in each of them what I have wanted to make clear of them as a whole: how each is itself; and how each is a shapener. (110)
... if these seem lists and inventories merely, things dead unto themselves, devoid of mutual magnetisms, and if they sink, lose impetus, meter, intension, then bear in mind at least my wish, and perceive in them and restore them what strength you can of yourself: for I must say to you, this is not a work of art or of entertainment, nor will I assume the obligations of the

artist or entertainer, but is a human effort which must require human co-operation. (111)

Though Godard is no humanist, Agee's problem is similar in that he embraces on the one hand empirical data, and on the other an insistent faith in and prayer for resolution: 'let us know, let us *know* there is cure, there is to be an end to it' (439). Like Melville, Agee strives to hold Narcissus and the voyeur in balance; and he insists upon a human significance which William Burroughs regards as superfluous.

The most inviting way to compare peeping Tommo to Agee as reporter-spy among the tenants is through Agee's Gauguin, who also goes to live 'intimately with the natives of the wilderness. . . gradually gain their confidence and come to know them', and is accused by the Tahitian governor of being a 'spy' (AF, II, 66-67). The painting, 'Where do we come from? What are we? Where are we going? ' which is Gauguin's record of the experience, 'isn't the ordinary thing – studies from nature, preliminary cartoon, and so on: it's all boldly done, directly with the brush, on a sackcloth full of knots and rugosities, and so, it looks terribly rough. . . They'll say it's loose... unfinished. But I believe not only that it outdoes my earlier paintings, but also that I shall never paint a better one' (AF, II, 112). Whether or not, as is tempting to believe, this is Agee commenting on LUNPFM, the book, like the painting, is a skeletal, diagrammatic cluster, unfinished in appearance, of sketches, studies and preliminaries. In terms, that is, both of his abstention from any attempt to resolve complementary modes of description, and of his moral effort, LUNPFM is the least he could do.

NOTES

1. James Agee, '1928 story', in Victor A. Kramer, 'Agee in the forties: the struggle to be a writer', *Texas Quarterly* XI (1) Spring 1968: 36.
2. Father J.H. Flye, *James Agee: A Portrait*. New York, Caedmon Records, 1971: side 4.
3. James Agee, *The Morning Watch*. New York, Ballantine, 1969: 22, 52, 24. Subsequent references are noted in the text (MW).
4. James Agee, *A Death in the Family*. New York, Bantam, 1969: 60. Subsequent references are noted in the text (DF).
5. James Agee, 'Dream sequence', in Victor A. Kramer, 'Agee in the forties: the struggle

to be a writer', *Texas Quarterly* XI (1) Spring 1968: 45-46.

6. W.M. Frohock, 'James Agee: the question of wasted talent', in *The Novel of Violence in America*. London, Arthur Barker Limited, 1959: 228-229.

7. James Agee, 'Noa Noa', in *Agee on Film*, volume II. New York, Grosset and Dunlop, 1969: 5, 42, 72, 102. Subsequent references are noted in the text (AF, II).

8. James Agee, 'Introduction', in Walker Evans, *Many Are Called*. Boston, Houghton Mifflin, 1966.

9. James Agee, *Agee on Film*, volume I. New York, Grosset and Dunlop, 1968: 95. Subsequent references are noted in the text (AF, I).

10. James Agee, 'Dream sequence', in Victor A. Kramer, 'Agee in the forties: the struggle to be a writer', *Texas Quarterly* XI (1) Spring 1968: 43.

11. James Agee, 'An essay by James Agee', in Helen Levitt, *A Way of Seeing*. New York, Viking, 1965: 3.

12. See particularly Normal N. Holland, 'Agee on film: reviewer reviewed', *The Hudson Review* XII, Spring 1959: 148-151; John S. Snyder, 'James Agee: a study of his film criticism'. Unpublished Ph.D. Dissertation, St. John's University, 1969; and Michael Sragow, 'Agree and film', *The Harvard Advocate* CV (4) February 1972: 39.

13. Edward Murray, *Nine American Film Critics: A Study of Theory and Practice*. New York, Ungar, 1975: 8-12.

14. James Agee, 'An essay by James Agee', in Helen Levitt, *A Way of Seeing*. New York, Viking, 1965: 6, 3.

15. John Russell Taylor, 'The last great silent director', *Take One* V (2) May 1976: 13.

16. James Agee, 'Pseudo-folk', *Partisan Review* XI (2) Spring 1944: 221.

17. James Agee, '1928 story', in Victor A. Kramer, 'Agee in the forties: the struggle to be a writer', *Texas Quarterly* XI (1) Spring 1968: 28, 30.

18. James Agee, 'An essay by James Agee', in Helen Levitt, *A Way of Seeing*. New York, Viking, 1965: 3.

19. James Agee, 'Pseudo-folk', *Partisan Review* XI (2) Spring 1944: 220.

20. Quoted in Victor A. Kramer, 'Agee and plans for the criticism of popular culture', *Journal of Popular Culture* V (4) Spring 1972: 763.

21. For an analysis of the book according to this distinction of 'levels', see Peter Ohlin, *Agee*. New York, Oblensky, 1966: 49-107.

22. Janes Agee, 'An essay by James Agee', in Helen Levitt, *A Way of Seeing*. New York, Viking, 1965: 7.

23. James Agee, ' "Surprise", an unused chapter for *A Death in the Family*', in Victor A. Kramer, 'Agee in the forties: the struggle to be a writer', *Texas Quarterly* XI (1) Spring 1968: 53.

24. Michael Sragow, 'Agee and film', *The Harvard Advocate* CV (4) February 1972: 38.

25. James Agee, 'Dream sequence', in Victor A. Kramer, 'Agee in the forties: the struggle to be a writer', *Texas Quarterly* XI (1) Spring 1968: 46.

26. James Agee, 'Religion and the intellectuals', *Partisian Review* XVII, February 1950: 109.

27. James Agee, 'Dedication', in *The Collected Poems of James Agee*, ed. by Robert Fitzgerald. New York, Ballantine, 1970: 15-16, 18.

28. James Agee, 'Art for what's sake', *New Masses* XXI (12) December 19, 1936: 48.

29. James Agee, 'An essay by James Agee', in Helen Levitt, *A Way of Seeing*. New York, Viking, 1965: 78.

30. James Agee, 'The nation', *Time* XLVI (8) August 20, 1945: 19.

31. James Agee, ' "Surprise", an unused chapter for *A Death in the Family*', in Victor A. Kramer, 'Agee in the forties: the struggle to be a writer', *Texas Quarterly* XI (1) Spring 1968: 55.

32. James Agee, Sonnet XX, 'Permit me voyage: 1934', in *The Collected Poems of James Agee*, ed. by Robert Fitzgerald. New York, Ballantine, 1970: 1.8, 56.
33. James Agee, 'Scientists and tramps', quoted in Victor A. Kramer, 'Agee in the forties: the struggle to be a writer', *Texas Quarterly* XI (1) Spring 1968: 12.
34. James Agee, ' "Surprise", an unused chapter for *A Death in the Family*', in Victor A. Kramer, 'Agee in the forties: the struggle to be a writer', *Texas Quarterly* XI (1) Spring 1968: 49, 47.
35. James Agee, 'Genius-à-la-king', *Time*, April 1, 1947: 74-75.

6

Watch Your Language:
Narcissus as Addict in *Naked Lunch*

"Say 'rich, chocolaty goodness.' "
"Rich, chocolaty, goodness," said Oedipa.
"Yes, " said Mucho, and fell silent.
"Well, *what*?" Oedipa asked after a couple
minutes, with an edge to her voice.
"I noticed it the other night hearing Rabbit do a
commercial. No matter who's talking, the different
power spectra are the same, give or take a small
percentage. So you and Rabbit have something in
common now. More than that. Everybody who says
the same words is the same person if the spectra
are the same only they happen differently in time,
you dig? But the time is arbitrary. You pick your
zero point anywhere you want, that way you can
shuffle each person's time line sideways till they
all coincide. Then you'd have this big, God, maybe
a couple hundred million chorus saying 'rich, chocolaty goodness' together, and it would all be the same
voice."
"Mucho," she said, impatient but also flirting with
a wild suspicion. "Is this what Funch means when
he says you're coming on like a whole roomful
of people?"
"That's what I am," said Mucho, "right. Everybody
is."

Thomas Pynchon
The Crying of Lot 49

POSTHUMANIST REPORTING

Although *Naked Lunch* is remarkably similar, in tactics and in epistemological approach, to LUNPFM, William Burroughs does not share Agee's humanism. When, in *Nova Express*, the Nova Police wish to question someone, they 'send out a series of agents — (usually in the guise of journalists) — to contact [that person] and expose him to a battery of stimulus units — the contact agents talk and record the response on all levels to the word units while a photographer takes pictures — this material is passed along to the Art Department — Writers write "Winkhorst", painters paint "Winkhorst", a method actor *becomes* "Winkhorst", and then "Winkhorst" will answer our questions'.[1] Whereas Agee enjoins upon his reader the task of human realization, Burroughs regards the assembly of data and habits to be all there is to Winkhorst: call me Ishmael. As Godard's Alpha-60 and Kubrick's Hal demonstrate, the human element is unspeakable, neglibible, finally an encumbrance — ' "a sort of fifth wheel to a wagon" ', as Elijah tells Ishmael (MD, 86). 'Man', Burroughs says in *Minutes to Go*, 'is virus. Kick the virus habit MAN'.[2] That is, among the various forms of habit dealt with in *Naked Lunch* is man's narcissistic addiction to his own image:

> The broken image of man moves in minute by minute and cell by cell. . . . Poverty, hatred, war, police-criminals, bureaucracy, insanity, all symptoms of The Human Virus.
> *The Human Virus can now be isolated and treated.* (NL, 168-169)

The attack, in *Naked Lunch*, on the Family-of-Man style of humanism, includes reports on the 'virus venereal disease indigenous to Ethiopia' (42); the gray and brown pigments found in mulatto skin because 'the mixture did not come off and the colors separated like oil and water' (57); the disease, Bang-utot, peculiar to 'males of S.E. Asiatic extraction' (71); the 'rutting season' of Eskimos (83); and the spontaneous amputation of the little toe 'in a West African disease confined to the Negro race' (224) — all of which suggests, as Locke and Berkeley suggest, that Man cannot be abstracted from individual men or racial characteristics. The heroin addict needs to increase his doses, in fact, in order 'to maintain a human form' (vi). As the Public Agent puts it in *The Soft Machine*, 'human' is a rigid formula, a ' "mold" ' or ' "die" ' (SM, 34); and the Professor in *Naked Lunch* insists that his students be '*male humans,* positively no Transitionals in either direction will be allowed in this decent hall' (NL, 85).

William Lee, the principal narrator of *Naked Lunch* (and Burroughs' early pen name), is a pusher who controls a clientele of boys (' "He force me to commit all kinda awful sex acts in return for junk" ' [7]) and who hides his stash from sick fellow junkies in jail (9). His associate, Dr. Benway, is 'a manipulator and co-ordinator of symbol systems, an expert on all phases of interrogation, brain-washing and control', who describes himself as ' "an anti-human enemy" ' of his victim's ' "personal identity" ' (21). They are a delightfully comic and brutally inhuman team, addicts to control and to heroin, which is defined as a form of control, who manipulate the addictions of others, whether to heroin or to symbol systems (again, a form of control), and whose peculiar freedom resides in their nonaddiction to the human image, their inability to be degraded: 'In the words of total need: *"Wouldn't you?"* Yes you would. You would lie, cheat, inform on your friends, steal, do *anything* to satisfy total need' (vii). When an attendant in his hospital summons squealing and grunting junkies with a hog call, Benway comments, 'Wise guy. . . . No respect for human dignity' (35).

THE WISE GUY VS. THE CONFIDENCE MAN

The wisdom of the wise guy is that of the witness, of one who has been around and come back to tell — wry, disillusioned, detached but not transcendent — whose comments are casual but brilliantly succinct, delivered as if out of an incapacity for surprise, shot from the hip rather than deliberated or sophistic: wise cracks. Since he has no existential or prophetic message, he is not related to the Shakespearean fool or to such derivative figures as Pip. He has no religious message, and so is not related to the Elizabethan punster. Urbane and traveled, he has little in common with the regionally located teller of tall tales, though he certainly puts his audience on. His closest relative and match for speed and impertinence is the Restoration wit, though the wise guy is never a gentleman unless, as in *Naked Lunch*, 'by an act of Congress. . . . nothing else could have done such a thing' (92). Ishmael, who sits in a Lima bar telling a tale without demonstrable substance, swearing to its truth on the biggest bible in town, offering casual, passing, semi-serious allegorical comments (as does

William Lee: 'And let me say in passing, and I am always passing like a sincere Spade. . . .' [230]), and ending inconclusively (' "Conclude? " ' says Benway; ' "Nothing whatever. Just a passing observation" '. [36]), is, though his icy and hilarious sarcasm is anticipated in some early passages of *Typee*, arguably the first wise guy, typifying the cool but not invulnerable stances of later reporters, detectives and spies. When Agee calls an actress' mugging before the camera 'as uningratiating, as if a particularly cute monkey, instead of merely holding his hand out for a penny... insisted that he was working his way through Harvard'; when he responds to Lauren Bacall by 'getting caught in a dilemma between a low whistle and a bellylaugh' (AF, I, 42, 121); and when he affects aggressive Brooklynese in LUNPFM — 'if you think da dialectic is going to ring in any conceivably worthwhile changes, you can stick that and yourself up after' (385) — he is speaking the language of the wise guy, the baggy-suited reporter, as Evans describes him, who has the facts but doubts his audience's ability to comprehend their significance, and so bullies, kids, insults and leads it on.

Burroughs' wise guys are occasionally confidence men, like the priests who control the Mayan calendar (SM, 24); like the 'smart operators' who think they are conning 'The Rube', a Nova agent who has perfected the gestures of a naive mark (' "There's a wise guy born every minute' " [NE, 70]); like the pliers of The Bill, 'a short change con' (NL, 199); like the 'Itinerant short con and corny hyp men [who] have burned down the croakers of Texas' (i.e., talked doctors into writing prescriptions [NL, 13]); like Christ, Buddha, Mohammed, Confuscious and Lao-Tze, of whom the vicious fruity old saint remarks, ' "why should we let some old brokedown ham tell us what wisdom is? " ' (NL, 115); like Benway, who claims to be 'a reputable scientist, not a charlatan, a lunatic, or a pretended worker of miracles' (NL, 20-21); and like 'Lee the Agent', laying down the game of the text, offering the 'tentative half-impressions' on his memory track as photographs, 'vibrating in the silent winds of accelerated Time. . . . Pick a shot. . . . Any shot. . .' (NL, 218). But the con man can never be a thoroughgoing wise guy by virtue of his own addiction to control. (Norman Mailer has opined that 'the hustler's *dignity* is that he controls the flow of experience. He considers it obscene if he doesn't'.[3])

Burroughs' con men, like Melville's, claim to represent authority in some form — a psychoanalyst, like Benway, or a policeman, like Bradley the Buyer, a narcotics agent 'so anonymous, grey and spectral' that he can score from and 'twist' any pusher before the latter knows what has happened, but who himself needs to be fixed by rubbing up against junkies: 'Nonusing pushers have a contact habit, and that's one you can't kick. Agents get it too' (NL, 15). In fact, the most frequently appearing con man is half of the tough-cop-con-cop team which alternately softens and bullies a suspect (NL, 195; NE, 26). This, Burroughs speculates, is a strategic form of virus attack (J, 187), and is the mode in which engrams are formed: an event or formula is associated with contemporaneous pain and thus rendered unavailable to conscious attention except through strenuous analysis. The verbal virus, which has taken up residence in the larynx and proceeded to control and direct attention ('First it's symbiosis, then parasitism — The old symbiosis con'[4]), involves the analogy pitch employed by Melville's Confidence Man, the encouragement of the mark's belief that verbal meaning is both fixed and indispensable: 'In the beginning was the word and the word was bullshit. The beginning words come out on the con clawing for traction' (TE, 85). In their addiction to control, con men exhibit a rigid horror of change, so that they 'don't change, they break, shatter — explosions of matter in cold interstellar space' (NL, 10).

More often, however, the wise guy is a critical agent who must learn to deploy his attention, and is pitted against the con man's game:

Now learn to sit back and watch — Don't talk don't play just *watch*. . . Learn to *watch* and you *will* see all the cards. . . . The house know every card you will be dealt and how you will play all your cards — And if some wise guy does get a glimmer and maybe plays an unwritten card:
    "Green Tony... Show this character the Ovens — This is a wise guy".
(TE, 159)

The controllers of information perpetuate myths, habits of belief, arguments — 'That's what they call it: "making a case" ' (SM, 45) — which the wise guy analyzes, and against which he guards his independence. Burroughs finishes his introductory remarks on addiction in *Naked Lunch* with the comment, 'A word to the wise guy' (NL, xvi).

Burroughs has himself worked as a reporter and as a private
detective, and appears in *Nova Express* as an agent of the Nova
Police: 'One of our agents is posing as a writer. He has written
a so-called pornographic novel called Naked Lunch' (NE, 54).
The Nova Police is to 'the parasitic excrescence that often travels
under the name "Police" ' what apomorphine is to morphine, a
nonaddictive antidote to a state of metabolic need (NE, 50),
and is comparable to the organization joined by William Lee in
The Ticket that Exploded, supervised by a man who talks

in a voice without accent or inflection, a voice that no one could connect
to the speaker or recognize on hearing it again. The man who used that voice
had no native language. He had learned the use of an alien tool. The words
floated in the air behind him as he walked.
  'In this organization, Mr. Lee, we do not encourage togetherness, *esprit
de corps*. We do not give our agents the impression of belonging. As you
know most existing organizations stress such primitive reactions as unquestioning obedience. Their agents become addicted to orders. You will receive
orders of course and in some cases you will be well-advised not to carry out
the orders you receive. . . . You will receive your instructions in many ways.
From books, street signs, films in some cases from agents who purport to
be and may actually be members of the organization. There is no certainty.
Those who need certainty are of no interest to this department. This is in
point of fact a *non-organization*'. (TE, 9-10)

The nonaddicted free agent and critic of verbal habits appears
throughout Burroughs' writing in various wise guises, his narrators
referring to themselves as 'Your Reporter' (NL, 73), 'Inspector
Lee', 'this investigator' (NE, 54, 137), and Joe Brundige of *The
Evening News* — like Agee, a spy travelling as a journalist (SM,85).
'The name is Clem Snide — I am a Private Ass Hole', a 'Private
Eye', ' "Dick Tracy in the flesh" ' (SM, 71, 79-80). In *The Wild
Boys*, he is ' "Fred Flash from St. Louis. Photographer" '.[5]
The wise guy spies out and exposes the secrets of control organi-
zations, is out, as Burroughs puts it, 'to wise up the marks' (WW,
174); so that Uranian Willy's program calls 'for total exposure —
Wise up the marks everywhere. Show them the rigged wheel —
Storm the Reality Studio . . .' (SM, 155).
  The description of Lee harassed by the authorities in *Naked
Lunch* suggests Spade or Marlowe dealing with pushy policemen:

'And how do we know that?'
'I gota affidavit.'

'Wise guy. Take off your clothes.'
'Yeah. Maybe he got dirty tattoos.' (NL, 171)

In the only episode with extended narrative shape in the book, comparable to the single extended episode in LUNPFM, Hauser and O'Brien, a tough-cop-con-cop 'vaudeville team' ordered to bring in all the texts they find in Lee's hotel room – 'all books, letters, manuscripts. *Anything* typed or written' – walk in on him as he is preparing a fix: he stalls by promising to betray a pusher, takes his shot, squirts alcohol into Hauser's eyes with the syringe, reaches his gun and eliminates the policemen, rescues the 'notebooks' they had been about to seize, and escapes (alone to tell thee). Like Agee, Burroughs regards the press as a device of control rather than dissemination, so the incident is not reported in the next day's newspaper; and when Lee calls the Narcotics bureau and asks for Hauser and O'Brien he is told that there are no such men in the department: the policeman on the phone repeats, ' "Who are *you*?" ' ' "Now who is this calling? " ' – a question that Lee is beginning to realize he cannot answer, for 'I had been occluded from space-time. . . . Locked out. . . Never again would I have a point of intersection. . . . relegated with Hauser and O'Brien to a landlocked junk past where heroin is always twenty-eight dollars an ounce. . . . Far side of the world's mirror. . .' (NL, 209-217). The point of intersection is the text: Lee has been occluded from plot or continuity, from knowledge of ultimate context or identity, and confined to a specific set of fragmented textual circumstances which he, like the reader, looks in upon, can neither transcend nor identify with.

The occlusion episode, as of which 'The heat was off me from here on out' (217), ends the book proper, to which are added an 'Atrophied preface' and an 'Appendix': the book begins with Lee on the run from a narcotics agent – 'I can feel the heat closing in' – whom he eludes when someone holds a subway train door for him, 'A square wants to come on hip', rewarded by Lee with the illusion of camaraderie: ' "Thanks kid. . . I can see you're one of our own." His face lights up like a pinball machine with stupid, pink effect'. Lee proceeds to lay down a shared-human-experience con, pointing out and explaining scenes in the subway and relating anecdotes until he leaves the square and continues his routine minus quotation marks. The square, that is,

'Young, good looking, crew cut, Ivy League, advertizing exec type fruit. . . . A real asshole' (1-4), stands in for the reader, sympathetic, eager, unreachable — so that the text is from the beginning a wry comment on itself, on the impossibility of communication, until it finally occludes both Lee and the reader: like Wittgenstein's propostions, it is a ladder which, once climbed, is thrown away. The forms of *Naked Lunch* include those of film and of the vaudeville act: jokes and drawn out anecdotes for which even Lee must stand still (172). Talking on without possibility of communication, Lee is throughout a wise guy, performing for and putting on an audience too stupid to see through the game of language, like that other wise guy and spy who has to restrain himself from methodically knocking people's hats off in the street: 'Call me Ishmael. Some years ago — never mind how long precisely — having little or no money in my purse, and nothing particular to interest me on shore, I thought I would sail about a little and see the watery part of the world. . . .'

VOYEURISM WITHOUT GUILT

The wise guy is a seasoned witness and examiner of his experience, from whom nothing empirically knowable is secret. Typically, in Burroughs' writing, he is a voyeur. If Lee winds up on the opposite side of the world's mirror looking in, he begins by describing to the square the injection of a ' "hot shot" ' — a syringe full of strichnine, which resembles heroine — watched from a similar point of view: 'We rigged his room with a one-way whorehouse mirror and charged a sawski to watch it. . . . The look in his eyes when it hit — Kid, it was tasty' (NL, 2). In the wise guy's survival-oriented world, details are rapidly computed, as Lee reads the personality of his latter-day Wedding Guest in terms of his appearance (2), as state police lay down 'practiced apologetic patter [while] electronic eyes weigh your car and luggage, clothes and face' (11) and as Fats's 'blank, periscope eyes [sweep] the world's surface' (206). Burroughs' characters repeatedly watch 'squirming at a keyhole' (NL, 143; SM, 137), peruse pornographic pictures (SM, 68-69), view 'actual films' of war and torture (SM, 83), and watch schoolboys with 'eight-

power field glasses. . . . I project myself out through the glasses
and across the street, a ghost torn with disembodied lust' (NL, 59).
A fifteenth-century sorcerer, accused of conjuring a succubus
who impregnates a young woman, is 'indicted as an accomplice
and rampant voyeur before during and after the fact' (NL, 112);
the attendant at the Ever Hard Baths spies in 'the dormitory with
infra red see in the dark field glasses' (NL, 216). Billy Budd's
hanging becomes an ' "exhibit" ', for the delectation of all hands,
and reveals Billy to have been a transvestite, so that the ' *"medical
fact"* ' of her physical response is explained by a matron (SM,
169-170). In *Exterminator!*, 'Audrey rapes a young soldier at
gunpoint while Lee impassively films the action' (E, 87-89).
And in *The Last Words of Dutch Schultz*, both the stenographer
who takes down the last words and Schultz's wiretapper are
played by Burroughs.[6]
    ' "There are" ', says the atomic professor in *Nova Express*,
' "no secrets any more" ' (76). But there is still shame – a response
manipulated by Benway when he takes over Annexia, makes
citizens liable to frequent inspection by 'the Examiner' and forbids the use of 'shades, curtains, shutters or blinds'. Police accompanied by a mentalist may burst into anyone's room in search
of something unspecified and subject 'the suspect to the most
humiliating search of his naked person on which they make
sneering and derogatory comments' (NL, 21-23). A citizen of
Freeland is similarly harassed by Benway's Chillingworth-style
' "cold interest" ' – 'Eyes without a trace of warmth or hate or
emotion. . . at once cold and intense, predatory and impersonal'
– and becomes aware that there is 'something. . . watching his
every thought and movement with cold, sneering hate' as he
masturbates into a specimen jar (NL, 189-192).

THE LANGUAGE GAME AND IMAGE IDENTITY

In 'Playback from Eden to Watergate', Burroughs theorizes that
'the spoken word as we know it came after the written word'
– that is, the recorded word: 'In the beginning was the Word,
and the Word was God – and the word was flesh. . . human flesh.
. . . in the beginning of *writing*. Animals talk. They don't write'.
But the 'written word is inferential in *human* speech'. Citing Dr.

Kurt Unruh von Steinplatz's theory that speech was made possible by a virus-induced mutation of the inner throat structure in certain primates (called Virus B-23 — hence the proliferation of that number throughout the post-*Naked Lunch* oeuvre), Burroughs suggests that 'in the electronic revolution a virus *is* a very small unit of word and image', which units 'can be biologically activated to act as communicable virus strains'. For example, arbitrary 'association lines' can be established by splicing together three tape recordings, one of the subject's speech, one of his sexual or defecatory activity, and one of 'hateful, disapproving voices'; so that, in terms of the edenic myth, tape recorders one, two and three are Adam, Eve and God, who plays back Adam's *'disgraceful behavior'* to him. For while there is nothing inherently shameful about defecation and intercourse, *'Shame is playback*: exposure to disapproval'. Martin Luther King's enemies bugged his bedroom: 'Kiss kiss bang bang. A deadly assassination technique. . . . So the real scandal of Watergate. . . is not that bedrooms were bugged and the offices of psychiatrists ransacked but *the precise use that was made of this sexual material'*. But the game of manipulative voyeurism is monopolistic, depends on keeping tape recorder three on closed circuit, for 'God must be *the* God': 'millions of people carrying out this operation could nullify the control system', each himself becoming God by taking over the splicing of tapes and creation of associations (J, 11-20).

This is precisely what is accomplished in the cutup method of writing which Burroughs derives from Gysin. Like Melville and Agee, Burroughs conceives of God as voyeur and eavesdropper: ' "never know who's listening in" ', says Benway (NL, 28); ' "Who is the third that walks beside you? " ' (TE, 163). The individual can co-opt that function by alerting his own attention to the programmed verbal habits which constitute self, and most readily by cutting up and scrambling a tape of his own voice: ' "What used to be me is backward sound track" ' (SM. 64). In fact, Burroughs plays with the meaning of 'Ishmael' in his description of an eleventh-century Persian general's hunt (we find him 'poring over his maps') for a Muslem leader who 'had committed the terrible sin referred to in the Koran of aspiring to be God. The whole Ishmaelian sect was a perfect curse, hidden, lurking, ready to strike, defying all authority'. This very man works for the General, who 'has stopped seeing him years ago', as a gardener, and 'peers at this through the orange leaves with laughing blue eyes': he who watches and listens becomes God — Ishmael, 'God who hears'. The General's unseeing madness as he is observed pacing, 'acting out a final confrontation with this Satan' (WB, 169-170), is like that of William Seward in *Naked Lunch*, about to unlock his 'word horde' — those words which come out clawing for traction, for like Ahab he likes things that hold: he will, as 'captain of this lushedup hash-head subway... cowboy the white whale. I will reduce Satan to Automatic Obedience. . .' (NL, 230, 225).

This recurrent Ahab-Narcissus figure cannot bear to have his self-image threatened. Audrey in *Exterminator!* and the tourist in *The Wild Boys* make the identical comment, ' "Other people are different from me and I don't like them" ' (E, 88; WB, 6). And he is, like Dr. John Lee, who encounters 'living organisms manifesting wills different from and in some cases flatly antagonistic to his own. . ."the situation is little short of tolerable" ', a humanist, 'a humane man who did not like to harm anyone because it disturbed him to do so and he was a man who did not like to be disturbed'. Unlike Ishmael and the multifaceted texts of LUNPFM and *Naked Lunch*, the doctor is 'not a man who argued with himself' (E, 52-54). The mirror image is a virus, for in 'all virus the past prerecords your "future". . . . the image past molds your future imposing repetition'; and any 'offer of another image identity is always on virus terms' (TE, 188-189). To the narcissist, the mirror's surface constitutes a barrier between self and image, against the possibility of identity: 'Far side of the mirror's surface moving into my past — Wall of glass you know' (NE, 38). Again, the breaking of glass almost invariably accompanies moments of orgasm and death.

But the voyeur sees only 'someone vague faded in a mirror' (E, 168): ' "Look in the mirror. You face dead soldier. The last human image" ' (TE, 188). And there is no meaningful eye contact in his 'relationships', so that Fred Flash meets the Frisco Kid's 'eyes... like I could see through them and out the back of his head' (WB, 94). Burroughs uses a passage from Carlos Castaneda to illustrate the fact that 'no two people can *really* look at each other and live, and remain people. We can of course biologically defend ourselves against something which we cannot assimilate. But when they'd taken a drug, as in this case, there's no way in which they could defend themselves against the knowledge of what they were and what they represented: they can't look at each other and they can't look in a mirror'.[7] In *The Job*, he remarks, 'As the Peeping Tim said, the most frightening thing is fear in your own face' (J, 183). Narcissism is the vain wish to stabilize identity, to render experience repetitive, symmetrical, controllable. But Burroughs regards even the intelligence as 'a useful instrument that will probably be laid aside eventually' (J, 97). Narcissus' addiction to self-image, a horror of chance and the arbitrary, is parodied in *The Wild Boys*, which closes with two youths casting dice by a fountain: the loser, in sexual deference to the winner,'bends over looking at his reflection in the pool', and the scene is exploded by orgasm and by laughter which 'shakes the sky' (WB, 184). *Naked Lunch*, then, is the record of its writer's struggle with the guilt involved in deviating from his preconceived self-image in order actually to look and describe:

> The writer sees himself reading to the mirror as always. . . . He must check now and again to reassure himself the The Crime of Separate Action has not, is not, cannot occur. . . .
> Anyone who has ever looked into a mirror knows what this crime is and what it means in terms of lost control when the reflection no longer obeys. . . Too late to dial *P o l i c e*. . . .(NL, 223)

SOLIPSISM AND TEXTUAL FRAGMENTATION

Like Agee, who considers the text of LUNPFM as a surrogate vision —

> Edgar, weeping for pity, to the shelf of that sick bluff,
> Bring your blind father, and describe a little;
> Behold him, part wakened. . . (LUNPFM, 5)

— Burroughs treats the printed word 'as extension of our senses to witness and experience through the writer's eyes', and supplies a list, comparable to Agee's collection of Anglo-saxon monosyllables, of *'non-pictorial'* words and bureaucratic phrases without referents, which confute understanding and render any text blind prose. It sees nothing and neither does the reader. Not an image in a cement-mixer of this word-paste' (J, 103-104). Like Ishmael, Burroughs is our guide in the junky's world: 'want to take a look

around with Honest Bill? ' (NL, xiv). His text is a paratactic
assembly of discrete phrases, clauses and sentences, sometimes
mutually elaborative, but in idiosyncratic rather than necessary
relation, solipsistic to the point of autism, and thus parodied in
the figure of the cocaine-sniffing policeman who hallucinates
being pursued by the 'Federals' and sticks his head in a garbage
can: 'Get away or I shoot you. I got myself hid good' (NL, 19).
Description has precedence over shape and arrangement: 'There
is only one thing a writer can write about: *what is in front of his
senses at the moment of writing.* . . . I am a recording instrument.
. . . I do not presume to impose "story" "plot" "continuity". . . .
Insofar as I succeed in *Direct* recording of certain areas of psychic
process I may have limited function. . . . I am not an entertainer'
(NL, 221). In 1969, Burroughs commented on this passage,
'One tries not to impose story, plot or continuity artificially, but
you do have to compose the materials. . . . So I will retract what
I said then. It's simply not really true'.[8] But he continues to point
out that the imposed control of verbal pattern is at odds with the
ability to see, as in 'Seeing red', in which an erotic picture of a
red-haired boy 'looking at somebody standing in front of the
picture' incapacitates the verbal apparatus of customs agents,
city police, Texas Rangers and the Royal Mounted, all of whom
stare with 'dumb stricken faces swollen with blood. None of them
can articulate a word' (E, 141).

The reader of *Naked Lunch* has everything in common with
the audience of the pornographic film fantasies described in the
text: 'The guests shush each other, nudge and giggle' (NL, 76).
The Great Slashtubitch, 'impressario of blue movies' in that book
(88), handles an actors' strike against undignified working conditions in *The Wild Boys* by introducing 'story, character development and background in which sex scenes are incidental', so that
sex will not occur as 'a mutilated fragment' (WB, 62); but the
text of *The Wild Boys* is punctuated by recurrent erotic presentations in 'The penny arcade peep show' on four screens surrounding
the solipsistic viewer, in discontinuous fragments, or, as one of
The Soft Machine's narrator's puts it, 'long process in different
forms' (SM, 177, 182). Since Burroughs directly records psychic
process, the text of *Naked Lunch* is his thinking, and the reader
quite literally looks into his thoughts, 'intersects', to use Burroughs
word, the same verbal space, as the ghost of Agee's father looks in

on his dream, as Carl's thoughts are watched, and as The Sailor trades heroin for a young junky's 'time': 'You have something I want... five minutes here... an hour somewhere else' (NL, 204). To be addicted to image sequence is to be addicted to time. Like Agee, Burroughs is preoccupied with the onlooking crowd — the children who 'stand watching with bestial curiosity' as an idiot is burned to death (25), jurors who 'fall to the floor writhing in orgasms of prurience' at a D.A.'s graphic harangue (105), diseased citizens who 'watch the passerby with evil, knowing eyes' (108) and, in *Sidetripping*, the photograph of an audience watching a girl masturbate: 'Substitute a car wreck, an epileptic convulsion, a lynching and the expressions would be equally appropriate'.[9] As for the indiscriminate clubbing by police of 'Yippies newsmen and bystanders' in Chicago 1968, 'After all there are no innocent bystanders. What are they doing here in the first place? The worst sin of man is to be born' (E, 94). Moreover, sex, Joe Brundige learns, is 'perhaps the heaviest anchor holding one in present time' (SM, 86); and Burroughs cites accounts of recent experiments indicating that 'any dream in the male is accompanied by erection' (J, 102). Thus the reader is an onlooker whose watching is always prurient. The narrator of *The Wild Boys* notes that 'The erect phallus... means... in Egyptian to stand before or in the presence of, to confront to regard attentively' (WB, 151).

That which is voyeuristic, as in Melville and Agee, is the indefinable attention which cannot be identified with the body: ' "What would believe it? " ' (J, 95). Such identification is regarded as addiction; 'In fact all longevity agents have proved addicting in exact ratio to their effectiveness in prolonging life' (NL, 54). Reference is made in *Nova Express* to experiments in sense withdrawal, wherein 'the subject floats in water at blood temperature sound and light withdrawn — loss of body outline, awareness and location of limbs occurs quickly, giving rise to panic in many American subjects' (NE, 135): thus the metabolism-regulating function of apomorphine is illustrated by Lee's leaving his body upon ingestion (NE, 86). Burroughs frequently plays with metempsychotic notions. Joe Brundige hires a Mexican doctor to perform an operation, accomplished through photography and orgasm, whereby ' "I" was to be moved into the body of this young Mayan': 'I came back in other flesh the lookout different, thoughts and memories of the young Mayan drifting through my brain' (SM, 88, 90), the obvious question being '*Who* lookout different? ' (50). A ghost is a watcher, the Vigilante in search of a body (NL, 8). 'The dead child' is the story of 'broken fragments' of consciousness: 'What is it that makes a man a man and a cat a cat? It was broken there', 'there' indicating both a place described and a point in the text. The narrator is caught with fellow workers in the 'magic net' of a Mayan control calendar, and, having 'watched and waited' for his chance to escape (WB, 110-111), dies in the forest, leaves his body — 'I could see and hear but I couldn't talk without a throat without a tongue' — and remains in the treetops for an unknowable duration, descending to watch Indian campers make love (117) and the son of a tourist family masturbate, entering the latter at the moment of orgasm, 'seeing... through his eyes'. (119), and from that viewpoint intersecting an earlier point in the text as a different person: 'I see myself standing on a street. . .' (102-103). Similarly, at the end of *Naked Lunch*, Burroughs lists his cast of characters, remarking that 'Sooner or later they are subject to say the same thing in the same words, to occupy, at that intersection point, the same position in space-time. Using a common vocal apparatus complete with all metabolic appliances that is to be the same person — a most inaccurate way of expressing *Recognition*' (NL, 222-223).

Like the text called Ishmael, *Naked Lunch* encodes the movement of more than one attention. There are numerous examples in Burroughs' work of multiple personalities encoded on the same text, larynx or strip of film — B.J., whose associate's 'voice has been spliced in 24 times per second with the sound of my breathing and the beating of my heart' (TE, 2-3), the astronaut Lykin through whom 'thousands of voices muttered and pulsed... pulling and teasing' (TE, 87-88) — programmed by verbal grammar and yielding, when exposed to the deconditioning of the Wild Boys, to a Pip-like reflection on 'person': 'I have a thousand faces and a thousand names. I am nobody I am everybody. I am here there forward back in out. . .' (WB, 140). The exercise is always to render propositions meaningless, to show the fly the way out of the fly bottle, to release the unspeakable witness, the voyeur 'at the window that never was mine' (NE, 75), from identification with spoken formulation. The recurrent narrative comment, 'But then who am I to be critical? ' (NE, 21; TE, 2), indicates precisely that indefinability of critical attention which is emphasized by Wittgenstein.

WITTGENSTEIN AND SUBSTANCE

The unimaginable 'content' of verbal 'form', of which Wittgenstein speaks in the *Tractatus*, is both the metaphysical subject, the content of 'sense' or understanding, and the 'colourless' world of objects. *Naked Lunch* incorporates Ishmael's formulation of substance as the 'colorless all-color' into the recurrent 'colorless no-smell of death' (NL, 8, 221; and NE, 149), associated with the world through which the Vigilante's ghost moves and indicating the limit of thought, defining substance by negation; so that the Vigilante 'winds up in a Federal Nut House specially designed for the containment of ghosts: precise, prosaic impact of objects . . . washstand. . . door. . . toilet. . . bars. . . there they are. . . this is it. . . . all lines cut. . . nothing beyond. . . Dead End' (NL, 8). The narrator of 'My face', awakening in a strange apartment, likewise suggests that understanding does not transcend the arrangement of objects and sensations: 'You understand his room chair by the bed three cigarettes in a shirt pocket garden outside in the afternoon light' (E, 31). As in 'The Tartarus of maids', the narrator of *Nova Express* is shown colorless sheets which 'are empty' and which 'are what flesh is made from − Becomes flesh when it has color and writing − That is Word and Image write the message that is you on colorless sheets' (NE, 25, 30).

   With no attempt to reconcile the two views, however, Burroughs also goes beyond the realistic notion of a 'substance' which confirms or denies propositions − the 'solipsism' which, in the *Tractatus*, 'coincides with pure realism' (TLP, 5.64) − to Wittgenstein's later position that 'true' and 'false' are merely the components of a particular language game. In his otherwise useful article, 'A picture is a fact: Wittgenstein and *The Naked Lunch*', R.G. Peterson insists that Burroughs' quotation of 'Heiderberg', whom Peterson assumes to be a combination of Heidegger and Heisenberg, profferers, he says, of 'Ways Out', is a 'slighting reference', whereas Wittgenstein is quoted 'with appropriate fanfare'.[10] Heisenberg, however, reiterates a solipsistic formulation similar to those of Wittgenstein and Burroughs, that scientific investigation is always self-interrogative, that man 'confronts himself alone'. Heisenberg offers no such Way Out, and is accordingly echoed in *Naked Lunch*: 'Defense is meaningless in the present state of our knowledge, said the Defense looking up from an electron microscope' (NL, 223).

Burroughs insists that 'the Aristotelian "either-or" ... does not even correspond to what we now know about the physical universe' (ER, 86), and explains his frequent reference to Hassan i Sabbah's dictum, '*Nothing Is True — Everything Is Permitted*', as a critique of realism: 'If we realize that everything is illusion, then any illusion is permitted. As soon as we say that something is true, real, then immediately things are not permitted' (J, 97). Like Wittgenstein, Burroughs holds that memory reaction cannot be abstracted from its verbal formulation, and suggests that splicing unrelated events into a film of someone's actions changes that person's memory, creates a 'hole in reality' (ER, 79). Thus his characters are not always sure of their memories: 'I don't know — Perhaps the boy never existed — All thought and word from the past' (NE, 88); 'I don't remember. Maybe it didn't happen like that' (WB, 107).

A Nova Police agent goes so far as to suggest that by the disintegration of 'verbal units' an atomic explosion might be retroactively prevented, 'could not take place in effect would never have existed' (NE, 41). The voyeuristic ghost of the Dead Child exhibits a Berkeleyan dissociation of sight and touch, registering people as 'pictures... that leave footprints' (WB, 118). And Burroughs himself opposes notions of levitation founded on a naive realism, regards it as 'a fundamental confusion to think of mental force as exerting any influence or pressure on matter. If I saw this cup in front of me as no more real than what goes on in my mind, then I could move it, or at least I could move the *image* of it, but I would not be moving the *matter* of it. That's the contradiction. Science is always being hampered by idealized concepts like this' (P, 122). Just as Wittgenstein defines pain as a linguistically derived concept, Burroughs defines it as 'damage to the image — junk is concentrated image and this accounts for its pain killing action — Nor could there be pain if there was no image' (NE, 49). Visual images are verbally controlled and prerecorded: 'Color is trapped in word — image is trapped in word — Do you need words? ' (TE, 45). Control systems make use of the fact that 'Word evokes image' (S), that 'What you see is determined largely by what you hear' (ER, 41): the human body, for example, 'is an image on the screen talking' (TE, 178). Subjectivity is verbally determined, caught in a syntactic prison, 'a sentence words together in and out... trapped in the sentence with full stop' (TE, 12): the verbal habit is a terminal addiction, and 'Junk is colorless no-smell of death as punctuation' (TE, 176).

THE VERBAL VIRUS AND THE MASS MEDIA

Since reality cannot be projected beyond verbal arrangement, 'there is no true or real "reality" — "Reality" is simply a more or less constant scanning pattern — The scanning pattern we accept as "reality" has been imposed by the controlling power of this planet' (NE, 51-52). The 'reality con', or 'reality film', is the 'instrument and weapon of monopoly': 'there is no real thing — Maya — Maya — It's all show business' (TE, 151, 77). Like other viruses — and Burroughs insists that 'this is not an allegorical comparison' (J, 201) — the verbal virus is a code message, 'a very small particle... precisely associated in molecular chains' (NE, 40), unscrambled by the body or nervous system, parasitizing the host and reproducing and passing itself on to another host: 'Subvocal speech *is* the word organism' (TE, 160) which controls the thoughts of the human host; ' "Compulsive verbal patterns are actually word viruses that maintain themselves in the central nervous system by manipulation of the speech centers, throat muscles and vocal cords" ' (J, 228); 'Word begets image and image *is* virus' (NE, 48). The verbal virus establishes its image in the human larynx through 'simple binary coding systems' (NE, 48), language being a scanning pattern or 'unscrambling device, western languages tending to unscramble in either-or conflict terms' (J, 181, 184-188). That is, Burroughs extends von Steinplatz' theory that Virus B-23 accidentally made speech possible by postulating a 'white word virus', the digital language of western culture (J, 13-14), which has become particularly malignant in the electronic age of mass exposure.

Beginning in *Naked Lunch*, Burroughs exhibits an interest in the 'Mayan Codices' (NL, 233), which 'contain symbols representing all states of thought and feeling possible to human animals living under such limited circumstances' (SM, 95), and which constitute the preplanned liturgical cycle or 'control racket' whereby the priest caste completely regulated the other ninety-eight per cent of the population: ' "they know what everybody will see and hear and smell and taste and that's what thought is and these thought units are represented by symbols in their books and they rotate the symbols around and around on the calendar" ' (SM, 23). Using L. Ron Hubbard's notion of the Reactive Mind, an unconscious repository of 'propositions that have command value on the automatic level of behavior', Burroughs suggests how the Mayan priests were able to precisely control 'what the populace did, thought, and felt on any given day', and thus 'to predict the future or reconstruct the past with considerable accuracy since they could determine what conditioning would be or had been applied on any given date'. Just as Melville's Confidence Man solicits a due faith in what is above, 'all control systems claim to reflect the immutable laws of the universe'. Moreover, 'the modern ceremonial calendar' constituted by the mass media 'is almost as predictable' (ER, 80, 82), so that people like the mathematician Dunne dream about future incidents and read about them the next day: 'Point is he discovered that his dream *referred not to the event itself but to the account and photos in newspaper*' (S).

Just as Wittgenstein asserts that spatial arrangement can express the sense of proposition, Burroughs suggests that, through layout, emphasis, selection and advertisement (which is 'the precise manipulation of word and image'), the mass media establish 'lines of association' which, since 'all association tracks are obsessional', condition patterns of thought[11] (J, 176, 166; ER, 82): 'A *functioning* police state', for example, 'needs no police. Homosexuality does not occur to anyone as conceivable behaviour' (NL, 36). Thus the *Time-Life-Fortune* complex, 'one of the greatest word-and-image banks in the world', is a form of 'police organization' (WW, 163), programming those thoughts from which the subject cannot be abstracted: 'An unreal paper world yet completely real because it is actually happening' (J. 176). In *Naked Lunch*, a pusher makes contact by strolling around humming a tune which is picked up by those concerned as if 'it is their own mind humming the tune' (NL, 6), much as 'The whisperer' in *Dutch Schultz* disseminates opinions by speaking barely audibly, sometimes saying his messages backward or otherwise scrambling them, so that the townspeople assume them to be their own thoughts (LWDS, 80-85). The reader of a newspaper likewise receives a 'scrambled message uncritically and assumes that it reflects his own opinions independently arrived at' (J, 179). Daily newspapers are ' "largely responsible for the dreary events they describe" ,' (J, 221), issuing contradictory 'reactive' commands 'implicit in the layout and juxtaposition of items':

Stop. Go. Wait here. Go there. Come in. Stay out. Be a man. Be a woman. Be white. Be black. Live. Die. Be your real self. Be somebody else. Be a human animal. Be a superman. Yes. No. Rebel. Submit. RIGHT. WRONG. Make a splendid impression. Make an awful impression. Sit down. Stand up. Take your hat off. Put your hat on. Create. Destroy. Live now. Live in the future. Live in the past. Obey the law. Break the law. Be ambitious. Be modest. Accept. Reject. Plan ahead. Be spontaneous. Decide for yourself. Listen to others. TALK. SILENCE. Save money. Spend money. Speed up. Slow down. This way. That way. Right. Left. Present. Absent. Open. Closed. Entrance. Exit. IN. OUT. Etc., round the clock.
    This creates a vast pool of statistical newsmakers. It is precisely uncontrollable, automatic reactions that make news. (ER, 82-83)

Understanding is habitual, need not be conscious; but scrambled media messages work on the level of waking suggestion which, while it directly addresses the 'unconscious or reactive mind', is 'not to be confused with subliminal suggestion... below the level of conscious awareness', for it 'consists of sounds and images that are not consciously registered *since the subject's attention is elsewhere.* If his attention were directed toward the source he would be able to see or hear it immediately' (ER, 80; J, 171).
    The salutary project which Burroughs shares with Wittgenstein (and, though in no directly derivative way, with Ogden, Richards and Agee) involves the deployment of attention, activation of the agent who analyzes the semantic environment: 'So I am a Public Agent and don't know who I work for, get my instructions from street signs, newspapers and pieces of conversation I snap out of the air' (SM, 31). Agent K9 of the Biologic Police calls in the Technicians because

A Technician learns to think and write in association blocks which can then be manipulated according to the laws of association and juxtaposition. The basic law of association and conditioning is known to college students even in America: Any object, feeling, odor, word, image in juxtaposition with any other object, feeling, odor, word or image will be associated with it — Our technicians learn to read newspapers and magazines for juxtaposition statements rather than alleged content — We express these statements in Juxtaposition Formulae — The Formulae of course control populations of the world — Yes it is fairly easy to predict what people will think see and hear a thousand years from now if you write the Juxtaposition Formulae to be used in that period. (NE, 78)

In *Naked Lunch*, Lee is an agent for the 'Factualist' group, which is opposed to attempts to 'control, coerce, debase, exploit or annihilate the individuality of another living creature' (NL, 146, 167). Control is an addiction, and *'can never be a means to any practical end. . . It can never be a means to anything but more control. . . . Like junk* (164). *Naked Lunch*, like LUNPFM, is about being awake, and begins, 'I awoke from the sickness at age forty-five. . .' (v); in that and subsequent books, Burroughs addresses the problem of being *'there'*, in present time, attending to what can be noticed: as in *The Soft Machine*, 'Total alertness is your card' (SM, 40). But the control machine acts to keep 'word and referent as far separated as possible' (J, 206), so the lunch is only naked when the reader can 'see what is on the end of that long newspaper spoon' (NL, xii).

Peterson's reading of the quotation of Heiderberg in *Naked Lunch* misleads because it ignores the importance that Burroughs gives to seeing: 'In the words of Heiderberg: "This may not be the best of all possible universes but it may well prove to be one of the simplest". If man can *see*' (NL, xii-xiii). Seeing is neither 'mystical identification', nor even 'familiarity', but a counteraction of the bombardment of 'images from passing trucks and cars and televisions and newspapers' which 'makes a permanent haze in front of your eyes' (ER, 78); this 'grey veil' is finally verbal, 'the pre-recorded words of a control machine' (TE, 209), and seeing is *'decontrol* of opinion... being conditioned to *look* at the facts *before* formulating any verbal patterns' (J, 138). Verbalization is compulsive, silence unattainable: 'Try halting your subvocal speech. . . . You will encounter a resisting organism that *forces you to talk'* (TE, 149).

CUTUP: COLLAPSING THE CON

Of the imagined cures for the verbal virus, including a 'powerful variation' of apomorphine (NE, 40) and a deconditioning program which, like the control systems, works by 'punishment and reward' (ER, 83), the most practical is Gysin's cutup method, whereby the individual records, splices, plays back and thus co-opts the function of programming the environment, for 'recording devices fix the nature of absolute associations' (TE, 170). Burroughs deals extensively with the tape recorder's potential for manipulating a public scene, particularly for programming riots, and Allen Ginsberg reports his creating an uproar in the Convention Hall at Chicago, 1968, with a tape of riot sounds from Tangiers.[12] Burroughs repeatedly quotes Wittgenstein on how this works: 'any number can play Wittgenstein said no proposition can contain itself as an argument the only thing not prerecorded on a prerecorded set is the prerecording itself' (TE, 166, 215; J, 168). The death con is the splicing together of subvocal speech with body sounds, so that 'You are convinced by association that your body sounds will stop if sub-vocal speech stops and so it happens' (TE, 160). The agent splices his body sounds in with other arbitrary sounds, and with those of other bodies, thereby promoting an unprecedented sense of intimacy: *'Communication must become total and conscious before we can stop it'* (TE, 50-51). But cutup is chiefly a textual device, the cutting a page of text into pieces which are rearranged and read as such, which emphasizes the word's status as thing, unidentifiable with sense; Academy 23 teaches its students 'to stop words to see and touch words to move and use words as objects' (J, 91).

Burroughs' extensive use of cutup begins only with *Nova Express*, which cuts in Joyce, Shakespeare, Rimbaud and Conrad; and such later stories as 'The Frisco kid' (WB) incorporate cutups of their own texts. But the idea is formulated in *Naked Lunch*: 'The Word is divided into units which be all in one piece and should be so taken, but the pieces can be had in any order being tied up back and forth, in and out fore and aft like an inaresting sex arrangement. This book spill off the page in all directions, kaleidoscope of vistas, medley of tunes. . .' (NL, 229). This suggests the method of LUNPFM and its proposal for the treatment of a sheet of newsprint. Since cutup counteracts conventional association patterns, apomorphine is a form of cutup, for it 'cuts drug lines from the brain' (NE, 50). Showing the fly the way out of the fly bottle involves the inducement of silence, extending 'levels of experience by opening the door at the end of a long hall. . . . Doors that open in *Silence*. . . . *Naked Lunch* demands Silence from The Reader. Otherwise he is taking his own pulse' (NL, 224). Among the possible methods of achieving vocally silent communication — such as 'a Morse code of color flashes — or odors or music or tactile sensations' (S) — is the use of hieroglyphic and ideographic script rather than Western syllabic language, which separates words 'from objects or observable processes': whereas seeing a picture of a rose allows the subject to 'register the image in silence', to see the written word 'ROSE' is to be forced 'to repeat the word "ROSE" to yourself' (J, 103, 59). Syllabic writing also imposes a left-to-right reading pattern, for its meaning depends on word order (J, 205, 207): the Chinese ideograph, which can be read in many possible ways, is 'a script derived from hieroglyphs' (J, 199), and thus 'is already cut up' (WW, 157). The recognition of word as image implicit in cutup counteracts those 'follow-falsifications' of syllabic language which Academy 23 proposes to reform:

Ths IS of Identity. You are an animal. You are a body. Now whatever you may be you are not an 'animal', you are not a 'body', because these are verbal labels. The IS of identity always carries the implication of that and nothing else, and it also carries the assignment of permanent condition. To stay that way. All naming calling presupposes the IS of identity. This concept is unnecessary in a hieroglyphic language like ancient Egyptian and in fact frequently omitted. . . .
  The definite article THE. THE contains the implication of one and only: THE God, THE universe, THE right, THE wrong. If there is another, then THAT universe, THAT way is no longer THE universe, THE way. The definite article THE will be deleted and the indefinite article *A* will take its place.
  The whole concept of EITHER/OR. Right or wrong, physical or mental, true or false, the whole concept of OR will be deleted from the language and replaced by juxtaposition, by *and*. This is done to some extent in any pictorial language where the two concepts stand literally side by side. (J, 200)

Watch your language.

THE EMPIRICAL ATTITUDE

The insistence, as in Hobbes and Locke (though here derived from Alfred Korzybski) that 'the verb *to be* can easily be omitted from any language', and the related critique of 'the whole concept of a dualistic universe' (J, 200, 96), are aspects of a consistent empiricism: institutional prose places its 'thesis beyond the realm of fact since the words used refer to nothing that can be tested... have no referent' (J, 107). Burroughs promotes the 'scientific investigation' of sex and language (S; J, 59, 111-119) and experimental attempts to 'map' the brain and the orgasm (P, 52, 122); Agent K9 constructs '*a* physics of the human nervous system or more accurately the human nervous system defines the physics I have constructed' (NE, 79). Like Richards, Burroughs recognizes no 'disease' beyond symptoms: 'Eliminate the metabolic symptoms of anxiety and you eliminate anxiety' (ER, 83; P, 46). His model of memory and conditioning is 'compliments of Pavlov': the 'human body', he says, 'is transient hotel memory pictures' (TE, 179, 181); for him, as for Locke (Essay, II, i, 15), 'Memory is not a matter of effort' (J, 208). He locates 'what we call the ego, the I, or the You. . . somewhere in the midbrain' (J, 113), and employs the mechanistic language of the empiricists, describing the human body, which is memory, the susceptibility to habit, as the soft machine, 'the soft typewriter' on which the message of personal identity is written (TE, 160-161), and playback or conscious memory as the 'Cerebral phonograph' (TE, 146). Benway points out that ' "The study of thinking machines teaches us more about the brain than we can learn by introspective methods" ' (NL, 24); and Burroughs advocates the therapeutic use of the machine in order to become aware of one's own association patterns: 'You can find out more about your nervous system and gain more control over your reactions by using a tape recorder than you could find out sitting twenty years in the lotus posture' (TE, 163). In *Naked Lunch* Lee compares the mind to 'thinking machines', and describes thinking as a 'sorting' process (215). The Professor's plan to 'disconnect' his queen 'synapse by synapse' (84) anticipates the undoing of Hal in *2001*.

The word is defined as 'an array of calculating machines' (TE, 146) with the force of logical tautology, like the Burroughs Adding Machine: 'no matter how you jerk the handle result is always the same for given coordinates' (NL, xvi). Heroin use eventually results in 'backbrain depression and a state much like terminal schizophrenia: complete lack of affect, autism, virtual absence of cerebral event' (NL, 34), since the front brain 'acts only at second hand with back-brain stimulation, being a vicarious-type citizen'; so that just before taking a shot, having momentarily awakened without connecting with the 'hypothalamus, seat of libido and emotion' (230-231), the junky issues 'some flat, factual statement' (120) without affective connotation, is in a space between, a state resembling that of the deconditioned mind, which moves in a 'series of blank factual stops' (J, 191; WB, 102). This suggests an analysis of the emotive and descriptive aspects of language similar to that of Berkeley and Richards: cutting up a tape recording or a text, for example, alters sense but leaves voice tone unchanged and salient (J, 178); telepathic communication, 'simply a matter of giving your full attention' to nonverbal signs (P, 46), is the mode of interview practiced by a psychoanalyst who has come to realize that 'nothing can ever be accomplished on the verbal level' (NL, 88). Emotions are 'soft spots in the host' whereby the word virus invades and manipulates, so that the Lemur People, who are 'all affect... that is blending of beauty and flesh', live and die 'in captivity' (NE, 100-101, 118). A black militant who can respond without violent emotion to the image of a Southern sheriff is 'infinitely better equipped' to deal with the situation (ER, 84). Factual, descriptive statements are encoded upon, but not to be identified with, configurations of emotion and feeling: 'It is a feeling', says the deconditioned ghost of the Dead Child, 'by which I am here at all' (WB, 106). Deconditioning issues, not in emotionlessness, but in the ability 'to identify and control the sources of one's emotions' (P, 122). Burroughs expects cutup to lead to 'a precise science of words and show how certain word-combinations produce certain effects in the human nervous system' (ER, 59): like Agee, he anticipates a 'merging of art and science' (WW, 158).

MELVILLE, AGEE AND THE LONG WAIT

Burroughs shares a great deal with Melville and Agee. He regards tribal and national units as outgrowths of the family, and rejects their validity as modes of identity (J, 72, 83, 126), insists that 'the apparency of authority *is* authority' (J, 99), denies that good and evil exist in any 'absolute sense' (J, 75), derives all knowledge from experience — ' "You see I *know* Mrs. Murphy... experienced along these lines" ' (E, 5) — and repeatedly makes the point that

' "Frankly we don't pretend to understand – at least not completely" ': ' "Our knowledge. . . incomplete, of course" ' (NL, 187-
188). Like Melville, he rejects the 'unwholesome states of love and
oneness with the all' made available by LSD (J, 134). Like Agee
(CSP, 162), he is interested in photographic cutups of the human
face (J, 114), and in semiologically 'mapping a photo' (NE, 33),
attacks ' "the provincial egotism of earth peoples" ' (E, 166),
regards symmetry, which is linguistic, as disease, is careful to
separate metaphor from fact – '(Note: this is not a figure. . .)'
(NL, 46) – and rejects the Zola-inspired codes of naturalism of the
'social consciousness novels of the 1930's', the 'idea that the more
brutality, the more poverty, the more real it becomes, which I
don't think is necessarily true' (ER, 87); in *Naked Lunch* he ridicules the notion of exact realism in the figure of the 'intellectual
avant-gardist – "Of course the only writing worth considering now
is to be found in scientific reports and periodicals" ' (NL, 38).
Like Agee, he frequently compares subjectivity and the narrative
point of view to a camera – a self-reflexive camera in 'Tio Mate
smiles' (WB); and *The Last Words of Dutch Schultz* is *A Fiction
in the Form of a Film Script.*

One of Agee's most consistent themes is that of waiting: the
'dead time between' which is the setting of *The Morning Watch*
(116); the ' "waiting in the dark" ', which is the central event in
A Death in the Family (121) and parallels the unresolved cognitive
tensions of all the characters involved; in LUNPFM, he suggests
that the trapped subjective condition is one of 'prisoners. . .
constantly waiting' (392), and sets up a series of such situations
as the 'terror and patience of waiting' in the storm (399). Gudger's
saving rhythm against 'the fear of waiting' (390), Agee's waiting
before the darkened Gudger house, men waiting to begin
work (431), the intense mutual waiting of the animal callers and
their listeners, and the long description of the predawn landscape
as it awaits the crescendo of rooster crow, 'is stretched: stretched:
stretched: and waits. . .: waits' (85). To wait is to submit to the
tension of the unresolved, to endure an unpredictable, unstable
experience – in Burroughs' terms, to be 'there'. *Naked Lunch*
is also about waiting, the Kafkaesque weeks of 'waiting around'
in the office of the Assistant Arbiter of Explanations (22), the
junky waiting to make a connection (55, 56), or for his body to

indicate a usable vein (65), the wise guy deceiving a friend –
' No matter how long, Rube, wait for me right on that corner.
Goodbye, Rube. . .' (11) – and the rule of 'Delay' in the heroin
business (ix): 'A junky... runs on junk Time and when he makes
his importunate irruption into the Time of others, like all peti-
tioners, he must wait' (200). Waiting is experience of one of those
spaces between which concern Burroughs as well as Melville and
Agee, such as the 'languid grey area of hiatus' at the frontier of
Freeland (68), 'Interzone' (84), the 'cold interstellar space' into
which con men explode (10) and 'the sex that passes the censor,
squeezes through between bureaus, because there's always a space
between, in popular songs and Grade B movies. . .' (133); the
point of stepping away from the heroin habit is 'a nightmare
interlude of cellular panic, life suspended between two ways
of being' (57), experience without controlling context or myth:
again, 'Cure is always: *Let go! Jump!*' (222).

Burroughs is constantly attacking myths of love (TE, 43-49),
of nirvana, of death, of the ' "wise saviour" ' (P, 52), of the
Royal Family and the Pope, who 'keep the marks paralyzed with
grovel rays' (E, 100-111), of Darwinian mutation over long periods
of time (P, 122), of an unchangeable past (ER, 78), of a Marxist,
technological or science-fiction future (J, 67-68, 72, 79), of
'salvation' and 'final resolution' (ER, 79) and of history, for
'history is fiction' (NE, 13). The availability of 'attention' depends
upon a subject's ability 'to move out of his own frame of reference',
to put aside 'compulsive preoccupations' (ER, 79), to reject all
certainty which isn't logical – that is, tautological: ' "Pry yourself
loose and listen" ' (NE, 19). Belief has no necessary relation to
'facts' (NL, 250), but 'once a formula on this planet gets started,
gets firmly established, it's very hard to change or replace it'
(P, 122); like Melville and Agee, Burroughs suggests that 'it is
probably necessary to resort to physical violence' to destroy
unchangeable verbal 'premises' (ER, 86) – hence the importance
of the explosion, and the sense of the title, *Minutes to Go. The
Ticket that Exploded* is the human body, colorless sheets carrying
a coded message of conditioning; more particularly, it is the larynx,
'laughing sex words from throat gristle in bloody crystal blobs'
(TE, 43): 'Last man with such explosion of the throat crawling
inexorably from something he carried in his flesh' (SM, 40).
Explosions proliferate throughout the work, especially in *Naked*

Lunch, and frequently end stories and episodes. Explosion is cutup: when everything 'goes up in chunks', identity is disintegrated,
the tape fragmented and 'word dust' falls from 'demagnetized
patterns' (NE, 17, 24-25) — thus, throughout *The Soft Machine,
Nova Express*, and *The Ticket that Exploded*, the repeated refrain,
'Word falling — photo falling — time falling' (TE, 104), for these
are the elements of the 'whole structure of reality' (SM, 164).
The physiological explosion referred to in *Naked Lunch* as 'the
flash bulb of orgasm' (229) likewise detonates context and liber-
ates attention, so that characters are often able to see things at
the instant of orgasm which had not previously been visible.

MOTIVE AND INTENTION

Burroughs, like Melville and Agee, addresses the issues of motive
and intention. *Naked Lunch* begins with the heat closing in and
ends when the heat is off, a colloquialism which yields a pun in
Nova Express: the Crab Nebula observed in 1054 is the result of
a nova or exploding star, which Burroughs portrays as the result
of Nova criminals sucking 'all the charge and air and color' out of
a location and then moving across 'the wounded galaxies always
a few light years ahead of the Nova Heat' (NE, 69-70). When the
heat closes in, one moves: motive cannot be abstracted from circumstance, which involves one's own agency. And just as the
cops-and-fugitives game proceeds according to rules — 'I can hear
the way he would say it holding my outfit in his left hand, right
hand on his piece. . .' (NL, 1) — there is no explaining the motive
to opium addiction, an 'illness of exposure' (J, 144-145), for there
is no 'pre-addict personality'. In fact, junk itself 'is a personality':
'The question,"Why did you start using narcotics in the first place?"
should never be asked. It is quite as irrelevant to treatment as it
would be to ask a malarial patient why he went to a malarial
area' (J, 149-150, 153-154). Intention, or will power, is as irrelevant to the opium addiction of several million Persians (NL,
259) as to Western emotional conditioning (ER, 84). Addicts
'do not "want" to be cured, since it is precisely the centers of
"wanting" that have been taken over by the drug'; nor do they
kick out of 'will power, whatever that is' (J, 148, 152), but as a

result of a 'cellular decision',[13] a rejection on 'a deep biological level' (J, 150-151). Do such control agencies as the American Narcotics Department intentionally aggravate the drug problem? 'Whether an agent acts deliberately or not is about as interesting as how many angels can dance on the point of a pin' (J, 146).

Motive and intention are myths manipulated by control agencies, as the American tourist is conned into a confident appraisal of his motives in 'Tio Mate smiles' (WB, 8), and young Dutch Schultz is convicted of ' "loitering with intent" ' (LWDS, 14). Cutup removes motive and intention − story and author − from a text: asked how he created the characters in *Naked Lunch*, Burroughs responded, 'Excuse me, there is no accurate description of the creation of a book, or an event' (WW, 160). Like the Ancient Mariner, *Naked Lunch* is attended to by 'those who cannot choose but hear' (87), and notions of authorial intention are treated satirically: 'Gentle reader, I fain would spare you this, but my pen hath its will. . .' (40). Intention is encoded upon the text as it is upon the writer's other gestures: '*I am never here*. . . Never that is *fully* in possession, but somehow in a position to forestall ill-advised moves. . . . Patrolling is, in fact, my principle [sic] occupation' (221). Like LUNPFM, *Naked Lunch* is a conceptual map of intention, 'a blueprint, a How-To-Book. . . Abstract concepts, bare as algebra, narrow down to a black turd or a pair of aging cajones' (224). That intention does not necessarily lead anywhere is suggested by the final statement of the narrative section: ' "Your plan was unworkable then and useless now. . . . Like DaVinci's flying machine plans" ' (217). *Naked Lunch* consists of 'many prefaces' which are unrelated to what follows, 'atrophy and amputate spontaneous' (224), and ends, like LUNPFM, with a statement of intention in the form of an 'Atrophied preface' (218).

While Burroughs employs the language of causality − unconsciously understood speech, for example, can 'cause an effect' (J, 181) − and approves Hubbard's definition of communication as 'cause, distance, effect, with intention, attention and duplication' (J, 206), he is pointedly tentative with it, speaks of concrete floors as 'a usual corrollary of abrupt withdrawal' (NL, 251), of alpha brain waves as 'correlated with a relaxed state' (ER, 83): 'If we can infer purpose from behavior. . .' (J, 202). And Benway sums up the inexplicable phenomenon of conditioning, ' "that's the way it is with the etiology" ' (NL, 36). The word virus is a metabolic disturbance, and ' "causal thinking never yields accurate description of metabolic process — limitations of existing language" ' (NL, 26); as Wittgenstein puts it, 'what the law of causality is meant to exclude cannot even be described' (TLP, 6.362). The 'incompetent' agent piloting the 'machine' of the human body (J, 115) cannot be spoken about, for metaphysical notions are meaningless in Burroughs' writing:

> The razor belonged to a man named Occam and he was not a scar collector. Ludwig Wittgenstein *Tractatus Logico-Philosophicus:* 'If a proposition is NOT NECESSARY it is MEANINGLESS and approaching MEANING ZERO'. 'And what is More UNNECESSARY than junk if You Don't Need it?' *Answer:* 'Junkies, if you are not ON JUNK'. (NL, xiv)

Commitment to necessity is addiction to a sequence which is merely logical, '*The Algebra of Need*' (NL, vii), a metabolic conditioning which is manipulated by control groups: 'the needs of our constituents are never out of our mind being their place of residence' (119). And the word virus is as redundant as the heroin virus: 'Wind up is you don't have to think anything' (J, 40).

THE MYTH OF TIME

Connected with the critique of necessity, and equally derived from Wittgenstein, is the rejection of continuous time, a myth which, like heroin, is a way of resisting change: old Opium smokers, in fact, die 'from an, overdose of Time' (NL, 6, 208). The addict's 'body is his clock, and junk runs through it like an hour-glass' (215), keeping him in 'a painless, sexless, timeless state' (249), so that he doesn't have to 'move around and waste TIME' (xiv). The Sailor has moved on from heroin and is ' "buying up TIME" ' (73). Time is a media control device: 'the Lord of Time is surrounded by files and calculating machines, word and image banks of a picture planet' (TE, 104). Time is a con laid down by The Rube of the Nova Mob: 'I am not one in space I am one in time. . . . So of course I tried to keep you all out of space — That is the end of time' (NE, 71). Whereas the myth of continuous time connects man with that ' "original nature which imposes itself on any human solution" ' — the killer instinct of the ' "aggressive southern ape" ' with the survival-of-the-fittest attitude of American expansionists (E, 103, 109), Burroughs cites evidence for a theory of sudden mutation (P, 122), and ruptures his narratives with 'perhaps something as simple as a hiccup of time. Empty room justlikethat' (WB, 136). According to Wittgenstein,

We cannot compare a process with 'the passage of time' — there is no such thing — but only with another process (such as the working of a chronometer).
　Hence we can describe the lapse of time only be relying on some other process. (TLP, 6.3611)

Like Wittgenstein, Burroughs deals with short, not necessarily related time spans, and regards time as verbal: 'Without words there is not time' (WB, 117). Since ' "time is getting dressed and undressed eating sleeping not the actions but the *words*... what we *say* about what we do" ', there would be no ' "time if we didn't say anything" ' (TE. 114). Joe Brundige travels in time 'with old newspapers folding in today with yesterday and typing out composites — When you skip through a newspaper as most of us do you see a great deal more than you know — In fact you see it all on a subliminal level — Now when I fold today's paper in with yesterday's paper and arrange the pictures to form a time section montage, I am literally moving back to the time when I read yesterday's paper, that is travelling in time back to yesterday' (SM, 85-86). Burroughs uses the notion of time travel, the without which not of all science fiction since Verne, self-reflexively, as a critique of the myth of time: ' "All out of time and into space. Come out of the time-word 'the' forever. Come out of the body word 'thee' forever. There is nothing to fear. . . . There is no word in space" ' (SM, 162). He regards the American space program and space travel as significant of the possibility of leaving 'the context of this planet' and its reinforcement of conditioning, of attaining 'an entirely different viewpoint' (P, 52), though he is impatient with the attitudes of the Houston scientists: 'Are these men going to take the step into regions literally unthinkable in verbal terms? To travel in space you must leave the old verbal garbage behind: God talk, country talk, mother talk, love talk, party talk. You must learn to exist with no religion no country no allies. You must learn to live alone in silence. Anyone who prays in space is not there' (J, 21).
　Intergalactic space, which does not conform to the Euclidian

geometry which Kant took to be an innate form of perception, is not amenable to habitual verbal contexts. The experience of space cannot be held together by the notion of a three-dimensional reality — which is time, the comparison and identification of temporally discrete points of view. 'Space *is* dream. Space *is* illusion' (J, 223). Whereas identification with the cumulative record or 'time track' which constitutes self is *ipso facto* a contraction of ' "terminal identity" ' (NE, 19), the General in *The Ticket that Exploded* advises his men, ' "It is time to forget. To forget time. . . . That point where the past touches the future is right where you are sitting now on your dead time ass hatching virus negatives into present time into the picture reality of a picture planet. Get off your ass, boys' (TE, 196). To be present is not to identify with the present but to attend to it, to be aware of the arbitrary nature of its connection with past and future: 'listen to your present time tapes and you will begin to see who you are' (J, 167). The old tycoon's obsession with immortality (WB, 168) exemplifies that uncritical acceptance of the metaphysical implications of language which Wittgenstein is concerned to combat; 'Or is some riddle solved by my surviving forever? ' (TLP, 6.4312):

If we take eternity to mean not infinite temporal duration but timelessness, then eternal life belongs to those who live in the present.
   Our life has no end in just the way in which our visual field has no limit. (TLP, 6.4311)

The present, for Wittgenstein, is spatial and infinite: 'A spatial object must be situated in infinite space. (A spatial point is an argument place.)' (TLP, 2.0131). Gysin connects this idea with Burroughs' use of space: 'It's EVERYBODY'S space and there is plenty of it. A point in space is an argument place says Wittgenstein. "No two anythings can occupy the same space-time position", mutters Burroughs. . . . Who says time? ' (MG, 45).

THE EMPIRICAL TEXT

Like *Moby-Dick* and LUNPFM, then, *Naked Lunch* is a text without a context, a report on the rules of a particular form of life which is finally its own subject. It is introduced by an affidavit — 'Deposition: testimony concerning a sickness' — and ends with an appended exhaustive listing of drugs and their characteristics, also published in *The British Journal of Addiction*. Like Ishmael on whales and Agee on tenant farming, Burroughs takes great care with definition, pointing out misuses of the term 'addiction' and restricting it to the description of biological, metabolic need (NL, 240-241): 'Because there are many forms of addiction I think that they all obey basic laws' (xii). He devotes considerable attention to the argots incorporated in the text — ' "Ever notice how many expressions carry over from queers to con men? " ' (3) — and parenthetically glosses twenty-nine terms '(Cowboy: New York hoodlum talk means kill the mother fucker wherever you find him. . .)' (20). Meaning is use in a context — ' "In the immortal words of Father Flanagan there is no such thing as a bad boy" ' (152) — and insistence upon precise verbal reference yields disturbing results, as when a young man pays a prostitute for ' "a piece of ass. . . So I switch my blade and cut a big hunk off her ass, she raise a beef like I am reduce to pull off one shoe and beat her brains out. Then I hump her for kicks" ' (119). Burroughs emphasizes that he does 'not presume to pass any final judgements, only to report my own reaction to various drugs and methods of treatment' (224), and pointedly restricts himself to that experience throughout: 'The author has observed. . .' (77); 'I saw it happen . . .' (233); 'My own experiences suggests. . .' or 'confirms. . .' (243, 247). And like *Moby-Dick* and LUNPFM, *Naked Lunch* is part travelogue, reporting on Ecuador, Sweden, Tangier and various American cities, and particularly on 'U.S. drag', the accumulation of American 'habits', which can be traced to no source:

But where does it come from?
    Not the bartender, not the customer, nor the cream-colored plastic surrounding the bar stools, nor the dim neon. Not even the T.V. (11-13)

These three peculiar books, which analyze forms of life and are pointedly not novels, might conveniently be considered as examples of the form, Menippean satire or anatomy, proposed by Frye, a form which 'deals less with people as such than with mental attitudes', 'presents us with a vision of the world in terms of a single intellectual pattern', is encyclopoedic and provides a 'creative treatment of exhaustive erudition'; Frye regards *Moby-Dick* as a combination of the romance and anatomy forms,[14] and it might be pointed out that both Agee and Burroughs invoke Swift as a model for their satiric savagery. But in making explicit use of the intellectual pattern or analytic mode of empiricism, these books are further distinguished by becoming reports on themselves, empirical inquiries into the nature of texts. In the Introduction, in the Atrophied Preface and throughout *Naked Lunch*, Burroughs, like Ishmael and Agee, discusses the method of the text; he not only regards everything in the empirical environment in terms of codes, providing a lengthy, Agee-style list from 'Breathing rhythm of old cardiac, bumps of a belly dancer, put put put of a motorboat' to 'cancer. :. at the door with a singing telegram' (207-209), but speaks of the text as a code, capitalizing phrases such as 'The Reader' which suggests roles in a predictable ritual, and attacking literary clichés (9-10).

Ginsberg describes *Naked Lunch* as 'a collage of routines'.[15] It focuses on the 'mosaic' of flotsam in the East River (4, 75-76), of 'sleepless nights and sudden food needs of the kicking addict' (8), of a city layout (53), of articles in a drawer (116), and of Aztec art (117); and it refers to itself as a composition of 'pieces', a 'kaleidoscope' (229). Shifts are sudden, as when, using Soneryl, 'You shift to sleep without transition, fall abruptly into the middle of a dream. . . . I have been years in a prison camp suffering from malnutrition' (67), announced by a filmic 'Fadeout' (104, 112) or 'Time jump like a broken typewriter' (94): and if the overall sense of the text is undercut, so is the identity of the first-person narrator, who reports as he reads the paper, 'I keep slipping away. . . . I try to focus the words... they separate in meaningless mosaic' (68).

Heroin clicks the user into 'junk focus' (204), and textual forms are evidence of addiction to habits of configuration: plot, for example, is 'continuity, beginning, middle, and end, adherence to a "logical" sequence and people don't think in logical sequences' (ER, 78). Self is a narrative device, a collection of words and images into logical sequence, as examples throughout the work suggest: 'Those pictures *are* yourself' (SM, 40); 'Remember I was the movies. . . . in the beginning there was no I am' (TE, 102); 'Who do you love? — If I had a talking picture of you would I need you? ' (S). In *Naked Lunch* a man has an affair with his 'Latah', a creature which precisely imitates all the words, gestures and mannerisms of anyone in its presence, and 'simply sucks all the persona right out of him like a sinister ventriloquist's dummy. . . . "You've taught me everything you are . . . . I need a new amigo". And poor Bubu can't answer for himself, having no self left' (141). The mythless, unidentifiable condition of attention is illustrated by the predicament of Marty (as in LUNPFM, just say he's from Mars and let it go at that), a space man, not a time man, who has been '*borned*' here as a human, and whose plans to leave are hampered by a policeman who dislikes in him ' "a certain furtiveness of person and motive after all where was he escaping to? *Who* was he escaping to? . . . Who was he? Could it be that he didn't need *friends*? " ' (E, 140). The story ('Friends') elaborates the question posed in *Naked Lunch*: ' "Where do they go when they walk out and leave the body behind? " ' (11).

The text encodes and prerecords the movement of attention, keeps 'I-you-me in the pissoir of present time' (SM, 126). The exercises outlined by Burroughs to pry attention loose from modes of identity, to direct the subject to '*as-is*' rather than ignore or '*not-is*' a problem (ER, 84), to be '*there*' during mundane activities (J, 108), to be '*on set*' in present time (E, 165), are critiques of habitual modes of reading, of understanding. Similarly, the method of paratactic discontinuity in *Naked Lunch* scrambles the memory tape of the narrator and mobilizes his liberated attention:

suddenly I don't know where I am. Perhaps I have opened the wrong door and at any moment The Man In Possession, The Owner Who Got There First will rush in and scream:
'*What Are You Doing Here? Who Are You?*'
And I don't know what I am doing there nor who I am. I decide to play it cool and maybe I will get the orientation before the Owner shows....So instead of yelling 'Where Am I?' cool it and look around and you will find out approximately . . . . You were not there for *The Beginning*. You will not be there for *The End* . . . . Your knowledge of what is going on can only be superficial and relative. (NL, 220)

The text is a memory track subject to lesions; if understanding is knowing how to proceed, then disruption of the memory track obviates understanding, directs the reader to a consideration of its nature. Benway exhibits patients suffering from Irreversible Neural Damage, who retain ' "reflexes" ' but are otherwise not present: ' "Over-liberated, you might say" ' (32). To be there is not to control but to witness. Like Lee ('Last night I woke up with someone squeezing my hand. It was my other hand' [66]), like The Professor, ' "rudely interrupted by one of my multiple personalities" ' (87) and like ' "the man who taught his asshole to talk" ' and had to struggle with another personality in the same flesh (131-132), *Naked Lunch* encodes a mosaic of intersecting personae, The Sailor repeating Lee's phrase in his own narration: 'Junkies tend to run together into one body' (219). Call me Ishmael.

The text is a form of addiction which is continually undercut and used against itself, so that one extended sexual fantasy is followed by a curtain call in which the actors are 'not as young as they appear in the Blue Movies. . . . They look tired and petulant' (103). It is a 'mind tape' that can be 'wiped clean – Magnetic word dust falling from old patterns' (NE, 168), a blueprint which is perhaps 'Craps last map' (E, 168). Most frequently, the text is compared to a film, as in *The Wild Boys* – 'On the screen an old book with gilt edges. Written in golden script *The Wild Boys*. A cold spring wind ruffles the pages' (WB, 184) – so that stories end with the camera being shot, the camera man joining the gun fight, or with the explosion of the screen (WB, 18, 184). The text is thereby assigned that 'instant present' which, Agee says, is the 'tense' of film (AF, I, 321-322), just as, like Ishmael, Burroughs' narrators date the text – ' "July 1962, Present Time" ' (TE, 100, 172) – indicating the intersection of the reader's present time with that of the persona, the spatial accomplishment of time travel. The reader comes out of time and into space by destroying the memory tape which, in present time, is his own mode of identity: 'Rub out the word' (TE, 169); 'Rub out the life I led' (TE, 177); 'Language of virus (which is these experiments) really necessary?' (TE, 100). This is one way in which language is made to report on itself in *Naked Lunch*, to disintegrate habits of narcissistic self-attachment, and to make a voyeur of the reporter.

NOTES

1. William Burroughs, *Nova Express*. New York, Grove, 1965: 37-38. Subsequent references are noted in the text (NE).
2. William Burroughs, 'Words dealth by William Lee Dealer', in *Minutes to Go*. San Francisco, City Lights, 1968: 59. Subsequent references are noted in the text (MG).

3. Norman Mailer, 'Aquarius hustling', interview by Richard Stratton, *Rolling Stone* 177, January 1975: 46.

4. William Burroughs, *The Ticket that Exploded*. New York, Grove, 1968: 85. Subsequent references are noted in the text (TE).

5. William Burroughs, *The Wild Boys: A Book of the Dead*. New York, Grove, 1973: 94. Subsequent references are noted in the text (WB).

6. William Burroughs, *The Last Words of Dutch Schultz: A Fiction in the Form of a Film Script*. New York, Viking, 1975: 57, 115. Subsequent references are noted in the text (LWDS).

7. William Burroughs, 'Penthouse interview: William Burroughs', *Penthouse* III, March 1972: 52. Subsequent references are noted in the text (P).

8. William Burroughs, 'Journey through time-space: An interview with William Burroughs by Daniel Odier', *Evergreen Review* XIII, June 1969: 85. Subsequent references are noted in the text (ER).

9. William Burroughs, *Sidetripping*, with Charles Gatewood. New York, Strawberry Hill, 1975. Subsequent references are noted in the text (S).

10. R.G. Peterson, 'A picture Is a fact: Wittgenstein and *The Naked Lunch*', *Twentieth Century Literature* XII, July 1966: 80.

11. William Burroughs, 'William Burroughs', interview in *Writers at Work: The Paris Review Interviews*. New York, Viking, 1967: 167. Subsequent references are noted in the text (WW).

12. Allen Ginsberg, 'John Tytell: A conversation with Allen Ginsberg', *Partisan Review* XLI (2) 1974: 261.

13. William Burroughs, *Junkie*. London: New English Library, 1972: 152.

14. Northrop Frye, *Anatomy of Criticism: Four Essays*. Princeton University Press, 1971: 304-313.

15. Allen Ginsberg, with Burroughs, *The Yage Letters*. San Francisco, City Lights, 1969: 60.

7

Opening the Private Eye:
Wittgenstein and Godard's *Alphaville*

> The definite attraction which cinematographic
> creation exercises upon many new novelists must
> be sought elsewhere. It is not the camera's objec-
> tivity which interests them, but its possibilities in
> the realm of the subjective, of the imaginary. They
> do not conceive the cinema as a means of expression,
> but of exploration, and what most captures their
> attention is, quite naturally, what has most escaped
> the powers of literature: which is not so much the
> image as the sound track — the sound of voices,
> noises, atmospheres, music — and above all the
> possibility of acting on two senses at once, the
> eye and the ear; finally, in the image as in the sound,
> the possibility of presenting with all the appearance
> of incontestable objectivity what is, also, only dream
> or memory — in a word, what is only imagination.
>
> Alain Robbe-Grillet
> *For A New Novel*

As the camera moves closer to a cup of coffee being stirred in a
Paris restaurant, the screen becomes completely black except for
swirling shapes which dissolve, re-form and dissolve again, as
Jean-Luc Godard whispers,

Where does it begin?. . . Where does what begin? God created the heavens
and the earth. Of course. . . but that's a bit simple, too easy. One should be
able to say more. . . Say that the limits of my language are those of my world.
That as I speak, I limit the world, I end it. . . and when logical and mysterious
death comes to abolish this limit. . . and there will be no more questions, no
more answers. . . everything will be amorphous.

The identification of 'the limits of my language' with 'those of my world' is one of several allusions to Wittgenstein's *Tractatus Logico-Philosophicus* in this film, *Two or Three Things I Know About Her* (1966), in which the heroine defines language to her son as 'the house in which a man lives', speaks of 'the ABC of existence' and repeatedly declares: 'I am the world'. The *Her* about whom two or three things are known is both a woman in particular socioeconomic circumstances, and the city of Paris; and the subject of the film, that which we are invited to become aware of, is not those two or three items, but how, through the cinematic medium, they are known. Paris is also the subject of Lemmy Caution's wrist-radio reports in the original treatment of *Alphaville, or A Strange Adventure of Lemmy Caution* (1965), which is exemplary of the Wittgenstein-derived epistemology that informs Godard's films, and which considers almost exclusively, in fact, the question of how things are known.

Film, for Godard, is report and analysis, the truth twenty-four times per second; and it is literally, not metaphorically, linguistic. Beginning with his attention to signs, billboards and advertising slogans in *Une Femme Mariée* (1964), and continuing through the political analyses in *La Chinoise* (1967) and *One Plus One* (1968), Godard has directed critical attention to the contemporary environment of word and image; in *La Chinoise*, for example, Véronique rejects the idea that a revolutionary should burn all books, since there would then 'be nothing left to criticize'. Like Agee and Burroughs, Godard wants to come to terms with the modern American dominated culture machine, more specifically with the languages of film, the Hollywood B-picture vocabulary of plots and attitudes of which several of Godard's early films make use, and which are those forms of thought which limit the world, impose upon the understanding. 'At the cinema', Godard once said, 'we do not think, we are thought'.[1] In fact, he regards film, just as Burroughs regards language, as disease, 'the virus, the capitalist microbe in its present form',[2] and, like Burroughs, recommends the setting up of de-intellectualization schools to combat conditioned mental habits.[3] Language, for Godard, has always the status of an arbitrary habit or skill, and even *Tout Va Bien* (1972), with its heavily didactic political tone, can only conclude with the advice to 'rethink yourself in historical terms', terms which may provide a strenuous and renewing mode of analysis but which have no ultimate or necessary purchase: 'With the probable exception of his view on Vietnam', Susan Sontag has written, 'there is no attitude Godard incorporates in his films that is not simultaneously being bracketed, and therefore criticized, by a dramatization of the gap between the elegance and seductiveness of ideas and the... opaqueness of the human condition'.[4]

The printed definition, in *La Chinoise*, of 'a word' as 'what remains unsaid', suggests Wittgenstein's distinction between the 'content' of sense and that 'form' or arrangement of appearances upon which it is encoded. The camera that filmed itself in the mirror would make the ultimate movie, would record the mechanics of its own recording, supply all information about itself without giving expression to the 'content' of the record, the collation of distinct frames, the understanding of the sense of the film. Moreover, affectless observation and record of what goes on in the mirror is voyeuristic rather than narcissistic, for it presumes no possibility of consummate identity with the image: Godard made *Le Petit Soldat*, he says, about 'a man who finds that the face he sees in the mirror does not correspond to the idea he has of what lies behind it', 'who analyses himself and discovers he is different from the concept he had of himself. Personally, when I look at myself in a mirror I have the same feeling'.[5]

Made in U.S.A. dramatizes the problem of identity in terms of language: a dictaphone recording of Paula's voice on the soundtrack says, as she shoots Goodis, 'Where am I? Is it I who am speaking? Can I say that I am these words I speak, through which my thoughts slide? Can I say that I am these murders I have committed with my own hands, actions which escape from me not only when I have finished, but before I have even started?' Is Ahab, Ahab? Is it I, God, or who that lifts this arm? Because, as Wittgenstein says, 'Language disguises thought... so, that from the outward form of the clothing it is impossible to infer the form of the thought beneath it', it is as impossible to identify Paula with her physiological equipment − 'Can I say that I am this life which I feel within me'? − as with the tape recorder which speaks her words. Godard's idea of filming the camera as it films is related to his declared wish to 'show − just show, not comment on − the moment when a feeling enters the body and becomes physiologically alive'[6]: meaning is encoded upon physiology −

feelings, laryngeal formations — as upon the mechanical operation of a camera; it is remarked in *Une Femme Mariée*, in fact, that 'memory is the first thing we teach a machine'. The young intellectuals in *La Chinoise*, who demonstrate their rejection of dualism by striking the word 'DESCARTES' with a suction arrow, recommend the confusion of words and things as a revolutionary activity; similarly, Godard edits his films 'on the basis of what's in the image and on that basis only... not in terms of what it signifies, but what signifies it'.[7] By holding to the image and to the shape of the word, he obviates any transcendence of, or, which is the same, identification with the empirically apparent.

Like Paula, we cannot regard speech, or rather the sense which it encodes, as an effect springing from an 'inner' identifiable cause. Godard's remark that *Pierrot Le Fou* (1965) 'is not really a film' but 'an attempt at cinema' illustrates this lack of necessary relation between intention and act or realization: the film is less misleadingly considered as a blueprint, for like LUNPFM and *Naked Lunch*, it is the record of an unfulfilled intention. In the same article on *Pierrot*, Godard quotes Claudel's statement that ' "This morrow does not follow the day that was yesterday" ', and explicates, 'This... sentence in movie terms means: two shots in sequence are not successive. Which holds for two that aren't in sequence'.[8] Godard uses montage, not as Eisenstein, to produce something greater than the sum of its parts, but to make two shots strip each other of irrelevant connections, and thus criticizes syntactic habits and causal thinking. The myth of continuous time and the causal nexus, which Wittgenstein characterizes as superstition, offers the possibility of an account of motive, which in Godard's films, as Sontag points out, is either simplistic or unexplained: 'An art which aims at the present tense cannot aspire to this kind of "depth" or innerness in the portrayal of human beings'; asked by Georges Franju whether he acknowledged ' "the necessity of having a beginning, middle and end in your films" ', Godard is said to have replied, ' "Certainly. But not necessarily in that order" '.[9]

If for beginning, middle and end can be substituted past, present and future, it is precisely this scrambling that is carried out in *Alphaville* (again, one thinks of Burroughs' cutup method of writing, a comparable antidote to paralysis of the understanding). The film begins as the computer Alpha 60 issues the self-interrogative statement, 'Some things in life are too complex for oral transmission. But legend gives them universal form'. Originally entitled *Tarzan versus IBM*, *Alphaville* proceeds as the mutual criticism of legends or myths, a confrontation between past and future. Lemmy Caution, the hero of a French series of detective novels, is rendered as a compendium of individualist myths, and is played by Eddie Constantine, an expatriate American veteran of French detective films; like the 'American trailing across the wounded galaxies' in *Nova Express*, Lemmy has crossed 'intersidereal space' in his Ford Galaxie to reach Alphaville, the totally programmed environment of the future, heralded by the traffic sign, 'ALPHAVILLE. SILENCE. LOGIC. SAFETY. PRUDENCE'. He wears a wrist radio like Dick Tracy's and behaves as a conventional tough guy, insulting and fighting with and finally shooting his hotel's procurer: 'I'm too old to sit around discussing the weather. I shoot. It's the only weapon I have against fate'. Lemmy loves 'women and money' more than anything else and is 'afraid of death... but for a humble secret agent fear of death is a cliché ... like drinking'. Natasha, daughter of Professor Nosferatu, alias von Braun, and thus a product of this future, knows no such fear, has been taught by Alpha 60 that 'death and life exist within the same sphere'.

Lemmy has, the computer points out, a 'tendency to dwell in the past', to 'think far too much of what has happened, instead of what is to become'; when an engineer mocks his old-fashioned camera, Lemmy sneers, 'Technology — keep it!' And his susceptibility to past formula is dramatized when, surrounded by the police, he is told joke number 842 and seized when he doubles up predictably with laughter. Lemmy's behavior, that is, is as programmed as that of the citizens of Alphaville: having instructed his Seductress Third Class to hold a centerfold nude over her head, he lounges on the bed reading *The Big Sleep*, a novel about the smashing of a pornography ring, and shoots two holes through the breasts of the pinup; and when Lemmy comments on Natasha's 'small pointed teeth', he is echoing Philip Marlowe, who repeatedly, in that book, notices Carmen Sternwood's 'little sharp predatory teeth' and the knife-like teeth of Vivian Regan.[10] Not only does Lemmy narrate his adventure in the first person as Marlowe does, but he is also associated with the array of tough-guy figures played on the screen by Humphrey Bogart: as he ignites his lighter with a shot from across the room, Anna Karina makes her entrance, like Lauren Bacall in *To Have and Have Not*, with the line, 'Anybody got a match? ' Lemmy is Secret Agent Number 003 whose mission is to gather information on Alphaville and to 'liquidate' von Braun, and travels as Ivan Johnson, reporter for Figaro-Pravda: 'Haven't you noticed', he says to von Braun's assistant, 'that Reporter and Revenger start with the same letter? ' Like Agee, and like many of Burroughs' characters, he is a spy travelling as a journalist, and as such is both an importunate investigator, asking, 'too many questions' and at one point forcing von Braun into an elevator to interview him, and a rampant voyeur, photographing von Braun's outraged staff, the hidden center of Alpha 60 and anything else that interests him. As Harry Dickson, an agent who has been broken by Alpha 60's control system, enjoys his last dalliance with a Seductress Third Class, Lemmy watches from behind a wardrobe and photographs the scene; and when the old man dies in orgasm, Lemmy photographs the body.

Godard's original treatment calls for Lemmy's reports on his wrist radio 'to compile a documentary on the town and its inhabitants', 'true documentary images of present-day life' in Paris, altered by 'a novel, rather strange, mysterious quality'.[11] Three years prior to the making of *Alphaville*, Godard told an interviewer, 'According to Truffaut, the cinema consists of the spectacle... and research. If I analyze myself today I see that I have always wanted, basically, to make a research film in spectacle form. The documentary side is this: a man is in such and such a situation. The spectacle side comes from making the man a gangster or a secret agent'.[12] There could be no more succinct summary of each of *Moby-Dick*, LUNPFM and *Naked Lunch* than as research plus spectacle. In this sense, all of Godard's films are reports: *Alphaville*, self-reflexively, is about a reporter. Like Burroughs, Godard puns on the phrase, *'agent secret'*, which suggests an active critical attention which cannot be spoken about or identified with the logical forms and habits of thought. Of course, the philosophical Pragmatists and Behaviorists assume the contrary, and Lemmy's subjectivism is regarded by von Braun as an anachronism: 'Your ideas are strange, Mr. Caution. Several years ago, in the Age of Ideas, they would doubtless have been termed... sublime. But look at yourself — men of your kind will soon no longer exist'. The presence of conscious attention, which distinguishes Lemmy from a computer, and to which he refers when he boasts to Alpha 60 of his 'secret', can be defined only negatively, or, as Lemmy defines it, with a riddle: 'Something that never changes with the night or the day, as long as the past represents the future, toward which it advances in a straight line, but finally closes on itself in a circle'. For Alpha 60 to find the answer to the riddle would mean its self-destruction, 'because you would become my equal, my brother' — the throwing away of Wittgenstein's propositional ladder. According to Godard, 'To look around one's self, that is to be free'[13] : when Lemmy insists that he is a 'free man', the Chief Engineer comments, 'This reply is meaningless. We know nothing... We record... we calculate... and we draw conclusions... Your replies are difficult to code and sometimes impossible'.

Lemmy finds Dickson in a shabby hotel where the clients loiter in the lobby reading detective novels — individuals who have been occluded, like Lee in *Naked Lunch*, from the logical system of Alphaville, and who await execution or suicide. Not only, Dickson reports, are Dick Tracy and Flash Gordon dead, but there are no more novelists, musicians or painters. In bed with his Seductress, Dickson speaks the illegal language of romantic love, and his last words are 'conscience... conscience... make Alpha 60 destroy itself... tenderness... save those who weep'. Weeping, too, is illegal; and the last words of a man who is executed for weeping at his wife's death, and thus for 'behaving illogically', are of love, faith and tenderness, things which cannot be codified and of which the citizens of Alphaville are ignorant. Like the artists of the past with whom he is associated, Lemmy speaks for what cannot be spoken about: when he tries to define 'love' ostensively to Natasha, she understands only the 'sensuality' which is its form. When someone says 'something metaphysical', according to Wittgenstein, it is demonstrable that he has 'failed to give a meaning to certain signs in his propositions' (TLP, 6.53; the pun is unavoidable):

Propositions can express nothing that is higher.
It is clear that ethics cannot be put into words.
Ethics is transcendental.
(Ethics and aesthetics are one and the same.) (TLP, 6.42, 6.421)

But if the metaphysical cannot be described, or embodied in the clichéed deportment of the individualist hero, neither can it be negated or reduced to the unambiguously logical. When Natasha defends Alphaville's total commitment to rational structure by remarking, 'we minimize the unknown', Lemmy renames the city 'Zeroville'; and he sneers at von Braun's opposition of 'my moral and even metaphysical sense of destiny with nothing more than a physical and mental existence created and dictated by technocracy'. The mythic totalitarian behavioristic future utterly crushes the independence which Lemmy so grandly overdramatizes: Alpha 60 dwarfs the individual intelligence by formulating problems for itself — train and plane timetables, electric power supply, war — which 'no one can understand because the methods and data used by Alpha 60 are too complex', Like Burroughs' control machine, it 'predicts the data which Alphaville obeys', and eloquently defends those more familiar forms of control which it represents: 'Nor is there in the so-called capitalist world, or Communist world, any malicious intent to suppress men through the power of ideology or materialism, but only the natural aim of all organizations to increase their rational structure'. Alphaville is the result of continuous growth in time, that evolutionary development to which Wittgenstein assigns the dubious validity of any other hypothesis in natural science, the logical movement from past, through present to future, which is the basis of the antisubjectivist myths of progress: all of Alpha 60's decisions are directed, it assures Lemmy, toward an 'ultimate' and 'universal good'; the inhabitants, whom Lemmy regards as 'slaves of probability', are 'the endproducts of a series of mutations', and those are excluded who 'don't manage to adapt'. According to the Chief Engineer, one must never say 'why', as Lemmy does, but ' "because". In the life of all individuals, as well as in the lives of nations, everything is determined by cause and effect'. Like Peirce, the Pragmatists and the Behaviorists, who base their thinking on Darwin's theory of evolution, von Braun's technicians regard final causation as alone primary, as the motive impetus from indeterminacy to the complete reign of law.

Those who are convicted of illogical behavior are executed, of course, at the Institute of General Semantics: thought is linguistically controlled. The hotel bible turns out to be the latest issue of the Alphaville dictionary ('But isn't it the same in the

Outerlands, Mr. Johnson?'), continually updated by the deletion and replacement of words. Natasha does not understand 'love' or 'conscience', and becomes frightened when she knows a word without memory of having heard or read it, for the limits of her language are those of her world. Symbols are completely arbitrary – in Alphaville a shake of the head means 'yes', a nod 'no' – and in this case Alpha 60 arbitrates them; its voice renders each word as a series of distinct metallic sounds without inflection, reducing language, as it is put in *La Chinoise*, 'to sounds and matter'. But Lemmy insists that words have meaning, refuses, for example, to 'betray the Outerlands'; he commandeers a car as he escapes the police, orders the driver, played by Godard, to 'Wait here and don't move', and on second thought shoots him dead: 'That's to be sure you'll keep your word, pal'.

However, in the course of his confrontation with the future, Lemmy is torn away from his attachment to the archetypal postures of the past, and is left on an uncomfortably ambiguous middle ground, struggling to derive meaning from arbitrary signs. Having killed von Braun and fired into the computer, Lemmy finds himself moving through darkened corridors, 'running along a straight line, which reminded me of the Greek labyrinth that Dickson told me about, in which so many philosophers had lost their way, where even a secret agent could stray from his course'. Inhabitants of Alphaville, cut off from the source of electrical energy upon which they depend, grope along the walls of these darkened corridors. In an essay written about and contemporaneously with the making of *La Chinoise*, Alain Jeffroy writes, 'Wittgenstein ecrit quelque part qu'un homme qui vit dans la confusion philosophique ne sait pas meme trouver la porte ouverte pour en sortir. A ce pauvre homme, il conseille de longer les murs, plutôt que se fracasser la tête contre eux: au bout, il trouvera fatalement la porte'.[14] Like Lee the Agent, Lemmy moves toward the door at the end of the long hall; his critical predicament, that is, suggests the Wittgenstein of the *Philosophical Investigations*, for whom 'language is a labyrinth of paths', and who regards 'meaning something' as going 'up to the thing we mean... so one is oneself in motion. One is rushing ahead and so cannot see oneself rushing ahead' – hence the straight-line, self-contained movement which Lemmy describes to Alpha 60 as his 'secret'.

Alpha 60: Is there a difference between the mystery of the laws of knowledge and those of love?
Lemmy: In my opinion there is no mystery in love.

But both meaning and love are inexpressible, since that which
advances cannot be codified or spoken about, must be passed over
in silence. The man condemned for weeping urges the necessity of
simply advancing 'in a straight line toward all that we love';
when Natasha responds to Lemmy with poetry, she says,

One need only advance to live, to go
Straightforward toward all you love;

and Lemmy taunts Alpha 60 with another paradoxical definition
of the human situation: 'Take a look at her and me! There's
your reply. We are happiness... and we are making our way
toward it'. This 'reply', of course, does not compute: Alpha 60
has specifically demanded a 'yes or no' answer.

If Lemmy is a 'security threat' to the computer's digital logic,
he is also threatened, the code of the past endangered by the
future, and it is in this context that his fear of death is interesting:
'I had the impression', he says 'that my life here was becoming a
shadow, a twilight memory... of a doubtless awesome destiny.'
Alpha 60 is not only a futuristic version of the 'IBM... Olivetti...
General Electric' computers of the 1960s, it is that ultimate memory machine which does turn Lemmy into a shadow, films death
at work: the moving camera. If Lemmy is an individual voyeur,
Alpha 60's camera eyes observe every act of every citizen in
Alphaville, so that it can deduce from his actions that Lemmy is
not who he says he is: when the latter comments that 'News
travels fast around here', von Braun replies, 'at about 186,000
miles per second', a speed appropriate to the 'Civilization of
Light' brought about by the film image. In its lecture on itself,
Alpha 60 makes the point that the 'future' as we know it, exists
in the present:

The Central Memory is given its name because of the fundamental role it
plays in the logical organization of Alpha 60. But no one has lived in the past
and no one will live in the future. The present is the form of all life, and there
are no means by which this can be avoided. Time is a circle which is endlessly
revolving. The descending arc is the past and the rising arc is the future.

Everything has been said. At least as long as words don't change their meanings and meanings their words... Nothing existed here before us. No one. We
are absolutely alone here. We are unique, dreadfully unique. The meaning
of words and of expressions is no longer grasped. One isolated word or an
isolated detail in a drawing can be understood. But the comprehension of
the whole escapes us. Once we know the number 1, we believe we know the
number 2, because 1 plus 1 makes 2. But we do not even know what 'plus'
means.

That this is a problem of film syntax, of how 'sense' is made of
sequence plus sequence, shot plus shot, frame plus frame, is
made clear in Godard's later *One Plus One*: as for Wittgenstein,
understanding is linguistic, an ability to add things together into
verbal contexts which cannot itself be understood. If the computer must be made to destroy itself, so must the film undercut the
narrative context which holds it together, the temporal progression from beginning through middle to end, or, in terms of its
'content', from past through present to future; so that Alpha 60's
last words before its destruction are a quotation of Borges' 'A
new refutation of time', an essay on Locke, Berkeley and Hume
which rejects the notion of temporal continuity[15]: 'The present is
terrifying because it is irreversible... because it is shackled, fixed
like steel. . . . Time is the material of which I am made. . . . Time is
a stream which carries me along. . . but I am Time... it is a tiger
which tears me apart, but I am the tiger'.

Lemmy leaves Alpha 60's lecture on understanding 'because
I couldn't understand a single word', but later, when Natasha
complains that since his arrival she can no longer understand what
is happening, he says, 'Me! — I'm just beginning to understand,
I think'. Like the other works discussed in this book, *Alphaville*
is about the irreducibly simple fact of being awake, and represents
sleep as the boundary bracketing an ineluctably subjective and
ambiguous experience; so that when Natasha finally awakens to
ask if she has slept for long, Lemmy replies, 'No... a mere fraction
of time'. Of central structural importance, then, is Chandler's
The Big Sleep, the title of which is Marlowe's euphemism for
death, and is related to Godard's statements about film; for one
falls into dream at the cinema, 'but people prefer to dream in the
first degree rather than the second which is the true reality': those
who cannot see what is in front of them 'because they are always
attached to what went before' are 'not dreamers, they are asleep
and lazy. To dream is to contemplate and to let one's self go'.[16]

Many of those who cannot adapt to Alphaville are electrocuted in their seats while watching a film, anaesthetized and passive in the midst of first-degree dream, the seats tipping up and depositing them into huge garbage cans; returning from this spectacle to his hotel, Lemmy declares his wish 'to sleep, perchance to dream', suggesting thereby his nascent willingness, despite his fear of death to liberate his attention by putting aside his stereotypical code, his attachment to what went before. Accordingly, he rejects von Braun's offer of all the money and women he wants and escapes into intersidereal space. But there is thereby no transcendence of logic, only an awakening of conscious attention to its limits, a dismantling and rearrangement of its component parts, as in the explosion of Alpha 60.

The final scene in *Alphaville*, in which Lemmy and Natasha drive away from the burning city, is modeled on a scene in Howard Hawks' film version of *The Big Sleep*, with Bogart and Bacall, as Marlowe and Vivian Regan, exchanging declarations of love as they drive away from a preliminary showdown at Eddie Mars's farmhouse:

Natasha: I don't know what to say. At least I don't
know the words. Please help me. . .
Lemmy: Impossible, Princess. You've got to manage by
yourself, and only then will you be saved.
Natasha: I. . .
love. . .
you. . .
I love you.

Lemmy insists upon that synthetic effort which cannot itself be spoken about or understood: the addition of 'I' plus 'love' plus 'you' expresses a sense, and, indirectly, the role of the conscious individual in speaking an arbitrary and habitual communal language, as in giving a film cliché 'meaning'. In terms of the temporal triptych, the fact that the prototype is not the last scene of the Hawks film suggests that *Alphaville* moves from beginning, through end, to middle: just as the past advances toward the future in a straight line, Lemmy, who represents the individualist past, advances toward Natasha, who inhabits the behaviorist future, so that the two meet on the middle ground of the self-conscious present, the tense of the film image.

NOTES

1. Quoted in Jean Collet, *Jean-Luc Godard: An Investigation into his Films and Philosophy*. New York, Crown, 1970: 6.
2. Quoted in Jean Collet, *Jean-Luc Godard: An Investigation into his Films and Philosophy*. New York, Crown, 1970: 97.
3. Peter Ohlin, 'Colours, Dreams, Shadows: Reflexions on the Narrative Crisis in Film 1960-1970', Unpublished manuscript, 1975: 85.
4. Susan Sontag, 'Godard', *Partisan Review* XXXV (2) Spring 1968: 310.
5. Jean-Luc Godard, 'Shooting *Le Petit Soldat*' and 'Interview with Jean-Luc Godard by Yvonne Baby', in *Le Petit Soldat*, trans. by Nicholas Garnham. New York, Simon and Schuster: 8, 12.
6. Jean-Luc Godard, 'One or two things', in *Jean-Luc Godard*, ed. by Toby Mussman. New York, Dutton, 1968: 282.
7. Jean-Luc Godard, 'Struggle on two fronts: a conversation with Jean-Luc Godard', *Film Quarterly* XXII (2) Winter 1968-1969: 23.
8. Jean-Luc Godard, 'Pierrot mon ami', in *Cahiers du Cinéma*, trans. by Joachim Neugroschel and reprinted in *Jean-Luc Godard*, ed. by Toby Mussman. New York, Dutton, 1968: 244.
9. Susan Sontag, 'Godard', *Partisan Review* XXXV (2) Spring 1968: 290-291, 307.
10. Raymond Chandler, *The Big Sleep*. New York, Ballantine, 1975: 3, 205, 130.
11. Jean-Luc Godard, 'Original treatment: *a new adventure of Lemmy Caution*', in *Alphaville*, trans. by Peter Whitehead. New York, Simon and Schuster, 1966: 77-78.
12. Jean-Luc Godard, 'An interview with Jean-Luc Godard', trans. by Rose Kaplin and reprinted in *Jean-Luc Godard*, ed. by Toby Mussman. New York, Dutton, 1968: 109.
13. Jean-Luc Godard, 'Interview with Jean-Luc Godard by Jean Collet', in Jean Collet, *Jean-Luc Godard: An Investivation into his Films and Philosophy*. New York, Crown, 1970: 141.
14. Alain Jeffroy, 'Une affaire à régler avec le monde entier', in *La Chinoise*. Paris, L'Avant Scene, 1971: 9.
15. Jorge Luis Borges, 'A new refutation of time', in *Labyrinths: Selected Stories and Other Writings*, ed. by D.A. Yates and J.A. Irby. New York, New Directions, 1964: 234.
16. Jean-Luc Godard, 'Interview with Jean-Luc Godard by Jean Collet', in Jean Collet, *Jean-Luc Godard: An Investigation into his Films and Philosophy*. New York, Crown, 1970: 141.